Rich with the voices of black and white southern workers, *From Rights to Economics* shows how ardently African Americans have had to continue fighting for economic parity in the decades since the civil rights legislation of the 1960s.

Using oral histories and case studies that focus on black activism throughout the entire South, award-winning historian Timothy Minchin examines the work of grassroots groups—including the Southern Regional Council and the NAACP Legal Defense Fund—who struggled with the economic dimensions of the movement.

While white workers and managers resisted integration, activists' efforts gradually secured a wider range of job opportunities for blacks. Minchin, however, shows that the decline of the manufacturing industry in the South has been especially difficult for the African American community, wiping out many good jobs just as blacks were gaining access to them.

Minchin also offers a detailed discussion of a major school integration battle in Louisville, Kentucky, and examines the role of affirmative action in the ongoing black struggle.

From Rights to Economics

NEW PERSPECTIVES ON THE HISTORY OF THE SOUTH

UNIVERSITY PRESS OF FLORIDA

Florida A&M University, Tallahassee
Florida Atlantic University, Boca Raton
Florida Gulf Coast University, Ft. Myers
Florida International University, Miami
Florida State University, Tallahassee
New College of Florida, Sarasota
University of Central Florida, Orlando
University of Florida, Gainesville
University of North Florida, Jacksonville
University of South Florida, Tampa
University of West Florida, Pensacola

From Rights to Economics

The Ongoing Struggle for Black
Equality in the U.S. South

Timothy J. Minchin

University Press of Florida

Gainesville Tallahassee Tampa Boca Raton Pensacola
Orlando Miami Jacksonville Ft. Myers Sarasota

Copyright 2007 by Timothy J. Minchin
Printed in the United States of America on recycled, acid-free paper
All rights reserved

12 11 10 09 08 07   6 5 4 3 2 1

Library of Congress Cataloging-in-Publication Data
Minchin, Timothy J.
From rights to economics : the ongoing struggle for Black equality in the U.S. South /
Timothy J. Minchin.
p. cm.—(New perspectives on the history of the South)
Includes bibliographical references and index.
ISBN 978-0-8130-3092-0 (alk. paper)
1. African Americans—Civil rights—Southern States—History—20th century.
2. Civil rights movements—Southern States—History—20th century. 3. Equality—
Southern States—History—20th century. 4. Civil rights—Southern States. 5. African
Americans—History—1964– 6. Southern States—Race relations—History—20th
century. 7. African Americans—Southern States—Economic conditions—20th century.
8. Discrimination in employment—Southern States—History—20th century. 9. Labor
movement—Southern States—History—20th century. 10. Southern States—Economic
conditions—1945– I. Title.
E185.615.M548 2008
331.6'396073075—dc22   2007004262

The University Press of Florida is the scholarly publishing agency for the State
University System of Florida, comprising Florida A&M University, Florida Atlantic
University, Florida Gulf Coast University, Florida International University, Florida
State University, New College of Florida, University of Central Florida, University
of Florida, University of North Florida, University of South Florida, and University
of West Florida.

University Press of Florida
15 Northwest 15th Street
Gainesville, FL 32611-2079
http://www.upf.com

For Natasha, my cherished daughter.

Contents

Acknowledgments

From Rights to Economics draws on research that I have conducted on more than twenty trips to the American South over the past fifteen years. In this time, I have always been struck by the warm hospitality of those I have met, and I have built many cherished friendships with people in the region. It is impossible to thank all those who have helped me over this time, but I would particularly like to acknowledge my friends in Chapel Hill, North Carolina, especially Richard Zieger, Rocco and Hatsy Nittoli, and the Leloudis family. I would also like to thank my friends in Mobile, Alabama, especially the late Chuck Spence, who would have been so pleased to see these essays in print. In carrying out interviews for this book, I was also helped greatly by Lamar Speights in Port St. Joe, Florida, Kent Spriggs in Tallahassee, and Clyde Bush in Roanoke Rapids, North Carolina. Staff at the Southern Labor Archives at Georgia State University and the Southern Historical Collection at the University of North Carolina went out of their way to assist a demanding overseas researcher.

Since I moved to Australia in 2004, I have enjoyed the support of colleagues and friends at La Trobe University, which provides a relaxed and open environment in which to carry out historical study. I would particularly like to thank Tim Murray and Richard Broome for their encouragement and guidance. I owe a great debt to John Salmond, a true friend and mentor over the last thirteen years. It was John who first suggested the idea for this book, and he has guided me in his warm and experienced manner through the writing process. I have also been enriched by my contacts with talented graduate students, particularly Sarah De Santis and Ross Brooks. I would also like to thank Bronwyn Naismith, a La Trobe graduate student who provided valuable and skillful research assistance for this project.

Several staff at the University Press of Florida deserve particular acknowledgment for their continued support of my research. Meredith Morris-Babb has consistently guided and supported me in a caring and efficient manner since I first came on board as a UPF author several years ago. I would also like to thank series editor John David Smith for his wholehearted backing of my work over the last few years.

I owe a great debt to my family, especially my parents for encouraging my love of history. My wife Olga has been unflagging in her support, especially during my prolonged research trips. This book is dedicated to the newest member of the Minchin family, my daughter Natasha. I shall never forget her birth in February 2006, as I was putting the finishing touches to the first draft of this work.

I would also like to thank those who have given me permission to draw on some previously published work here. Parts of chapter 1 were earlier published as "Beyond the Dominant Narrative: The Ongoing Struggle for Civil Rights in the U.S. South, 1968–1980," *Australasian Journal of American Studies* 25, no. 1 (July 2006): 65–86. An earlier version of chapter 4 was previously published as "'A Brand New Shining City': Floyd B. McKissick Sr. and the Struggle to Build Soul City, North Carolina," *North Carolina Historical Review* 82, no. 2 (April 2005): 1–31, while the original version of chapter 7 appeared as "'There Were Two Job in St. Joe Paper Company, Black Job and a White Job': The Struggle for Civil Rights in a North Florida Paper Mill Community, 1938–1990," *Florida Historical Quarterly* 78, no. 3 (Winter 2000): 331–59. Finally, parts of chapters 2 and 3 draw on material in my *Hiring the Black Worker: The Racial Integration of the Southern Textile Industry, 1960–1980* (Chapel Hill: University of North Carolina Press, 1999) and *The Color of Work: The Struggle for Civil Rights in the Southern Paper Industry, 1945–1980* (Chapel Hill: The University of North Carolina Press, 2001). While chapters 5 and 6 are substantially new, there are brief summaries of the legal cases that they cover in these two books.

Introduction

In May 1970 a band of protesters walked for over one hundred miles across the black belt of Georgia in a "march against oppression." Responding to police killings of six African Americans, over three hundred people set off from the small town of Perry, a mule-drawn coffin leading their way. As they walked through small towns and isolated rural areas, the group kept up their spirits by chanting freedom songs. When the march reached the State Capitol of Atlanta, it gathered force. A "liberation train" of supporters arrived from Washington, D.C., while chartered buses brought in sympathizers from across the nation. At the conclusion of the protest, a massive rally took place in the streets of Atlanta, with more than ten thousand people walking four miles on a warm southern day. With the mood triumphant, the leaders of major civil rights organizations and U.S. senators addressed the group.[1]

The march bore a striking resemblance to the famous Selma-Montgomery trek of 1965—both were inspired by the killing of black protesters at the hands of white law enforcement officials, both were organized by the Southern Christian Leadership Conference (SCLC), and both drew mass participation, particularly on their final legs as participants walked into the heart of major southern cities. Yet while the Selma march is so well known that the name of the small Alabama town is indelibly associated with the civil rights movement, the Perry-Atlanta march of 1970 is hardly recognized. The protest received only limited press coverage, a reflection of the fact that national papers scarcely reported racial activism after 1968, when Martin Luther King Jr. was murdered. Reflecting a lack of sources, historical scholarship has also generally concentrated on civil rights protest before 1968, and much less is known about the important period immediately after it.[2]

Over the last twenty-five years, historians have produced many fine studies of the key racial protests of the 1950s and 1960s, establishing the field of civil rights studies as one of the most active in American history. To date, most historical

attention has focused on the struggle to secure equal rights legislation—specifically the 1964 Civil Rights Act and the 1965 Voting Rights Act—rather than
looking at how these new laws affected race relations in the South. Many works
fail to go beyond the high point of 1965 or have only short sections on the years
after it. Some standard histories of the movement, such as Fred Powledge's *Free
at Last?* and Juan Williams' *Eyes on the Prize*, fail to consider events after 1965
at all.[3] Other studies draw the line with King's death in 1968.[4]

By concentrating on the struggle to enact national legislation, scholars have
been able to emphasize the movement's successes. Many historians have identified openly with the civil rights struggle, even titling their books with phras-
es plucked from Martin Luther King's inspiring rhetoric.[5] The movement's
achievements certainly need to be recognized. Rightly identified as the most
significant social movement in American history, the civil rights revolution
was able to end legal segregation quickly and with relatively little loss of life, a
remarkable accomplishment.[6]

It is important to realize, however, that in most of the South the passage
of civil rights laws only marked the start of the fight for racial justice. In the
last few years scholars have increasingly pointed to the need to look more at
the impact of equal rights legislation. In an overview of the field published in
November 2000, leading civil rights historian Charles Eagles commented that
"more attention needs to be paid to the period after 1968 and the legacies or
ramifications of the movement." In 2005, Organization of American Historians president Jacquelyn Dowd Hall noted that a "dominant narrative" that
"celebrates the decade between *Brown v. Board of Education* and the passage of
the Voting Rights Act" has heavily influenced civil rights historiography. This
narrative obscures both the movement's "rich antecedents" and the important
ongoing struggles that took place after 1965.[7]

Examining the period after 1965 is especially important, because real racial
change did not occur in the South until federal civil rights laws were passed.
Seeing segregation as immutable, few white southerners were willing to accept
integration until forced to act by federal legislation. As southern historian Elizabeth Jacoway noted in 2004, "Until the passage of the Civil Rights Act of 1964
and the Voting Rights Act of 1965, the South saw very few concrete changes in
its patterns of racial interaction."[8]

It is not difficult to illustrate Jacoway's point. A full decade after the *Brown
v. Board of Education* decision of 1954 had supposedly outlawed segregated
schools, less than two percent of southern schools had offered even token
compliance with the decision. Real progress in school integration only oc-

curred in the late 1960s and early 1970s, and even then many whites vehemently resisted it. The southern work place was also overwhelmingly segregated until the 1964 act initiated a long process of change, while black disenfranchisement in the South also only *began* to be tackled once the 1965 Voting Rights Act became law. At the end of 1966, King himself told a closed gathering that the movement had failed to defeat what he called "the monster of racism." He added that the integration of public facilities and better protections for black voting rights "were at best surface change, they were not really substantive changes."[9]

The essays that follow provide an insight into some of the important racial struggles that occurred in the South in the era after the dominant narrative. They concentrate on the ongoing struggle for black equality in the southern states, because the national civil rights legislation was designed to overcome the legacy of legal racial segregation in these states.[10] All eight essays show that the fight for black equality was far from over when Lyndon Johnson signed the historic Voting Rights Act. While some national groups did decline after 1965, local struggles continued, especially in the thousands of small towns that dotted the region. National or regional organizations that had never depended exclusively on mass activism, such as the Southern Regional Council (SRC) and the NAACP Legal Defense Fund (LDF), also fought vigorously to enforce federal civil rights legislation at the local level.[11]

In many ways, the time is now right to carry the civil rights story forward in time. Over the last twenty years, scholars such as Beth Tompkins Bates, Robert Korstad, Nelson Lichtenstein, and Patricia Sullivan have emphasized that a great deal of important civil rights activism occurred in the 1930s and 1940s. These historians have established that the civil rights movement cannot be contained within a narrative that privileges the events of the 1955–65 era. In particular, they have shown that black pioneers in the 1930s and 1940s laid the groundwork for later protests by surging into the NAACP and by registering to vote in record numbers. In the World War II era over half a million African American workers also joined progressive unions that fought to break down segregation. Although postwar anti-communism later damaged the Left, Jim Crow had been irrevocably weakened during the war, which was the "seedtime" for the modern civil rights movement.[12]

Building on this scholarship, which emphasizes the long trajectory of the movement, historians have also begun to explore black activism after the mid-1960s.[13] Tired of the limitations of the leading narrative, scholars are reshaping the field to include a broad chronological focus. Drawing on newly released archival sources, recent case studies by Emilye Crosby, Christina Greene, Cynthia Griggs Fleming, Bobby L. Lovett, J. Todd Moye and Timothy B. Tyson all pay close attention to events after 1965 and specifically challenge the idea that the black struggle was over by the mid-1960s.[14] In her finely grained examination of Claiborne County, Mississippi, Crosby speaks out against what she calls an "outdated narrative of progress," with its "accompanying assumption that our nation has actually confronted and solved the problems generated by segregation and white supremacy." Fleming similarly shows that the fight for civil rights in the rural South is a "continuing" one, concluding her analysis of Wilcox County, Alabama, by insisting that "the struggle to realize the promises made by the civil rights movement over a generation ago continues." J. Todd Moye extends his coverage into the 1980s, showing how African Americans in Sunflower County, Mississippi, had to engage in a "forty-year struggle for civil rights."[15]

Drawing on his childhood experiences, Timothy B. Tyson's gripping account of race relations in Oxford, North Carolina, shows that little had changed by 1970 when the white community closed ranks behind two local whites who had brutally murdered a black resident. Many facilities in Oxford remained strictly segregated and whites continued to expect little retribution when they beat or even killed blacks. Tyson skillfully draws broader lessons from the story of the murder. "It speaks volumes about the racial situation in the United States in 1970," he notes, "that virtually every African American in the county believed that white men could butcher a black man in public and not even face arrest and prosecution, let alone conviction." Blacks in Oxford only began to make some gains after the killing galvanized them into action, and they did so not through the transforming force of non-violence but by "a complex mixture of violence and non-violence, economic coercion and moral appeal."[16]

From Rights To Economics builds on these case-studies and spotlights the wide range of activism that occurred in the years immediately after 1965. The broadly conceived opening essay sets the stage by summarizing some landmark events. Many marches and racial disturbances occurred in the 1970s, a decade that has often been dismissed as a time when "nothing happened."[17] Historians such as Peter Carroll and Bruce Schulman have now challenged this traditional view of the 1970s and have shown that a great deal of activism occurred in the decade, especially with the rise of the environmental movement and the emergence of the women's and gay rights movements. The black struggle itself inspired other racial minorities, including Native Americans and Latinos, to become more assertive and demand civic equality. While the efforts of these groups are beyond our focus here, they do indicate that a broad fight for social justice took place during the later years of the civil rights movement.[18]

The 1970s witnessed plenty of volatile black protest. In 1970 alone a race riot in Augusta, Georgia, left six blacks dead, while in Jackson, Mississippi, police killings of two black students precipitated a statewide boycott of white businesses. In Wilmington, North Carolina, deadly racial violence in the early 1970s became the spark for the case of the "Wilmington Ten," a long-running controversy that severely embarrassed the Carter administration. In 1975 and 1977 the SCLC also staged major protest marches to dramatize the disproportionate number of African Americans who remained mired in poverty.

As the SCLC marches highlighted, after 1965 black activism increasingly focused on economic issues, and it is this shift that is the main concern of *From Rights to Economics*. After they had gained legal equality, blacks became more aware of their continuing economic inequality, and they consistently fought to gain a bigger slice of the American pie. Targeting enforcement of Title VII of the 1964 Civil Rights Act, which prohibited discrimination in employment, black community activists worked with the NAACP Legal Defense Fund and challenged whites to make the promise of the law a reality.[19]

Seeing litigation as the only way of breaking up entrenched patterns of workplace segregation, blacks brought thousands of Title VII lawsuits in the two decades after the law became effective in July 1965. Focusing largely on two major southern industries, textiles and paper, the second essay shows how these Title VII lawsuits opened up more jobs for African Americans. These industries have been selected because they played a central role in the southern economy and because they both witnessed a large amount of Title VII litigation. Between 1965 and 1980 almost every major company in both industries was sued under Title VII by groups of aggrieved black workers.[20]

The second essay spotlights the importance of federal intervention, especially the 1964 Civil Rights Act, which finally broke up discriminatory employment practices in southern industry. In paper and textiles, however, the process of integration only started in 1965, and it was both long and torturous. In textiles, where less than 5 percent of the workforce was black in 1965, African Americans gradually began to get access to production positions in the late 1960s, while in the paper plants they had to fight even longer to weaken entrenched notions of "white" and "black" jobs. Even the formal segregation of facilities and unions lingered on into the early 1970s.

The LDF was not the only civil rights group that fought for black economic rights after 1965. Although it has been active in the civil rights struggle since the 1940s, the Atlanta-based Southern Regional Council is the most neglected of all equal rights organizations. Drawing on the group's copious files, the third essay shows that the SRC pioneered a range of initiatives aimed at lifting southern blacks out of poverty. In addition, Council researchers fought hard to document that the struggle for equal rights was far from over after 1965. While some of the Council's initiatives had a limited impact, the group deserves recognition for its long lasting commitment to racial justice.[21]

The subsequent essays are close-grained community studies that draw on both written and oral sources. The former president of the Congress of Racial Equality (CORE), Floyd B. McKissick, was one of several high-profile leaders who remained active in the black struggle long after the mid-1960s. The fourth essay shows that McKissick's efforts to build the new town of Soul City, North Carolina, were a reflection of the movement's renewed interest in giving blacks stronger economic rights. The North Carolina native attracted over $27 million of federal and state funding for the project, but he still confronted damning criticism from local whites. Although it was a major initiative that consumed McKissick's energies for over a decade, Soul City's story has remained largely untold. While the pioneer community was not the success that McKissick had envisaged, it did leave behind some positive legacies, including a new water system, a community health clinic, and a core of determined residents.[22]

The next three essays all vividly illustrate how blacks fought for their economic rights well into the 1970s. Detailed studies of Roanoke Rapids, North Carolina, St. Marys, Georgia, and Port St. Joe, Florida, chart the slow pace of racial change in the small-town South and show the importance of continuing black activism in order to ensure that any improvements occurred. Port St. Joe and St. Marys were paper mill communities, while Roanoke Rapids was a textile town. In each location whites had traditionally monopolized the best-paying jobs in the plants and were keen to defend their racial privileges. In all three towns black activism opened up more job opportunities for succeeding generations. Without pressure to enforce the mandate of Title VII, progress toward integration in these communities would have clearly been much slower. Although layoffs and plant closures eventually negated some of these gains, activists had helped make the southern workplace a much fairer environment. They worked with federal agencies and civil rights groups to push employers' adoption of affirmative remedies to employ more black workers and promote them more fairly.

These stories of black workers' efforts engage with the broad scholarly debate about black economic progress since 1965 and the role of affirmative action in helping racial minorities. Economic data indicate that black income levels rose vis-à-vis whites between 1965 and 1975; in 1964 U.S. blacks made 62 percent of what whites made, but this number had risen to 72 percent by 1975. Some economists have argued that this improvement had little to do with Title VII or affirmative action but was more a reflection of general economic growth and labor market pressures. In recent studies, both Paul Moreno and Robert Weiss have been generally pessimistic about the impact of affirmative action, insisting that it has created damaging racial divisions.[23]

Other scholars have been much more positive about affirmative action's effect on black economic progress. In her recent landmark study, Nancy Mac-Lean argues that the main cause of the "opening of the American workplace" was "the black freedom movement's fight for jobs and justice." Working at the community level, black activists themselves prodded employers to make affirmative action effective and ensured that the workplace gradually became much more diverse. Similarly positive in tone, political scientist Ira Katznelson has outlined how affirmative action has been necessary in order to "right particular past wrongs." In a detailed econometric study, John J. Donohue III and James Heckman credit Title VII with a central role in improving black economic performance. "Federal civil rights policy," they conclude, "was the major contributor to the sustained improvement in black economic status that began in 1965."[24]

Building on this scholarship, *From Rights to Economics* shows how grassroots activists used Title VII to forge a fairer workplace. At the same time, however, these essays also highlight that black grassroots activism had its limits. As the Port St. Joe and Roanoke Rapids case studies demonstrate, black activists and federal agencies found it difficult to tame the most intransigent employers. In addition, broader economic forces have disproportionately hurt blacks and circumscribed their gains. The decline of manufacturing industries wounded an African American community that was heavily dependent on these staple jobs. By the mid-1970s, many important southern industries were already shedding jobs. As the U.S. Commission on Civil Rights carefully documented, new manufacturing and service industries also tended to locate in the lily-white suburbs, cutting off blacks in both inner-cities and rural areas. After 1975 black economic gains slowed; in the South, black income levels relative to white stagnated between 1975 and 1981. Many studies indicate that, since the late 1970s, a black "under-class" has grown in size.[25]

The community case studies presented here also highlight the importance of gender to understanding the dynamics of the civil rights struggle. In recent years historians have produced an enormous amount of quality scholarship on women and gender during the civil rights and black power movements, showing how the black freedom struggle intersected with the emerging feminist movement. Gender also shaped the character of the grassroots struggle for civil rights in the textile and paper industries. In textiles, where large numbers of women toiled, black women fought hard to gain access to production jobs that promised to free them from the drudgery of working as domestics in private homes. In *Sledge v. J. P. Stevens* and other cases, they used Title VII to gain access to the plants. Male workers, in contrast, already had access to the plants; in both industries their struggle was to use the law to try to upgrade to better-paying, "white" jobs. Many of these male workers were also proud of their role as breadwinners, and this motivated them to fight for improved opportunities.[26]

The final essay focuses on a neglected but important school integration crisis that occurred in Louisville, Kentucky, in 1975. After the Supreme Court case of *Swann v. Charlotte-Mecklenburg County Board of Education* (1971), which mandated the use of busing to achieve racial balance in schools, busing was used in over one hundred southern cities, including Little Rock, Jacksonville, Nashville, Tampa, Dallas, Norfolk, and Louisville. The Louisville study gives us a revealing insight into a controversial issue that helped to define racial conflict in the 1970s. Across the region busing led to discord, because it was deeply unpopular with many whites, who argued that the education of their children would suffer. By 1978, when busing had been used across Dixie, one Gallup poll showed that just 5 percent of whites endorsed it. The busing controversy was again related to economic issues, as both blacks and whites grasped that education was a key passport to gaining economic rights. As the United States Commission on Civil Rights commented in a November 1983 report, "Education has always been the key to greater employment opportunities and successful participation in society at all levels."[27]

Louisville was the first metropolitan area in the country to carry out the court-ordered, cross-district busing of children between the central city and the suburbs. The busing plan led to serious violence that was spearheaded by the local union movement. Although the Kentucky National Guard eventually restored order, marches and efforts to boycott the schools continued for many months. Events in Louisville illustrate how civil rights were still being violently contested in the 1970s. In all of the case studies, in fact, whites resisted change for many years and only sustained black activism forced them to give some ground. The Louisville story, however, offers the most detailed insight into the continuing white opposition to equal rights. Events in Louisville also demonstrate that racial conflict was not confined to small towns in the Deep South but also occurred in the "progressive" border states.[28]

In Port St. Joe, St. Marys, and Louisville, workers used majority-white local unions to help organize their opposition to civil rights. The three essays all spotlight the conflict between national unions and local branches over civil rights. In 1974, AFL-CIO Civil Rights director William E. Pollard asserted that the federation's unions were "fully and completely irrevocably committed to the task of rooting out every vestige of discrimination against any human being in every area of American life." Unions, he added, had done more to "make equal rights a reality than [had] any other institution." Local unions had considerable autonomy, however, and national non-discrimination policies were often flouted on the ground. These essays vividly highlight the large gap that existed between labor leaders' rhetoric and local conditions.[29]

The battle for school integration illustrates the long struggle for civil rights particularly well. Realizing that most blacks were afraid to enroll their children in white schools, whites were able in the late 1960s to use "freedom of choice" plans to stall integration. In 1968 77.5 percent of black students in the South went to schools that were 90 percent or more black. Real progress in desegregating schools did not occur until after 1968, when the Supreme Court finally forced southern school officials to take decisive action.[30] Even then many whites were not willing to accept integration. In 1976 a study by the National Institute for Education concluded that Americans were still "grappling" with the complex legacy of *Brown*. "The controversy surrounding the social merits, the legal requirements, and the educational effects of desegregation remains intense, and displays no sign of abating in the near future," it warned. "The fact is that more than twenty years later, there is still much racial segregation in American public education."[31]

Much still remains to be learned about black activism after the mid-1960s, and this collection does not attempt to cover all aspects of the ongoing struggle for equal rights. I do not try to examine the impact that increased black voting had on the political landscape, an important story that has already been skillfully charted by political scientists and journalists.[32] In sharp contrast, the battle for economic justice has been neglected but is central to understanding black activism outside the confines of the dominant narrative. I also concentrate most of my focus on the decade and a half after 1965, when blacks fought hard to make the mandate of civil rights laws a reality in their own communities.[33]

Right through the 1970s blacks were acutely aware that despite the breakdown of legal segregation, they still had to battle for economic parity with whites. When the civil rights laws were passed, African Americans earned much less than whites and closing the gap proved very difficult, especially after the mid-1970s. Blacks were hit hard by the economic downturns of 1969–71 and 1974–75, and by 1976 they were twice as likely to be unemployed as whites.[34] In July 1975 Republican Senator Edward W. Brooke declared that the "great majority of black people still live on the margin of economic existence." While blacks represented just over ten percent of all Americans, they comprised about thirty percent of those living in poverty.[35] In 1977 a report from the National Urban League showed that white high school dropouts had lower unemployment rates than blacks youths with a college education.[36]

As these essays highlight, African Americans repeatedly took action to try to improve their economic plight. The rising workload of the Equal Employment Opportunity Commission, which monitored compliance with Title VII, is a good indicator of how African Americans increasingly complained about workplace discrimination. In 1966 the commission received 8,700 complaints, but this number rose steadily to 71,000 cases in 1975. Although it took on more staff, the EEOC was still unable to cope and soon had a considerable backlog. As the EEOC took up to two years to process complaints, black workers who were seeking racial justice knew they were unlikely to secure quick results. EEOC complaints often acted as a prelude to Title VII cases that themselves took many years to resolve. Gradually, however, black activists forged a new workplace that was free of the worst vestiges of racial discrimination.[37]

In the 1970s blacks across the South also launched grassroots projects designed to try to improve their desperate economic position. Like Soul City, these initiatives struggled to change deep-seated patterns of economic inequality but secured some tangible results. Richard A. Couto has examined how blacks in scores of southern communities fought to establish community health care centers. Funded by War on Poverty programs, the centers provided basic health coverage to thousands of poor people.[38] In the Mississippi Delta, Charles Evers also became a powerful civil rights leader by using federal and private money to attract industries and launch economic self-help projects.[39] In central Georgia, activists similarly organized East Central Committee for Opportunity, Inc. (ECCO) in order to help local blacks achieve their "economic and political rights." Until ECCO was formed, explained Chair Ruby C. Clayton, "a near-state of apartheid existed in the county."[40]

Comparable initiatives occurred across the South. Deep in the Mississippi Delta, Fannie Lou Hamer, the black campaigner who had fought for the right to vote in the 1960s, turned away from politics after 1968 and concentrated on economic development. In the 1970s Hamer poured her energies into a "Freedom Farm" project that strove to help blacks buy land and market their produce.[41] In nearby Greenville, a group of local blacks complemented Hamer's efforts by organizing Delta Enterprises, a $10 million business that ran four manufacturing plants and a large farm.[42]

Economic concerns also inspired protest. In the 1970s Hamer herself organized a series of "Walks Against Hunger," while the SCLC headed several protest marches and conferences to demand full employment.[43] The shift to economic issues marked a major reorientation of civil rights activism. As NAACP labor director Herbert Hill claimed in 1977, the focus of the civil rights movement had moved from simple integration as "economic issues" assumed a "greater priority."[44] In the same year, the *New York Times* noted that black activism had switched "from rights to economics." Black economic problems, noted the *Times*, were "intractable," and were the key area that the movement now needed to tackle. As the *Atlanta Journal* suggested, the slogan of the civil rights movement had changed from "We Shall Overcome" to "We Want Full Employment."[45]

At the grassroots level, African Americans frequently commented on the failure of the civil rights movement to bring them economic equality and were keen to refute notions of real progress in race relations. Blacks especially did not like media reports that hurriedly declared the dawn of a "New South" that was free from racial inequality.[46] "We can vote now and we got a few colored people into office," commented Alabama farmer Bill Grant in 1975, "but we still got real problems getting food and buying clothes and shoes and things." In 1974 black leader David Franklin similarly declared that "The fact is that the masses of black people have not made it. We don't want to see stories saying, hey, look, black folks are doing well there. It is embarrassing how little we do have."[47]

Above all, *From Rights to Economics* shows us the importance of taking a long view of the civil rights struggle. While positive changes did occur in race relations after 1965, much remained to be done. Contemporaries often made this point. In the spring of 1979, prominent black and white thinkers gathered in Oxford, Mississippi, for a conference to commemorate the twenty-fifth anniversary of the *Brown* decision. The fact that the conference was held at the University of Mississippi, which had only admitted its first black student in 1962, itself indicated how much race relations had improved.[48] Speakers noted that segregation was rapidly becoming a distant memory, as a new generation of southerners was emerging that had never even seen a Jim Crow sign. By the time of the conference, thirteen blacks were sitting in the Alabama state legislature in Montgomery, a city that had always prided itself on being "the cradle of the confederacy."[49]

At the same time, however, participants did not feel that the South had truly surmounted its crippling legacies of segregation and racism. Scholar Robert H. Wiebe agreed with prominent southern historian Charles P. Roland's judgment that the two races were "as far apart in the 1970s as they had been in the 1940s." Pondering the question "have we overcome?," black journalist Lerone Bennett Jr. was cautious. "We crossed a river," he declared, "and now we've got to cross a sea."[50]

Bennett's dictum sums up how many African Americans felt about the limited progress of civil rights after the mid-1960s; despite some changes, they fiercely disputed the idea that further struggle was not necessary. "People . . . make the statement that the civil rights movement is dead," fumed Floyd Mc-Kissick in 1978, "You mean to tell me that every person I see no longer wants any rights—no longer wants economic success—no longer wants his schooling and housing?" SCLC president Ralph Abernathy had made a similar point a few years earlier. "The Movement," he declared, "is far from dead—no matter what you read or hear."[51]

Even before the law, African Americans were hardly equal, as federal legislation now decreed they should be. In the mid-1970s, police officers in many southern communities continued to shoot blacks and yet be cleared of any wrongdoing. Protected by a law that allowed them to open fire on felony suspects, police in Memphis killed three or four blacks a month until the mid-1970s, when pressure from the black community led to the law being overturned. As the opening essay shows, police killings often provoked militant and violent protests by southern blacks. On July 20, 1979, for example, blacks in Birmingham launched one of the largest marches in the city's history to protest the killing of an African American resident by a police officer. Anger over the shooting helped elect Richard Arrington as the city's first black mayor.[52]

In the post-civil rights South, then, clear progress occurred but a great deal of racial inequality also remained. While some whites were keen to put the past behind them, many more clung to it. It is important to look behind the South's façade of progress and analyze whether race relations really did change after 1965. In January 1971, for example, new Georgia Governor Jimmy Carter took office and famously declared, "the time for racial discrimination is over." Many observers saw Carter's address as a sign that a New South had arrived; the *New York Times*, for example, hurriedly declared that a "new era" had arrived in the region. Equally revealing, however, was a comment made by a white man in the crowd after the speech. Leaning forward, the listener warned the newly elected Governor that he did not speak for many southern whites. "I don't think," he declared defiantly, "the people of Georgia agree with him on what he said about the races being equal."[53]

1

Beyond the Dominant Narrative

The Ongoing Struggle for Civil Rights
in the U.S. South, 1965–1980

Over the last twenty-five years, the field of civil rights historiography has been one of the most active in American history. Much of the literature has focused on Martin Luther King Jr., the charismatic leader who has been the subject of numerous biographies and interpretive studies. King-centered books have shown how the eloquent leader was able to mobilize both blacks and whites, creating the pressure that led to the passage of effective equal rights legislation in 1964 and 1965.[1] Anxious to keep King's role in context, scholars have also written a plethora of case studies that remind us of the importance of local activism and mass participation in ensuring the success of civil rights protest. Synthesizing this national and local scholarship, several writers have produced fine general histories that have become widely adopted in courses at both schools and universities.[2]

A "dominant narrative" that privileges the 1954–65 era has powerfully shaped the historiography of the civil rights movement.[3] In recent years, many scholars have become increasingly dissatisfied that this narrative overlooks a great deal of important black protest. Most have stressed the importance of African American activism before 1955, arguing that the civil rights movement built upon an upsurge in black militancy that began in the New Deal and World War II eras.[4] In the last few years, however, some historians have also called for more inquiry into recent civil rights history. Robert Norrell's *The House I Live In*, an up-to-date overview of southern race relations, argues that the civil rights struggle is an ongoing one and cannot be contained within the dominant narrative. "The story of the civil rights movement," he concludes, "is a much longer and richer narrative than we have often thought."[5]

In many ways, the period after King's demise is central to a full understanding of the civil rights movement. It was in these years that much of the equal rights legislation reshaped southern society. As well as exploring the events that led to the passage of this legislation, we also need to see how the laws were implemented and how whites and blacks reacted to them. At this stage, it is important to sketch out the contours of black activism and identify broad themes. This analysis will focus on the southern states, as the civil rights legislation was aimed at the South, the only part of the United States where legal segregation had existed. In addition, most racial protests occurred in the South, and the region was home to the majority of the nation's African American population.[6]

Overall it is clear that while many national civil rights groups did decline after 1965, local struggles continued.[7] At the local level, African Americans continued to take part in mass marches and protests, especially in response to incidents of police brutality. As blacks turned away from nonviolence, many of these protests ended in bloodshed. Civil rights activism also took on a strong economic focus, as African Americans realized that the equal rights legislation of the mid-1960s had done little to address their continuing economic inequality. In the late 1960s and early 1970s, blacks made some progress in closing the income gap, but significant disparities remained. In 1974, for example, whites earned $5,548 per year more than blacks did. In the post-King era, addressing this economic inequality became a major concern of African American leaders. As a black leader in Alabama commented in the late 1970s, "Until people become economically strong, political power alone won't do."[8]

The notion of decline applies most accurately to national groups, as many did fall on hard times after 1965. Previously one of the most active organizations, by 1969 the Student Nonviolent Coordinating Committee (SNCC) was defunct, having been torn apart by conflicts over "black power." At the end of the 1960s, the SCLC continued to exist, but it had been hit hard by King's death. In the years immediately after their leader's assassination, King's former lieutenants argued among themselves, and new president Ralph Abernathy lacked King's ability to unify the warring factions. Arguably the most talented of King's assistants, Jesse Jackson left the SCLC in 1971 to set up a rival organization. In the mid-1960s, the SCLC had a staff of 150 and a budget of over $1 million a year, but by 1972 its income was down to $917,000, and just 61 staff remained.[9]

Other groups that had led the civil rights movement during its classic phase also experienced problems. Although it continued to exist, CORE suffered from declining membership levels and a loss of influence, especially at the national level. The NAACP, America's oldest civil rights organization, also struggled. In the early 1970s, aging president Roy Wilkins, who had led the group since 1955, came under increasing attack from younger members who felt that he had failed to move with the times. Rather than addressing the organization's increasing financial problems, Wilkins clung to power and resisted calls for modernization. In 1976 the NAACP lost a boycotting case in Mississippi and almost went bankrupt, being saved by a $1.5 million loan that was underwritten by the American Federation of Labor–Congress of Industrial Organizations (AFL-CIO).[10]

In many ways, these groups were victims of their own success. During the 1950s and early 1960s, they had focused their attention on breaking down legal segregation and fighting for improved black voting rights. They had been largely successful in achieving these goals, as pressure from black interest groups had influenced the passage of both the 1964 Civil Rights Act and the 1965 Voting Rights Act. These laws brought tremendous improvements to black lives, as African Americans could now travel freely through the region using the same facilities as whites. Blacks who moved back to the South after 1965 were astonished by these changes. "I'm not afraid about anything happening now," declared Howard Spence, an African American who returned to Mississippi from Chicago in the mid-1970s. "When I was here before, I was afraid. The big difference is I feel free. I'm much more in control. I can make a decision without being afraid. I can go downtown, anywhere I want to. I can talk to anybody."[11]

Such freedom of movement helped to attract many other blacks back to Dixie; in eleven southern states, the African American population increased by almost two million between 1970 and 1980, reversing a pattern of out-migration that dated back to World War I. The Voting Rights Act also brought about what scholars Chandler Davidson and Bernard Grofman have called a "quiet revolution" in the region, allowing for a steady increase in black political power. In 1979 African Americans held 4,607 elected offices, 66 percent of them in the South. By this time, there were 191 black mayors and 313 state legislators.[12]

These laws failed to directly address black economic inequality, however, and after 1965 the movement increasingly focused on economic issues. Despite the well-publicized progress that some African Americans had made, as the country celebrated its bicentennial African Americans made up less than 3 percent of all doctors, lawyers, dentists, and engineers. The gross revenue of all the nation's black businesses was also less than the annual earnings of the Sears Roebuck Company. Tackling economic injustice was difficult, however, as such campaigns brought few quick or easy victories. While segregated public facilities could easily be abolished by taking down signs, the problems of unemployment and poverty were deep-seated and defied quick solutions.[13]

In order to address these complex issues, civil rights groups needed large treasuries that would enable them to conduct long, detailed campaigns, but instead their funding contracted. King's death had a negative impact on fundraising, as no other African American leader proved as effective at swelling the coffers. The economic recession of the early 1970s also hit black interest groups hard. Following a downturn between 1969 and 1971, in 1973 the U.S. economy entered a prolonged recession. Inflation hit double digits in 1973 and 1974, and for the rest of the decade the economy suffered from "stagflation," a simultaneous burden of inflation and unemployment. By 1975 unemployment stood at 8.5 percent, and it rose even higher in the latter part of the decade. The downturn hurt civil rights organizations, because most relied on income from foundations and wealthy individuals whose fortunes rose and fell with the nation's economy. The Ford Foundation, for example, no longer gave as generously to black interest groups as it had in the past.[14]

Lacking a clear focus and ample funding, direct action campaigns by national groups became less common. While national organizations no longer engaged in as many high-profile battles, at the local level African Americans continued to take to the streets in surprising numbers. Their protests revealed that many blacks remained profoundly frustrated with the pace of change and felt that they still needed to fight to address deep-seated racial inequalities.[15]

Mass protests were often triggered by white violence, especially killings of blacks by white police officers. In the post-King era, these protests increasingly turned violent. As Timothy Tyson's recent work has shown, police killings provided a catalyst for frustrated blacks who increasingly rejected nonviolence as ineffective and self-defeating. Even when King was alive, southern blacks had often questioned the wisdom of being nonviolent, but they usually deferred to the wishes of national groups. After King's death, many blacks were no longer willing to bite their lips. "All non-violent ever got Martin Luther King was dead," commented armed marcher Eddie McCoy to Tyson, "or else he'd be out here with us. We wasn't gonna start nothing but we was ready." Many were now determined to hit back, and they did so in a variety of locations.[16]

These protests reflected a general mood of frustration in the black community. Many felt angry due to the failure of civil rights legislation to bring real change, especially as increased voting had failed to deliver greater economic equality. "The civil rights movement," notes Tyson, "knocked down the formal and legal barriers to equal citizenship, but failed to give most African Americans real power in this society." Increasing black voter registration was often canceled out by increasing levels of white registration and by white flight, which meant that black elected officials often presided over economically depressed, majority-black communities. In 1972 around seventy black mayors set up the Southern Conference of Black Mayors to try to tackle what executive director Bernard M. Porche called "the impoverished condition of their cities and constituents." The group lobbied hard for funds, but African American mayors still struggled to cope with intractable economic problems and poorly funded government bureaucracies.[17]

In the early 1970s, there were some serious outbursts of racial conflict that have yet to receive detailed treatment from scholars. In May 1970, rioting broke out in Augusta, Georgia, after over five hundred blacks marched to protest the treatment of juvenile prisoners at the Richmond County jail, where a 16-year-old black youngster had been beaten to death. Prison officers claimed that Charles Oatman, a black teenager awaiting trial, had died after falling from his bunk, but the undertaker noticed that Oatman had suffered systematic torture, including cigarette burns and skin punctures from a fork. Violence broke out when marchers burned the Georgia state flag, and police killed six blacks in a night of shooting. All were shot multiple times in the back.[18]

Civil rights leaders insisted that Oatman's death was simply the spark that ignited a desperate community, and the violence was concentrated in the poor black neighborhoods of the east Georgia town. "This is the result of years and years of white racism," declared black city councilman C. S. Hamilton. Little improved for the African American community as a result of the violence; the predominantly white city council shelved a report into the causes of the riots, and the Augusta police were later cleared for the deaths of the six protesters. By the end of the 1970s, the city's sheriff had acknowledged that racism was still endemic among his overwhelmingly white force.[19]

The Augusta violence acted as the catalyst for the mass march from Perry to Atlanta that ended in what the *New York Times* called a "massive rally" in the streets of the state capital. With a mule-drawn wagon leading their way, up to ten thousand people walked four miles through the streets of Atlanta. Organized by the SCLC, this self-styled "march against oppression" was reminiscent of the mass marches of the 1960s.[20]

In other small southern towns and rural districts, blacks increasingly stood up to whites. In the early 1970s, violence was particularly prevalent in rural districts where whites refused to yield ground to militant blacks. In 1971, for example, the remote farming area around Marianna, Arkansas, was rocked by interracial gunfire, fistfights, and numerous incidents of arson. Here, blacks battled to get a fairer share of economic wealth and to break down white political control.[21] In the eastern North Carolina town of Ayden, around nine hundred blacks were arrested in the autumn of 1971 following marches triggered by a racial killing. The Ayden protests, however, raised broader demands about discrimination in housing, schools, and the workplace.[22] In Oxford, North Carolina, where race relations had been largely unaffected by the civil rights movement, blacks repeatedly took to the streets to complain about the racially motivated murder of Henry Marrow, a black man. In May 1970, around one thousand determined activists from Oxford even marched to the door of the state capitol building in Raleigh. To the disgust of the group, however, Governor Robert Scott refused to meet them.[23]

Similar episodes occurred across the rural South. In the early 1970s, acute racial tensions in Sparta, Georgia, led blacks and whites to engage in an arms race, while in the nearby town of Wrightsville, Georgia—where the local sheriff still called black men "boys"—there were exchanges of gunfire and racial brawls on the courthouse lawn. As an SCLC analysis highlighted, violence in the rural South reflected white reluctance to cede power to increasingly impatient blacks. In addition, the group claimed that the economic recession had caused "a Southwide retrenchment in racial attitudes" that was particularly acute in remote areas. A region-wide Klan revival was one indication of this shift, with some black leaders claiming that the renegade group's membership had tripled over the course of the 1970s. The Klan had certainly not died out, and in the late 1970s the clandestine organization was involved in violent confrontations with civil rights groups in Decatur, Alabama, and Greensboro, North Carolina.[24]

During the 1950s and 1960s, the African American population had become increasingly urban, and much of the ongoing racial conflict occurred in cities. In urban communities, African Americans usually lived in poor, segregated neighborhoods and frequently clashed with the white police officers who patrolled their crumbling streets. Events in Mississippi's state capital were illustrative of broader trends. In May 1970, police killed two black students and wounded nine others at the predominantly black Jackson State College. In all, reporters counted more than 140 bullet marks on a student dormitory and dining hall. Forming a coalition called the United Front, around thirty civil rights organizations insisted that the police action had been unprovoked, an argument disputed by local whites. African Americans, however, responded to the shootings by launching a statewide boycott of white businesses and by pushing hard for the integration of Mississippi's National Guard, where blacks made up just twenty-one of the thirteen thousand troops. Pressure from civil rights groups eventually helped to secure greater black representation in both the state's police force and National Guard.[25]

These were not isolated incidents. In 1969 and 1971, alleged police brutality triggered race riots in Jacksonville, Florida. Again, the Jacksonville violence was sparked by the killing of a black youth by a white police officer but reflected broader problems, as much of the city's black community was cut off from good jobs and adequate services. Although booster-minded white leaders expressed concern about the violence, after the riots subsided there were few reforms, and conditions in the disintegrating neighborhoods of east Jacksonville failed to improve.[26] In 1972 a police move to break up an impromptu black protest rally in Baton Rouge led to an exchange of gunfire that killed four and wounded thirty-one. Although whites and blacks varied in their accounts of who fired first, the violence confirmed that many blacks were willing to carry arms. In Birmingham, Alabama, scene of famous civil rights protests in the spring of 1963, there was also a resurgence of racial violence in the late 1970s after the mayor refused to fire a white police officer who had killed a black woman by shooting her three times in the back.[27]

Racial conflict in Wilmington, a city of around sixty thousand people on the coast of North Carolina, sparked a major civil rights case that has yet to receive an authoritative study.[28] During racial clashes generated by school integration, blacks barricaded one of the city's major streets and posted armed guards, because they claimed that police had failed to prevent white night riders from shooting in the area. Influenced by Black Nationalist ideas, many young African Americans had clearly abandoned nonviolence. As high school student Barnabus Johnson recalled, "Sometimes whites would start fights and say things like: 'What are you niggers up to today?' And almost every time, we ended up chasing them down and kicking their asses. We called them 'search and destroy missions.'"[29]

Following a series of bitter racial battles that left two people dead, police arrested ten black youngsters. The charges against the so-called Wilmington Ten derived from the February 1971 burning of Mike's Grocery, a small white-owned store that was located in the black neighborhood. Composed largely of high school students, the group had become trapped in a church near the store, and its members were later convicted of conspiring to burn the store and of assaulting police officers. They received some of the heaviest sentences in the state's judicial history, with alleged ringleader Benjamin Chavis landing up to thirty-four years in prison.[30]

Following their conviction, black attorney James Ferguson repeatedly point-ed out irregularities in the case against the Ten. Although the group clearly had participated in some violence, Ferguson argued that they had been framed by state officials who wanted to stop the protests. The state press also reported that key documents had been kept from the defense, that key witnesses had been paid for their testimony, and that the prosecution's star witness had later recant-ed his original version of events. Fearing the consequences if he spoke out, the minister of the black church at the center of the controversy also stayed silent, even though he was with Chavis when Mike's Grocery was in flames. Failing to get the group's convictions overturned in the lower courts, Ferguson took the highly publicized case to the Supreme Court. Despite his untiring efforts, in January 1976 the Supreme Court declined to review the convictions. Black leaders rallied to the group's side, organizing a 143-mile march from Charlotte to Raleigh in order to ask Governor Jim Hunt to free the defendants. Hunt, however, refused to intervene. Members of the Congressional Black Caucus and the National Conference of Black Lawyers also demanded the group's release, and national and international criticism of North Carolina's judicial system increased the pressure on the governor. "The case," noted London's *Financial Times*, "has called into question whether racial equality really has been achieved in the new south." The events in North Carolina even came to the attention of Soviet leaders, with news agency Tass calling the Wilmington Ten "political prisoners."[31]

In February 1978, the National Wilmington Ten Defense Committee or-ganized a demonstration in front of the White House that put considerable pressure on the Carter administration to intervene in the case. President Carter also received around forty thousand signatures urging him to pardon the group, with some petitions coming from sympathizers in Greece and Germany.[32] The case became a test of Carter's commitment to civil rights, especially as the president was a passionate advocate of human rights abroad. With his popular-ity waning, Carter did not want to lose the black vote, and the pressure even-tually told. While remaining publicly neutral, officials from the U.S. Justice Department quietly influenced North Carolina governor Jim Hunt to slash the group's sentences. In January 1978, after several of the key witnesses recanted their original testimony, Hunt gave way and reduced the terms. In December 1980, the case was finally resolved when the Fourth Circuit Court of Appeals overturned the convictions.[33]

Over the course of the 1970s, the slow pace of school integration also trig-gered protests.[34] As James T. Patterson's study of the "troubled legacy" of *Brown* shows, Jim Crow continued to "flourish" in southern schools until the late

1960s, when the Supreme Court finally adopted the forceful line that was necessary to bring about substantive change.[35] As a result, the real battle over school
integration took place in the late 1960s and early 1970s. Again there was violence; in Lamar, South Carolina, mobs turned over and smashed buses filled
with black elementary school students, while in Charlotte extremists bombed
the offices of the civil rights lawyers who had brought the key busing case
of *Swann v. Charlotte-Mecklenburg County Board of Education*. Busing evoked
powerful opposition from many whites, but the controversial remedy was still
adopted by around one hundred southern school districts over the course of
the 1970s. Whites rallied behind the call for "neighborhood schools," a solution
supported openly by President Gerald Ford and implicitly by Jimmy Carter.
"Nobody's busing me just so some niggers can get a better deal," declared one
white student. "I didn't set up the schools. . . . Niggers don't like their schools,
let them change 'em, but they don't have the right to tell me what to do. . . .
The only right we got is to go to school near where we live."[36]

Many whites responded to "forced" integration by withdrawing their children from the public schools, ensuring that these schools simply "resegregated."
In Mobile, Alabama, where busing was widely used, white flight from the public school system reduced the student population by 20 percent between 1970
and 1975. In 1970 Richmond's city school population was 35 percent white, but
as the pace of integration quickened this fell to less than 20 percent in 1976.[37]
Many whites sent their children to the new private schools that mushroomed
across the region in the 1970s. By May 1972, there were 168 "segregation academies" in Mississippi, 163 in South Carolina, and 224 in Georgia. Ironically,
many of the white parents who opposed busing now proved willing to bus their
children long distances in order to get them to the private schools. In May
1970, a survey of ten academies found that students were traveling 17.7 miles
each way, compared to 10.1 miles for those who were bused to the local public
schools.[38]

Although white parents frequently denied that they were racists, many new
private schools were connected to segregationist groups. In 1972, for example,
the Southern Regional Council found that 396 schools in seven southern states,
which together had an enrollment of 176,000, were formally linked through
their membership in the Southern Independent School Association with the
segregationist Citizens Councils of America. The SRC asserted that the all-white
private schools were leading to a new "dual school system," a judgment that
proved to be highly accurate. By 1977 the U.S. Commission on Civil Rights
reported that "most black children in America attend predominantly minority

schools that are intensely segregated," a situation that was largely the product of white flight from the public schools.[39] When the twenty-fifth anniversary of *Brown* was celebrated in 1979, activists at a civil rights seminar in Washington were quick to point out that much remained to be done, as de jure segregation had been replaced by de facto segregation that was "spreading" across the country. In Summerton, South Carolina, where local blacks had helped bring the original *Brown* case, the public schools soon became almost entirely black. In 1979 just one white student went to classes with 2,029 blacks.[40]

Despite the turn away from nonviolence, many peaceful protests also occurred in the late 1960s and 1970s. Some were inspired directly by black demands for greater economic rights. In this sense, blacks had not simply shifted from "rights to economics," as the *New York Times* claimed, but were now using direct action to try to gain economic equality. In 1969 a strike by black hospital workers in Charleston sparked a major nonviolent movement that resulted in nearly one thousand arrests. As well as forcing city leaders to recognize their union, the strikers' struggle cemented the interest of civil rights groups in labor issues, especially as the SCLC and black churches became heavily involved in the battle. In April 1975, the SCLC also led a peaceful protest march through Mississippi, America's poorest state. Many of Mississippi's blacks continued to live in desperate poverty, and as the economy slumped there were few signs of improvement. Marchers urged President Gerald Ford to declare the state a federal disaster area, but the consensus-seeking Republican refused. Ford's response disappointed civil rights leaders, who continued to press him to embrace both full employment and compensatory affirmative action.[41]

In January 1977, several thousand African Americans also walked through the streets of Atlanta to demand full employment. The protest was a culmination of a three-day full-employment conference that had been held at the Martin Luther King Center in Atlanta. As president of the center, Coretta Scott King continued to coordinate a program of activities that had a strong economic focus, including events organized around the late leader's birthday each January. Anniversaries provided a spark for activism; in March 1975, for example, Coretta Scott King led around two thousand protesters across the Edmund Pettus bridge in Selma to commemorate the Selma-Montgomery march of 1965. At the conclusion of the trek, she declared that America was in a "critical state," because "there are no jobs for those who need them and people are hungry."[42]

These protests highlight the strong economic focus of black activism after 1965. While the bulk of writing on the movement has focused on direct action protests, it is important to realize that civil rights groups also carried out a great deal of other work, including litigation and lobbying. After the mid-1960s, organizations that had never relied heavily on direct action came to the fore to represent black interests, and they focused heavily on economic concerns.[43] The NAACP Legal Defense Fund, for example, carried out vital work to ensure that the Civil Rights Act did lead to real improvements for African Americans. By 1979 the fund was the nation's largest black advocacy law firm, with a caseload of one thousand. The fund's lawyers brought hundreds of cases to tackle discrimination in employment, education, and housing, although they shifted in the 1970s to prioritize workplace litigation.[44]

Class actions brought under Title VII of the 1964 Civil Rights Act, which prohibited discrimination in employment, were particularly effective in gaining African Americans compensation for discriminatory practices. In 1978, for example, awards for Title VII violations cost businesses nearly $30 million. Many firms were also pushed to adopt affirmative action plans in order to settle or avert litigation.[45] The LDF put particular pressure on the trucking industry, which had traditionally hired whites for the lucrative "over the road" jobs, and on textile companies, who were pushed to hire more and more blacks. Between 1960 and 1978, the percentage of black textile workers in the South increased from 3.3 percent to over 18 percent. In the late 1960s, civil rights litigation also opened up the Mississippi and Alabama highway patrols to blacks for the first time. In Alabama, where white troopers were a symbol of the established racial order, federal judge Frank M. Johnson Jr. ordered that the state's Department of Public Safety had to hire "one Negro trooper for each white trooper until approximately twenty-five percent of the Alabama state trooper force is comprised of Negroes." Under Johnson's strict edict, the number of black troopers increased from none to 20 percent within a decade, and by 1992 Alabama's police force was the most integrated in the country. The case was a graphic illustration of the remarkable progress that strong affirmative action remedies could bring about.[46]

Other civil rights organizations also continued to perform important work. Again, bodies that did not depend heavily on direct action protest carried on in much the same fashion as they always had, monitoring the state of black America and pressing federal agencies to enforce equal rights laws. Set up by the overlooked 1957 Civil Rights Act, the U.S. Commission on Civil Rights continued to issue regular reports that graphically reminded white Americans that racism had not been eliminated by equal rights legislation. In December 1972, for example, a thorough commission study outlined how black Americans were continuing their "search" for equal education. Although the commission's reports were well publicized, the federal body lacked enforcement powers and politicians frequently ignored its recommendations.[47]

The National Urban League, a historic civil rights group that eschewed street protests, also continued to lobby for black interests. Through the 1970s, the league closely monitored the effects of the economic downturn upon African Americans, refuting notions of civil rights progress by documenting rising levels of black poverty.[48] The group's reports were influential, especially as league leaders had cultivated close links with power brokers in Washington. By the late 1970s, civil rights organizations had united behind a program of full employment, pressing the Carter administration to act. As Carter aide Jack Watson informed the president in September 1977, "Clearly, reducing Black unemployment is the *highest priority* for the Black interest groups." The pressure eventually helped to secure the passage of the Humphrey-Hawkins Full Employment Act in 1978, although only in a watered down form.[49]

Some of the most effective efforts to tackle black economic inequality came from Jesse Jackson, the former SCLC staffer who set up Operation PUSH (People United to Save Humanity) in 1971. By the end of the 1970s, PUSH had over seventy chapters in both the northern and southern states. PUSH's projects had a strong economic focus, with Jackson often threatening boycotts against firms if they did not do more to hire and promote African Americans. The energetic leader negotiated landmark agreements with major corporations such as General Motors, Coca-Cola, Burger King, and Anheuser-Busch. Under the Coca-Cola accord, the soft drink giant agreed to spend $14 million with minority vendors, a goal it later surpassed. By the early 1980s, Jackson's success in PUSH had helped him to launch a national political career.[50]

Like Jackson, who had been with King when he was killed, many veterans of the civil rights movement continued their careers in a variety of different organizations. In 1970 former SNCC chair John Lewis became director of the SRC's Voter Education Project and carried on a massive campaign to register black voters. Other movement warhorses, including Fannie Lou Hamer and Julian Bond, helped him. Like Lewis, who later entered Congress, black activists such as Andrew Young, Walter Fountroy, Marion Barry, and Charles Evers moved successfully into politics. Many African Americans indeed had hopes that political power would lead to greater economic power, hopes that were often dashed.[51] Bayard Rustin, who had worked closely with King and had been one of the principal organizers of the 1963 March on Washington, later became director of the A. Philip Randolph Institute, an AFL-CIO–sponsored body that promotes a racially progressive agenda. During Rustin's presidency, the institute concentrated particular attention on registering blacks to vote and lobbying for the interests of the two million African Americans that belonged to trade unions. By 1974 the institute had 110 chapters in thirty-five states, and during the 1976 presidential election, when the black vote swung behind Jimmy Carter, it took credit for registering close to one million African Americans.[52]

In the decade after Selma, African Americans continued to fight for their rights, and their efforts increasingly focused on economic issues. It is vital for us to learn more about the ongoing black struggle, especially as fresh scholarship has highlighted that a great deal of social activism occurred after 1965. In recent years, work on the black power movement has documented "an African American . . . political renaissance" in the 1970s, with advocates of black political power demanding urban reform.[53] Outside of the South, new studies of the civil rights struggle by Hugh Davis Graham, Herbert Hill, and Paul Moreno have shown that the major issues revolved around equal employment opportunity. These books, moreover, do not end at 1965.[54] Work on the gay rights and women's movements has also documented that these struggles were at their peak in the 1970s and were inspired by the civil rights movement's example. Organized to commemorate the fiftieth anniversary of women's suffrage, the Women's Strike for Equality was arguably the largest women's rights demonstration ever. The 1970s also saw the passage of feminist landmarks such as the Equal Rights Amendment and *Roe v. Wade*, while small "consciousness-raising" groups sprang up from coast to coast. Women's historian Sara M. Evans indeed estimates that over three hundred nationally reported feminist events took place in 1975. Inspired by black militancy, Native Americans and Latinos also demanded better treatment after the mid-1960s.[55]

In the civil rights context, significant marches and conflicts also took place that deserve recognition. In these years, however, whites frequently argued that racial issues were no longer relevant, because equal rights had been assured by federal legislation. Whites also tended to emphasize the considerable progress that southerners had made to eradicate racism. As early as 1971, Alabama journalist H. Brandt Ayers proclaimed a "postracial South," while writer Willie Morris asserted that the region could offer "more than a few crucial lessons to other Americans." Some felt that the civil rights movement was "over" because legislation now guaranteed black equality.[56]

Black leaders dismissed the idea that the civil rights issue was resolved, stressing that the struggle for equality would always be an ongoing one. In a series of speeches, Floyd McKissick emphasized the "failures of the civil rights movement." Blacks were still "at the bottom of the economic ladder in this country," and "final emancipation" could only come with greater economic power.[57] Around the same time, Coretta Scott King asserted that rather than ending, the civil rights struggle had entered a "new stage." These differing perceptions confirm that race was continuing to divide Americans long after 1965.[58]

As historians have recognized, the civil rights movement was remarkably successful, as within a decade it was able to overthrow a system of legal segregation that had existed since the late nineteenth century. While it is important to recognize the magnitude of this achievement, it is equally vital to understand that the struggle the movement ignited was an ongoing one. Black activism in the post-King years reminds us that a great deal of racial injustice remained to be addressed. Historian William H. Chafe, who has praised the civil rights struggle as "the most significant social movement in all of American history," has also acknowledged that it left largely untouched "profound problems" of "institutional racism, unemployment [and] absence of capital," all problems that defied "easy solutions."[59]

Between 1955 and 1965, civil rights leaders chose to concentrate on gaining individual rights such as voting and equal access to public facilities. Once these rights had been guaranteed in law, it was natural that African Americans should fight for economic equality, especially as many realized that the right to eat at restaurants or ride buses meant little if blacks did not have the resources to take advantage of their new opportunities. As Louisiana civil rights activist David Johnson put it, "if you've got the dollar you can go where you want to." The move away from nonviolence was also a natural outgrowth of earlier struggles, especially as national groups that had promoted the tactic were losing influence. Rather than ending, the civil rights struggle took on new forms. With new sources becoming available, scholars can now start to write a complete history of the ongoing, long, and torturous struggle for racial justice in the United States. The essays that follow utilize these sources to provide insight into the continuing struggle for black equality in the southern states.[60]

2

"They didn't want you around them"

The Battle to Integrate Southern Industry in the Post-1965 Era

In 1965 Gladys Trawick started work as the first African American machine operator at a textile mill in rural Alabama. Soft-spoken but determined, the young high school graduate was part of a group of four women selected by company officials to be the first black production workers. Over thirty years later, Trawick clearly recalled the tension of her first day. "It was weird," she related, "walking in there with everybody looking at you and everybody whispering. People would hear things in the community that was said about the four of us that would make our parents afraid." Despite threats of violence from local whites, Trawick was committed to fulfilling her role as a black pioneer. "I felt that the community was depending on me," she explained, "and I had to, because a lot of them . . . would come to me and ask me would I be considered as one of the first; a lot of the black community, they just thought I could do it."[1]

Trawick's story is representative of a broader process that was taking place across the piedmont South in the mid-1960s. Before then, the textile industry had employed only whites in production positions.[2] Textile work, as Michelle Brattain has argued recently, was racialized, with the bulk of jobs reserved for whites.[3] This situation only began to be changed after 1965 as African Americans entered production jobs in large numbers for the first time. Still, many whites resisted the influx of African American women like Trawick, because they had grown up in a segregated society and wanted to keep the workplace "white." Both workers and managers also worried that if black women secured textile jobs, they would no longer be willing to work in private houses. In *Hicks v. Cannon Mills*, for example, a Title VII case filed in 1970, one of the main complaints was that "Negro females employed as housemaids may be refused employment on that account."[4]

Trawick's story also highlights how the fight to integrate the South's largest industry only started in 1965, after the Civil Rights Act had been signed into law. Over the next decade, African American workers had to battle hard to make the mandate of the law a reality. Across Dixie, "colored" workers were restricted to menial, heavy jobs in industrial plants. In 1962 NAACP labor secretary Herbert Hill testified that employment discrimination in the South was the worst in the entire United States. "I realize," he declared, "that civil rights represent the great unresolved social problem of the whole American society, but there can be no doubt that in the Southern States there currently exists the most extreme, rigid, and systematic pattern of employment discrimination to be found anywhere in the United States." In the same year, civil rights leader B. Tartt Bell also told a congressional hearing about the severity of employment discrimination that still prevailed in Dixie: "In industry after industry and company after company, in town after town, across the Southeast, there is the pattern of vicious discrimination on the basis of race and religion."[5]

In the early 1960s, as blacks engaged in civil rights protests across the region, the South's system of employment discrimination remained fully intact. The Southern Regional Council (SRC), which conducted case studies of employment patterns in the region in 1961–62, concluded that African Americans did not face a level playing field. "The evidence strongly indicates," concluded the civil rights group, "that discrimination in employment against Negroes is practiced in a wholesale manner throughout the entire South."[6] The SRC found that this situation was the result of many factors, especially the unequal provision of vocational training and resistance to change from employers, trade unions, and state employment agencies. Companies and unions tended to blame one another for the persistence of segregation, and both claimed that they were merely conforming to local customs.[7]

The costs of employment discrimination were considerable, dragging down white wages and contributing to black out-migration from the region. In Chattanooga, where the SRC carried out one of its case studies, poor job opportunities helped to ensure that up to 65 percent of black high school graduates quickly left the city to live elsewhere. "How much longer," pondered the SRC, "can Chattanooga afford to sustain and support a policy that fosters youth migration and forces those who stay at home to accept a permanent rung at the bottom of the employment ladder?" By the early 1960s, a similar mood of frustration was felt by African Americans across the region.[8]

Several federal initiatives were important in integrating southern industries. Executive orders 10925 (1961) and 11246 (1965) began the process by prohibiting discrimination by federal contractors. As only a minority of firms held these contracts, however, it was the passage of the Civil Rights Act in 1964 that was much more significant. Title VII of the act, which became effective on July 2, 1965, outlawed discrimination in employment, making it an unlawful practice "to fail or refuse to hire or to discharge any individual, or otherwise to discriminate against any individual with respect to his compensation, terms, conditions, or privileges of employment, because of such individual's race, color, religion, sex, or national origin." The act created the Equal Employment Opportunity Commission (EEOC) to enforce compliance. The new agency was authorized to solve job discrimination complaints through "conference, conciliation, and persuasion." If the commission failed to achieve voluntary compliance within sixty days, however, it was required to notify the complainant that they were permitted, within the next thirty days, to bring civil action. While the sheer number of complaints soon overwhelmed the fledgling agency, the law did offer aggrieved workers a constructive mechanism that they could use to tackle racial discrimination.[9]

That most of the important Title VII cases did not occur until the late 1960s and early 1970s was partly a reflection of the political context. The Civil Rights Act was originally signed during Johnson's presidency, but after 1968 President Nixon was centrally involved in winning congressional backing to give the EEOC authority to advance a strong affirmative action agenda. Although often appealing to a "silent majority" that was largely opposed to civil rights, Nixon also fostered initiatives to strengthen blacks' economic position. While the Republican leader certainly hoped to increase strife between blacks and organized labor, he was also genuinely interested in trying to help talented individuals rise to the top.[10]

Title VII litigation also emerged as the main mechanism for integrating southern industry after the Supreme Court decided in the crucial 1971 *Griggs v. Duke Power* case to give full support to the EEOC's affirmative action program. In *Griggs* the Supreme Court applied Title VII to invalidate general intelligence tests and other criteria for employment—unless dictated by business necessity—that disproportionately excluded blacks. The decision struck down many practices that were widely used by major southern employers, such as word-of-mouth recruiting and allowing relatives of current employees to be given preference in hiring. *Griggs* emboldened the lawyers from the NAACP Legal Defense Fund, who were using Title VII to redress fundamental patterns of job discrimination. Defense fund attorneys represented the plaintiffs in most cases, and they concentrated particular attention on important southern industries such as steel, textiles, and paper. By 1971 the LDF had brought more than 150 Title VII cases in U.S. district courts, almost all of them in the South.[11]

Blacks concentrated much of their effort on the battle to integrate the textile and paper industries, and both sectors witnessed a large amount of Title VII litigation in the two decades after 1965. The South's biggest employer, the textile industry was an obvious target. By the 1960s and 1970s, the American textile industry employed between eight hundred thousand and one million workers, over 80 percent of them in the southern states. The industry dominated the economy of the Carolinas, where it accounted for 45 percent of all manufacturing jobs in 1966. Textile jobs were also easily learned, making the industry particularly attractive to civil rights lawyers who were looking to improve black job opportunities. For these reasons, textiles became what Nancy MacLean has termed the "premier site" of the civil rights movement's jobs campaign in the South.[12]

The paper industry was smaller than textiles, yet it still played an important role in the region's economy in the civil rights era. Employing around seven hundred thousand people, the paper industry ranked on a par with steel. By the 1960s, the South had become the leading paper-making region in the United States, accounting for around one-half of national production. The paper companies began moving south on a large scale in the 1930s, a shift aided by the shorter growing time required for southern pine trees to reach maturity. As the industry offered some of the highest wages available in the region, it was crucial to the broader struggle for black economic equality. The paper industry was also a major employer in the rural South, where black poverty remained particularly prevalent.[13]

There were several major differences between the two industries, and these influenced the character of Title VII litigation. The textile industry was low-paying and predominantly non-union, whereas the paper industry offered some of the highest manufacturing wages in the region and was over 90 percent unionized. These differences reflected the fact that the industries had very different economic structures, with the paper industry being far more capital-intensive. As a result, employers feared costly labor stoppages and often recognized unions in the hope of securing labor peace. The textile mills also employed large numbers of women but, in the paper plants, where many jobs required physical strength, the work force was overwhelmingly male. In the 1960s, women made up close to half the southern textile work force, but in the paper factories they only worked in clerical jobs or in a very small range of production positions.[14]

Paper mills also contained more black workers than textile plants. African Americans had historically been excluded from the southern textile industry, which developed in the southern piedmont by drawing on white labor. The desire to tie blacks to agricultural labor, and the taboo against bringing black men into association with white women, contributed to the textile industry's exclusion of blacks. In 1940 only 2.1 percent of textile workers were black, and they were restricted to a small number of non-production positions. The industry became characterized by its reliance on white labor; as the pathbreaking *Like a Family* study explains, "The most striking feature of the labor system in southern mills was the exclusion of blacks from 'production jobs.'"[15]

In the paper industry, by contrast, there was a long tradition of black employment that stretched back to when the first mills were built in the region. Still, opportunities for blacks were strictly circumscribed. African Americans were only hired for heavy, laboring jobs, mainly in the wood yard where raw lumber had to be moved around by hand. Blacks were locked into these jobs by separate lines of progression and segregated local unions. The physical nature of these jobs meant that they were assigned to black men, who were seen by whites as being naturally suited to such work. Citing blacks' lack of educational opportunities, one executive asserted in 1971 that they were "not good prospects for skilled jobs."[16]

In the paper industry, the higher rate of unionization had an important impact on the civil rights struggle, because black activists had to fight unions as well as employers. Unions such as the International Brotherhood of Pulp, Sulphite, and Paper Mill Workers (IBPSPMW) were largely beholden to the interests of the white majority and did little to challenge the status quo. The companies and white unions acted together to set up segregated unions and lines of progression. Black lines of progression always covered only a small number of undesirable jobs, and transfer into the white lines of progression was prevented by a number of factors, including discriminatory seniority provisions.[17] Keeping the best jobs for their members, white unions repeatedly refused to merge the lines of progression. The situation was frustrating for black union leaders such as Alphonse Williams, a short, determined man who worked at International Paper Company (IP) in Mobile between 1942 and 1987. "Our line of progression," he reflected shortly before his death, "was like a short ladder up the side of a tall building. If you stayed on that ladder, it would never get you to the top jobs because you see the top jobs was represented, ranked into the jurisdictions of the other locals, and of course they never consented to merge the lines of progression."[18]

As companies and unions had colluded to restrict black opportunities, activists in the paper industry ended up suing both parties. In the textile plants, however, unions were rarely present and plaintiffs consequently targeted their efforts on companies. In some cases, the Textile Workers Union of America

(TWUA), which was trying to organize in the region, even expressed support for black workers' claims because it reasoned that African Americans were more likely to join labor unions. In 1970 TWUA organizing director Paul Swaity wrote president William Pollock describing how the "climate" for organizing southern textile workers had improved due to the entry of black workers who had been radicalized by the civil rights movement. The TWUA began to employ black organizers, and it recruited considerable support from African American employees, who usually had more grievances than whites.[19]

On the ground, however, majority-white TWUA local unions also opposed civil rights. Where textile plants had been organized for some time, unions usually represented the interests of the white majority. Bruce Raynor, a textile union leader who started working in the TWUA's education department in 1973, admitted in the 1990s that many grassroots union officials had resisted black civil rights. "The textile union in 1973 in the South," he reflected, "was a heavily white-led union, and the locals were led by whites, even though by that time there were lots of blacks in the plants." In some cases, such as *Ellison v. Rock Hill Printing and Finishing Company*, both the union and company were sued, just as they were in most paper plants.[20]

Overall, however, the textile unions responded more favorably to black demands than their counterparts in the paper industry. In a series of influential publications, former NAACP labor director Herbert Hill charged that organized labor reacted to Title VII with "ambivalence, resistance, and finally opposition." Validating Hill's criticisms, unions in the paper industry were certainly slow to embrace Title VII. As the Port St. Joe and St. Marys essays highlight, however, Title VII litigation did push the unions to belatedly embrace change, and their reaction to black demands was more nuanced than Hill's strident critique allows for.[21]

On the surface, black workers made a lot of progress in both industries after 1965, especially in textiles. In 1960 only 4.5 percent of American textile workers were black, but by 1978 African Americans held one-fourth of all operative positions. Pushed along by the pressures of federal legislation and a labor shortage, the industry made significant strides in integrating its workforce. The pace of change was also accelerated because of pressure from African Americans, who filed many lawsuits to open up the industry. In addition, some savvy employers soon grasped that they could use the introduction of blacks to lower wage rates, no small consideration in a labor-intensive industry.[22]

In the paper industry, the pace of black entry was not as rapid. As most jobs paid well, whites were not leaving en masse, and blacks faced a harder struggle to gain even entry-level posts. The chief battle for blacks, however, was to secure high-paying jobs rather than to get into the industry, and whites that were used to monopolizing the best positions were slow to accept the need for change. Over the 1960s and 1970s, the numbers of African Americans working in the industry increased slowly. By the late 1990s, around a quarter of the southern paper work force was African American, up from 15 percent in 1965.[23]

In both industries, however, the statistics conceal the resistance that blacks faced on the ground. Although complex in nature, white opposition was motivated by two different factors. In some cases, whites feared direct economic competition from blacks, fears that were greatest when blacks were promoted into higher-paying "white" positions. In other cases, whites who had grown up in the Jim Crow South simply desired to remain socially separate from African Americans. A native of Alabama who had worked in the textile plants, black union representative Sammy Glover summed up the situation well. "I think that there was this fear of competition," he stated in the 1990s, "that the black worker would take their job from them, and then there was this attitude that they were . . . superior to the black worker, and they just, they didn't want to work with them. They didn't want to share a restroom facility with them, they didn't want to share a water-fountain with them. . . . I think it was a fear of competition and just a superiority complex."[24]

Across the textile South, resistance was especially notable when social facilities were integrated. While company officials often tried to hide problems, many of the first African American workers had retained vivid memories of whites who bitterly resented the desegregation of bathrooms and water fountains. At Columbus Towel Mill in Columbus, Georgia, African American employee Jacob Little recalled that when the water fountains and bathrooms were integrated in 1966, there was a widespread boycott of facilities by whites. "When they first started, first integrating it right after I got there," he related, "the white people they quit drinking water out of the water-fountain, they quit changing clothes in the bathrooms because we were changing clothes with them. For a long time that went on. . . . A lot of them quit using the facilities, you know." Across the South, contemporary investigators dutifully recorded that similar problems were occurring. At the West Point Pepperell plants in the Chattahoochee Valley area of Georgia and Alabama, the company reported in 1969 that their "greatest difficulties have been in integrating restrooms." In the same year, whites at a Du Pont plant were boycotting the integrated cafeteria.[25]

In some textile plants, managers tried to pacify whites by providing paper seats and cups in the restrooms. Fearing racial violence, some supervisors also allowed facilities to remain segregated. In *Adams v. Dan River Mills,* filed in 1969, black worker Henry Wilson testified that in his department little had changed. "They taken the sign down," he acknowledged. "Still we go in like it was at first. Colored go on their side. White go the other side." In *Seibles v. Cone Mills,* a case brought against one of the largest southern textile companies, the court even found that company officials had "maintained segregated locker, toilet and shower facilities until 1973."[26]

In paper mills, white resistance to integrated facilities was even stronger; in May 1967, for example, Office of Federal Contract Compliance (OFCC) director Edward C. Sylvester told the main employer organization in the industry that ongoing segregation of "eating and sanitary facilities" was one of the most frequent problems his agency had encountered in southern mills.[27] In the all-male environment of the paper mills, many whites threatened their black counterparts if they dared to use "white" facilities. Following the passage of the Civil Rights Act, blacks at Crown-Zellerbach's mills in Louisiana remained afraid to venture into the "white" areas. Although restrooms had been integrated by having a door cut into the partition between them, blacks would not go through, believing that "the first black head that goes through it won't come back." At Crown, random attacks took place upon blacks when they did try to use "white" facilities. Disgruntled whites even attempted to drop metal weights on blacks who dared to use "white" bathrooms.[28]

Under pressure from federal agencies, most paper mills did integrate their facilities in the late 1960s, but whites often responded by refusing to use them. At International Paper Company in Mobile, a group of black workers bravely sat down in the "white" side of the cafeteria, causing whites to launch a long-lasting boycott. In a mill where African Americans made up no more than a quarter of the work force, the action was so damaging that company officials were forced to close the cafeteria. When the mill eventually shut down over thirty years later, the cafeteria was still closed.[29] In 1966 a similar boycott occurred at neighboring Scott Paper Company, although after fifteen months some whites started coming back. During this time, noted the company's manager of administrative services, Scott ran the cafeteria at a "very large economic loss."[30] At Crown-Zellerbach, where federal officials demanded that the company do more to integrate facilities, some whites even responded to the integration of the mill's bathroom by renting a building across the street and constructing shower and locker facilities there. The amenities were run as an all-white private club, with members paying six dollars a month to use them. Mervin Taylor, who was involved in establishing the club, recalled that most whites never used the mill facilities again: "We give that bathroom to the blacks, whites never did go back in there." As black worker David Johnson confirmed, "We moved in, they moved out."[31]

In both industries, white resistance to the integration of facilities coexisted with fears about economic competition. White opposition was most intense when African Americans were hired into non-traditional positions. In textiles there was vehement opposition to blacks becoming weavers, one of the highest-paying production jobs. In *Foster v. Fieldcrest*, filed in 1977, plaintiff Robert H. Foster was the first and only black weaver at a mill in Eden, North Carolina. In a detailed letter to the EEOC, Foster related how "the supervisors, forman [*sic*] and fixers were determined to prevent me from earning top pay as a qualified weaver. Because of their ingrained prejudices they acted as if I should accept the lower-paying, physically exhausting job of cloth doffer." Foster claimed that his coworkers and supervisor harassed him, tampering with his machine in order to ensure that he was fired for low production. In 1974 a black weaver at a Cone Mills plant also filed a Title VII lawsuit after confronting similar problems.[32]

Across the textile South, African Americans who were hired into well-paying production positions in the 1960s and 1970s remembered that whites refused to train them. Willie Long, who was hired in 1972 at the Columbus, Georgia, Eagle and Phenix Mill, related that blacks were only being placed in the low-paying jobs at the time, and most whites wanted to keep it that way. "They really didn't want to show you anything about the job," he explained, "because that's the way you had to get your experience. . . . They didn't want you around them." Supervisors and white workers, he added, "just wanted to make sure that the blacks stayed on the lower wage jobs."[33] Supervisors often supported white employees as they tried to restrict black progress into the better jobs. At Bloomsburg Mills in Abbeville, South Carolina, Joann W. Calhoun managed to secure a production position in the early 1970s but complained that she had to work with "old white ladies" who harassed her. One night one of the women "threw a Bobbin and tried to hit me and she called me a damn nigger. So I told my supervisor so he told me if I couldn't get along with people he would fire me." Like many other workers, Calhoun soon came to the conclusion that she would have to file a lawsuit in order to obtain fairer conditions.[34]

Blacks who were placed in white jobs had to endure verbal abuse, threats, and isolation. White employee Fletcher Beck candidly recalled that his coworkers were reluctant to train blacks at Rock Hill Printing and Finishing Company in Rock Hill, South Carolina, where blacks filed a suit in 1972 to address their complaints. "They [blacks] come on the machines," he related, "and they wanted us to teach them, and a lot of the white men wouldn't tell them what to do and show them what to do. They resented the fact that they had put the black guys out on the production jobs. . . . They would cuss about it. . . . They would use the term 'nigger.'" African American textile worker James Johnson charged that it took many years before attitudes started to change. "The better jobs," he insisted, "really didn't come along until the very late seventies. . . . There was a great deal of resentment on behalf of whites when this began to develop. . . . They didn't accept it at all, really, they were very bitter. They made racial slurs toward the black workers, things of that nature."[35] On a few occasions, the introduction of blacks even caused whites to walk out, although most disgruntled employees stayed on the job and instead tried to limit black advancement as much as they could.[36]

White opposition played a role in slowing the pace of black advancement, especially as many African Americans were afraid to try for higher-paying positions or reasoned that it was simply not worth the effort involved. Data from across the textile industry confirms that although blacks were being hired in greater numbers after 1965, they were still much more likely to toil in lower-paying positions. In April 1973, white men at Dan River Mills, one of the biggest textile firms, made an average of $2.77 an hour, but black males took home just $2.36. Half of all white men at the sprawling mill complex made more than $2.80 an hour compared to just 6.2 percent of their African American counterparts. At J. P. Stevens the situation was similar; in December 1973, black men at the textile giant made $2.71, but whites earned $3.01.[37]

In the textile plants, whites were particularly opposed to blacks securing supervisory positions. Many whites felt that integration was happening too fast, and they could not accommodate themselves to having to take orders from blacks. Elboyd Deal, a white man who worked at Cannon Mills between 1961 and 1991, admitted that whites struggled to adjust to changing racial roles. "I hate to say it, but they [blacks] were even kept lower than the white people's wages," he reflected in 1996. "We were slow to really accept that black people could work their way up to supervision and stuff like that, and I know a lot of people that resented a black man being over them." Black worker Joe Gaines, another veteran of the textile industry's integration battles, had similar memories. "I have seen some more or less concerted activity," reflected the native of Sylvester, Georgia, "on behalf of the whites when they felt like a black was getting into a position that meant he or she had authority to tell them what to do. They would sort of form their little sit-in group, they would make sure they would go to the top man, to the supervisor, or manager, and just lay it on the line; it's okay to have this guy in a position but don't put him in a position where he's going to start telling us how to do our jobs and things like that. . . . That happened on many occasions."[38]

Sherrill v. J. P. Stevens, a major Title VII case brought in 1973 by a group of plaintiffs at a plant in Stanley, North Carolina, illustrates the problems that blacks faced in securing supervisory positions. The main issue in the case was the harassment of A. C. Sherrill, an outspoken and gifted man who was the highest-paid African American in the plant. After Sherrill asked for a supervisor's job in 1971 (the company refused), white workers responded by launching a campaign of harassment against him. They placed trash in his car, subjected him to verbal abuse, and threatened him with a knife. Whites also told Sherrill that if he were given the supervisor's job they would all leave. In the end, Sherrill had to resort to litigation to improve opportunities for blacks at the Gaston County mill.[39]

In the paper industry, federal agencies pushed for more integration but confronted opposition from white workers, union leaders, and managers. Again, the process of desegregation only started after 1965, as government officials began to prod firms to adhere to Title VII. In 1968 the U.S. Justice Department initiated a landmark case when it sued Crown-Zellerbach, a major paper employer based in Bogalusa, Louisiana. The United Papermakers and Paperworkers, which represented most Crown workers, were co-defendants in the case. In its March 1968 decision in *United States v. Local 189, United Papermakers and Paperworkers*, which the Fifth Circuit Court of Appeals upheld sixteen months later, the District Court for the Eastern District of Louisiana laid down the principles that were to be the basis of integration in the southern paper mills. It ruled that a neutral seniority system could be illegal if blacks had historically been restricted to less desirable jobs and if their ability to rectify their status was impeded by the seniority system. It designated an "affected class" of black workers who were those hired prior to January 16, 1966, the date when all jobs had been theoretically opened to blacks at Crown. The court ruled that the members of the affected class should be allowed to use their mill, rather than job, seniority in matters of promotion, demotion, and layoff. This decision meant that the court accepted that members of the affected class could be promoted to their "rightful place" in the seniority hierarchy, or the place where they would have been had they not been discriminated against. In simple terms, blacks who had been trapped in poorly paid, segregated jobs could now transfer to "white" jobs without forfeiting their seniority rights.[40]

In an industry that was heavily unionized, this decision proved to be a watershed. Led by the OFCC, federal agencies were successful in applying the principles of *Local 189* across the South. They started their efforts by targeting the largest company in the industry. Because of its sheer size, International Paper Company had traditionally acted as a pattern-setter, and government officials were aware that other paper companies would likely match any agreement they could hammer out with IP. In August 1968, OFCC chiefs met with IP executives and the unions in Jackson, Mississippi, devising an agreement known as the Jackson Memorandum. A complex document, in essence the memorandum applied the principles of *Local 189* across International Paper's twelve southern mills, giving African Americans much-improved promotion rights.[41]

Feeling that federal officials were moving too fast, the memorandum was not popular with most whites. Throughout the Jackson conference, the OFCC's representatives took a strong stance, threatening to take away lucrative federal contracts if managers and unions did not implement the desired changes.[42] This uncompromising position paid off, as both sides accepted the federal government's proposals with few modifications. Although many of their members disliked the memorandum, union leaders felt that they could not oppose the agreement. "If we didn't settle it ourselves," commented white union leader Frank Bragg, "the feds was going to settle it for us."[43]

As the Jackson Memorandum applied to all IP's southern mills, implementing it would be no easy task. The facilities were scattered right across the region, and the company's management structure was decentralized. In fact, IP's records reveal that the number of black workers who were promoted under the memorandum was very limited. On September 1, 1972, out of 218 workers in the Mobile mill who were eligible to transfer, the vast majority (153) had refused. Of the 65 who had not declined, only 16 were still working in their new posts.[44] The situation was little better at other mills; in a Pine Bluff, Arkansas, mill employing 1,500 workers, only 8 blacks held positions in formerly white jobs by November 1971. As the EEOC concluded in 1978, the Jackson Memorandum clearly "fell far short of its intended goal."[45]

So what went wrong? Again, the main problem was that disgruntled whites discouraged blacks from transferring and harassed those who did move. Horace Gill, a determined African American who worked at IP between 1957 and 1994, explained that experienced black workers declined to transfer because they were scared of the white reaction. "When they integrated the jobs," he clearly recalled, "the older blacks, and it was pitiful, the older blacks that didn't have much education and was sort of shy, they harassed them. So I would say ninety-five percent of them signed off on the bottom jobs because they were afraid to move up because they would be harassed. For example, if they trained one on a job, you had to be trained by a white; they would show you totally different from what the jobs supposed to be. . . . They would totally harass you. . . . They weren't shown proper training." Bearing out Gill's statements, in 1971 blacks at the Mobile Mill filed *Stevenson v. International Paper Company*, a title VII case in which they claimed that they had been "harassed in attempting to exercise their rights" under the Jackson Memorandum. In 1975 the Fifth Circuit Court of Appeals largely supported the plaintiffs' case, asserting that while the memorandum had provided "some opportunity" for blacks to advance to their "rightful place," it was also fraught with "inadequacies."[46] At Pine Bluff, blacks also returned to court with similar complaints and again won a ruling that strengthened the provisions of the memorandum.[47]

Despite these legal victories, black workers at IP continued to be harassed by whites. The experience of blacks at the largest company in the paper industry reveals much about the tortured process of job integration in the South. Hired at IP-Mobile in the summer of 1977, military veteran Arthur Williams encountered resistance when he secured a job on the paper machine. Williams saw himself as part of a younger generation of African Americans who were no longer willing to accept second-class treatment. "When I first started out there, I wanted to be the best," he recalled proudly in 2004. "But then after a while you saw all this prejudice and stuff like that, it kind of put you in a different mood, a defensive mood. When you want to learn something, you open your mind up to people, but if you opened your mind up, they started playing tricks on you. So after a while you get in that defensive mode because you know they tell you something when they know it ain't right. So I had to go through all of that." Williams felt that whites "really didn't want us there on the machines. . . . They didn't want to really train us on the job. I learned most of my stuff looking over people's shoulders. . . . They didn't want you to have the knowledge."[48]

Other blacks who were hired at IP in the 1970s had similar experiences. Starting out in 1973, strongly built Grover Stewart succeeded in holding down a paper machine job for many years, but it was no easy task. "There was some prejudice problems there," he recalled matter-of-factly. "I had a guy that called me a Nigger one time. . . . When I first got on the paper machine, they tried to run me back. . . . But see I was young and strong, and all that work they put on me, I could handle it. . . . When I got up there (the paper machine), they really got their heads together; run that black guy back where I came from. I stood my ground."[49]

Not all the problems arising from the Jackson Memorandum can be blamed on whites. Often poorly educated, many of the older African American employees were not equipped to cope with skilled operating jobs. Williams himself acknowledged that some of the senior black workers, hired in an era when only menial jobs were available, "didn't have the skills to move up." Some were close to retirement and chose to see out their time in "black" jobs rather than try to transfer. With a few exceptions, however, most whites did nothing to encourage blacks to seek promotion, ensuring that only the most determined and able would even try for a transfer. Problems continued into the twenty-first century. "There's still that mentality," commented another former IP worker in 2004, "especially with the older generation out there, I guess that kind of separate type thing."[50]

The experience of the black IP workers was far from unique. Across the southern paper industry whites bitterly fought black advancement, feeling that the concept of the "rightful place" was robbing them of their own entitlement to hold high-paying jobs. At Union Camp in Savannah, another important paper producer, whites were upset when the company applied *Local 189* and gave blacks much stronger promotional rights. White worker Joe McCullough recalled that most of his friends viewed this granting of mill seniority to blacks as "reverse discrimination." The issue soon dominated union meetings, where McCullough faithfully took the minutes for over thirty years. "I used to go to the first couple of meetings where we had membership meetings explaining the affirmative action program," related McCullough. "They thought it was the end of the world, they did."[51] The reaction was typical. As was the case in the textile industry, fierce battles raged in the plants as whites strove to limit black advancement. In *Gilley v. Hudson Pulp and Paper Company* (1976), black workers at a Florida mill complained that they were persecuted when they tried to secure white jobs. As plaintiff George B. Williams commented, "They didn't want a black man to operate nothing out there, nothing." Bearing this out, lead plaintiff Edward Gilley painfully recounted how he bowed to white opposition and agreed to surrender his crane operator position. "I figured the Lord blessed me to go along as far as I did," he rationalized in 1980, "so I was going to go back. . . . I . . . told the company that I would go back and be the crane helper."[52]

Even in the 1980s and 1990s, black paper workers had to be extraordinarily determined and patient in order to secure lucrative positions. As Louisiana paper worker Bubba McCall commented, blacks could only succeed if they were "super-operators."[53] Across the region whites were strongly opposed to blacks becoming millwrights, skilled mechanics who could command high salaries.

At Mobile Paperboard, another Gulf Coast mill, Willie Ford encountered vicious opposition when he became the first black millwright in the mid-1970s. "The problem I had," he recalled vividly, "they didn't really want me to be a millwright because I was the only black. I had a hard time with them white folks over there, sure did. . . . I couldn't do nothing right. . . . Them fellas rode my back until I left there. . . . I tell you what, I felt so scared I thought some of them would come to my house and try to kill me. That's the kind of way I felt, because they didn't want me to have the job." Although he stayed in his new post for several years, Ford retired early because of the hostility he encountered at the plant, and his experiences haunted him even then. His story was typical in many respects. "Here in Mobile and Mississippi," recalled union representative Donald L. Langham, "different mills . . . we had problems. The white union members fought these decrees, or just resisted, strenuously resisted being forced to integrate."[54]

While whites fought to limit black advancement, they were unable to stop it completely. In both industries, class-action litigation was successful in achieving a number of important advances, including forcing companies to hire more African American women. In the paper industry the number of women workers remained small, but in textiles both black and white women were hired in large numbers after 1970.[55] Many cases were also settled by consent decrees that compelled companies to abolish discriminatory practices. In *United States v. Southern Weaving*, for example, the decree mandated that the company could not give preference to job applicants who had relatives or friends working at the plant. This was significant, because white employees had often been able to secure jobs for their family or acquaintances, especially in small communities.[56] On other occasions, simply the filing of EEOC charges pushed company officials to start hiring more African Americans into non-traditional jobs.[57]

In the paper mills, litigation was most important in breaking up discriminatory seniority systems. By the end of the 1970s, all of the major southern mills had adopted the main features of *Local 189*, either voluntarily or as the result of litigation. Mill seniority did allow many blacks to gradually move into higher-paying positions, and by the 1980s small numbers had become millwrights, mechanics, and even supervisors.

Black activists emphasized that they had had to struggle for decades before job opportunities improved significantly. In 1997 retired Union Camp worker George Sawyer reflected on his efforts to integrate Savannah's largest employer, which had included taking part in a major Title VII suit in the 1970s. The suit was necessary because many whites had initially fought the company's efforts to implement *Local 189*. "A lot of the young fellas that came behind us," he commented in his Savannah kitchen, "they don't realize how rough it was to get that road paved. And even now, even now in 1997, there's still some bumpy spots. It's not all smooth sailing. . . . What we have gained, we've fought for it. It wasn't anything handed to us on a silver platter."[58]

In the paper industry, lawsuits also pushed unions to abolish segregated locals, helping blacks to move into non-traditional posts. Again, however, the pace of change was slow, and it only began after the Civil Rights Act sounded the death knell for separate unions. In some cases change took many years; at Georgia Kraft Company in Rome, the black and white locals were only merged after a court order in 1972, and at Scott Paper Company the amalgamation was also delayed until the same year. While whites often opposed mergers, in some cases blacks also slowed proceedings by fighting for guaranteed representation within the joint unions. As an international union brief asserted in 1980, the efforts to combine racially separate locals had been "met by the resistance and even defiance of both black and white members."[59]

Since the 1980s, the economic decline of the textile and paper industries has limited blacks' ability to take advantage of their hard-won rights. As was the case in the steel and tobacco industries, the desegregation of textiles and paper occurred at a time of declining employment opportunities.[60] The pace of decline has been particularly rapid in the textile industry. Between 1994 and 2003, for example, the number of workers employed in textile manufacturing tumbled from 477,600 to 260,300. Hit hard by increasing competition from cheap imported goods, many of the companies that blacks had fought so hard to integrate ended up going out of business. By the opening years of the twenty-first century, the southern landscape was littered with empty and crumbling mill buildings.[61]

In the paper industry, employment levels have not fallen as fast, but firms have still cut labor as they seek to improve efficiency. Since the mid-1990s, a process of consolidation has also seen smaller companies bought out by the big players such as IP and Georgia Pacific. In 1995 the industry employed 639,000 people, but by 2004 the figure had slumped to 499,000. Paper mills, however, remain an important part of the southern economy, especially along the Gulf Coast.[62]

In a broader sense, the litigation that activists brought in these two industries has also helped all workers. The lawsuits broke up the region's system of employment segregation and ensured that today's young people enter a much fairer workplace. As Nancy MacLean has shown, a "veritable revolution" has transformed the American workplace into a much more diverse place than it was in the 1960s. Of course, racial discrimination still remains, and workers continue to bring suits that draw upon the case law established by the first generation of Title VII class actions. In late 2004, a Gallup poll found that 15 percent of all respondents said that they had been discriminated against at work during the past year. Four decades after the establishment of the EEOC, black and Asian workers were much more likely to complain about unequal treatment than whites were, and women had more grievances than men. On the same day that the poll was released, workers launched major Title VII suits against Best Buy and Auto Nation, carrying on the ongoing struggle for equal workplace rights.[63]

3

"Soberly, responsibly, never noisily"

The Southern Regional Council and the Struggle
for Equal Employment Opportunity

At the start of 1944, a new civil rights group was granted its charter in an Atlanta courtroom. Formed by more than two hundred liberal activists, the Southern Regional Council was a successor to the Commission on Interracial Cooperation, which had striven since 1919 to speak out against the worst forms of racial injustice in the former Confederate states. Like its predecessor, the SRC was an interracial organization that attempted to address the southern race problem. According to its founding document, the SRC's aim was "to attain, through research and action, the ideals and practices of equal opportunity for all peoples in the South." The SRC has fought to realize this goal for over sixty years. No civil rights group better illustrates the need to take a long view of the movement, as the SRC has used the same methods of action throughout its extensive existence. In many ways, the SRC became more prominent in the fight for racial justice after 1965 than it was in the heyday of the civil rights movement when its moderation and emphasis on research saw it overshadowed by groups that embraced more confrontational tactics.[1]

Lacking an organizational history, the SRC is one of the most neglected of the South's civil rights groups. Historians have been naturally drawn to organizations that led direct-action protests against segregation in the South.[2] In contrast, the SRC was a moderate body that generally sought to improve race relations through research and education. In 1955 SRC executive director George S. Mitchell summed up the group's method of operation: "We have carried along soberly, responsibly, never noisily; getting out to people all over the South the facts on health and housing and employment and farm ownership and educational opportunity." The Council did, however, also organize some innovative projects that secured concrete results, and its long contribution to the struggle for racial justice needs to be recognized.[3]

As an organization that consistently supported equal opportunity for all the South's citizens, the SRC struggled to change the racial order in the region. Despite its educational efforts, most whites resisted racial change until they were forced to accept it by federal law. At the same time, however, other civil rights groups also found it hard to secure immediate results. SNCC, whose efforts have been much studied, put a lot of emphasis into patient grassroots organizing that yielded few quick results. At the end of the 1960s, most of the NAACP's agenda, which included a federal ban on lynching and the abolition of all barriers to voting, remained unfulfilled. Even the SCLC, which was able to generate the national pressure that helped secure the passage of equal rights laws, encountered savage opposition at the local level and experienced its fair share of failures. For civil rights groups, victories were rarely easy or swift.[4]

The council's dual emphasis on research and action has been consistently reflected in its efforts to secure equal employment opportunity. Between the 1940s and the 1990s, SRC staff closely monitored southern working conditions and carried out a great deal of research into them, but they also launched projects to tackle employment discrimination. Most civil rights studies, however, have concentrated more on the fight to integrate public facilities or the struggle for black voting rights rather than the desegregation of the workplace. The period after the mid-1960s, when activists fought to break down entrenched patterns of job segregation that were outlawed by the 1964 Civil Rights Act, has been particularly overlooked. In this period, the council's interest in economic justice fused with that of blacks across the South.[5]

From its inception, the SRC showed a strong interest in fighting for equal employment. In the 1940s, southern blacks were restricted to working in a limited number of low-paying, menial jobs. They were strictly segregated from whites, who monopolized the better-paid positions. As a result, on average whites earned twice as much as blacks. Both employers and union leaders were reluctant to challenge the status quo, often claiming that white workers would strike if more blacks were hired or insisting that they were only following "local custom" in enforcing the color line.[6] In 1944 the original Durham Conference Statement, written by a group of black leaders instrumental in the founding of the council, noted that economic discrimination was a central part of the American race problem, particularly in the South. The statement called for greater job opportunities for African American workers and equal pay. While deploring those unions that discriminated against blacks, it also supported unionization as a way of achieving its aims. The response of white delegates, as expressed in the Atlanta Conference Statement, was more cautious, but it also supported equal pay for equal work. "If we cannot plan for a well-trained, well-employed, and prosperous Negro population, the economic future of the South is hopeless," they explained.[7]

In the context of the times, the SRC's endorsement of equal employment opportunity was significant. Prior to the 1960s, most southerners saw racial discrimination in employment as natural and were opposed to change. During World War II, the council sent field agents out across the South, and they carefully recorded resistance to change among managers in the textile industry, the region's largest employer. In 1941 the southern textile work force was 98 percent white, and the handful of black workers were restricted to menial, non-production jobs as service or janitorial staff. In the late nineteenth century, boosters had promoted the mills as the salvation of poor whites, and well into the twentieth century most southerners viewed textile work as a white domain. Executives also continued to claim that their white employees would strike or riot rather than work next to blacks. In the 1960s, as the passage of civil rights laws finally promised change, the SRC concentrated renewed efforts on a campaign to secure African Americans a greater share of southern textile jobs.[8]

The council's survey of the southern textile industry reflected its broader interest in securing greater job opportunities for southern blacks. At the end of World War II, SRC researchers produced "The Negro in Our Economy," a report which, like the textile survey, recorded that southern blacks had made some tentative employment gains during the worldwide conflict. "Fortunately, some of the changes brought about by the war have increased the economic opportunities of the Negro," noted the report. "As a result, large numbers of Negroes had their first chance to demonstrate abilities in the skilled and semi-skilled occupations of industry." After proudly documenting cases of blacks upgrading into non-traditional positions, the SRC noted that the South could reduce its poverty rates if it utilized both black and white labor. In reality, however, these hopes were not realized; most blacks hired during the war were laid off once the labor shortage had ended, and, as in the southern textile industry, the pre-war status quo was reinstated. "It is now clear," reported the Fair Employment Practices Commission in June 1946, "that Negro workers have lost large parts of their wartime employment gains and are finding that peacetime industry offers only the traditional openings of the years before 1940." The SRC was one of the few voices in the South that spoke out in favor of equal employment and tried to stop the revival of segregationist attitudes after the war.[9]

At the end of World War II, the SRC's interest in equal employment opportunity was also expressed through its Veterans Services Project. In the project, council staff investigated the employment possibilities for ex-military personnel in the South. Across the region, field agents examined the percentage of black and white veterans who were utilizing their rights under the 1944 GI Bill of Rights, which offered a range of potential benefits including loans for job training.[10] On their visits, they encountered considerable resistance from employers to training or hiring blacks in anything other than unskilled positions. In January 1946, agent Roscoe E. Lewis reported from Hampton, Virginia, that on-the-job training programs were "off to a good start—except for Negroes. . . . Many firms will offer such training to white boys, but not Negroes. Most, if not all, of the Negro men around here are in training as janitors or cooks."[11] Agents tried to ensure more equal opportunities for African American veterans, yet they found that company and union officials blamed each other for the absence of black trainees.[12]

Agents also reported that federal and state officials were failing to protect black access to the training benefits provided by the bill. Over the region as a whole, only 7.5 percent of veterans who received such training were black, even though African Americans comprised 33 percent of southern servicemen.[13] When representative Harry L. Wright visited the Veterans Administration in Mississippi, he found that staff were "suspicious" of him and were keen to avoid discussing racial issues. Much to Wright's anger, the Mississippi VA itself failed to employ any blacks in its staff positions. "The situation at the VA in Mississippi toward the fair employment of Negro personnel is plain rotten to the core," he fumed. "The only way Negroes will ever get anything that approaches a fair share of employment in the VA in Mississippi is for Washington authorities to absolutely demand a fair share of employment opportunities for Negroes. There is nobody in Mississippi who has enough influence and goodwill to put pressure toward VA's employment of qualified Negroes in their fair proportions."[14]

Council leaders understood that if black workers were to secure a fairer share of job opportunities, white attitudes had to change. Looking to break down resistance to civil rights, throughout the 1950s and 1960s SRC labor director Emory Via carried out much of the group's economic agenda. A native Virginian and graduate of Emory University, Via crisscrossed the region promoting racial tolerance. Seeking to develop what he called a "positive attitude," Via conducted many educational classes with white union members.[15] In March 1957, for example, Via organized a conference of southern labor leaders "to meet and to discuss the problems that unions face in the field of race relations." The gathering was attended by thirty-six union officials from a wide variety of industries and involved "frank discussions" of the race issue.[16] In front of hostile audiences, Via argued that most segregationist politicians were anti-union and did not represent the true interests of organized workers.[17]

Via found that union leaders and rank-and-file members reacted differently to the civil rights movement; leaders were generally supportive of equal rights, hoping that black enfranchisement would undermine conservative anti-labor groups and thereby strengthen organized labor's position in the South. Rank-and-file workers, however, usually defended segregation because it delivered them significant benefits, including better jobs with higher wages, more political rights, and better schools. Union leaders, in fact, helped fund the SRC, but their members often gave their hard-earned money to segregationist groups such as the White Citizens Council and the Klan. As Via acknowledged, most white union members were very opposed to school integration and held "antagonistic feelings toward Negroes."[18]

Although most union policy makers supported the SRC, Via also complained that they lacked "firmness" on the race issue and were reluctant to confront their members' racial views. While giving verbal support to civil rights at the national level, in the South labor leaders generally refused to challenge segregated work assignments. At the same time, contracts were negotiated locally, and they often locked blacks into the worst jobs. As Via found, there was a considerable gap between unions' national policies and actual racial practices on the ground.[19]

Via was more than aware of the barriers facing his work, yet he insisted that his educational efforts did secure some valuable results. He pointed out that few other civil rights groups worked extensively with labor on racial problems. He also noted SRC conferences provided "the first inter-racial living experience" for most white and black attendees. These contacts led to "growth," as they highlighted "that inter-racial experiences were possible without any damage to the persons involved."[20]

After a spell with the University of Wisconsin's School for Workers, in 1965 Via returned to permanent employment with the SRC. The veteran activist continued his work in labor education, conducting many programs in cooperation with both unions and universities. "Our effort has been to get union members to think," he wrote, "to accept the significance of important social developments and to begin to view the changes about them in a new perspective. It is hoped that they can begin to shake away from a negative and antagonistic view of civil rights progress and find an understanding that can hold some promise of a South of decency, equality and mutual progress." Via admitted that his task remained a difficult one, but he insisted that his goals were "sometimes achieved."[21]

Via worked quietly but persistently, gradually breaking down white opposition to civil rights. He corresponded extensively with union heads and frequently sent them educational literature that promoted the SRC's creed of racial tolerance and moderation. Reasoning that they were powerless to oppose federal law, some whites came to grudgingly accept blacks as coworkers. As Mississippi paper worker Allen Coley recalled, most whites "didn't necessarily like it [integration] but ninety per cent of them, ninety-five percent of them knew it was the law, and knew it was something they had to live by." Union leaders were more enthusiastic, and Via cultivated a close relationship with Mississippi AFL-CIO president Claude Ramsay, a former paper worker who was a committed supporter of equal rights. Working quietly behind the scenes, Via, Ramsay, and other moderate leaders helped to ensure that the integration of the workplace was generally not accompanied by serious violence.[22]

In addition to these educational efforts, Via was keen to involve the SRC in projects that secured more jobs for southern blacks. Pressure from SRC members helped to increase the number of black police who were hired in several southern cities. In the mid-1960s, Via also pressed for more African Americans to be employed in the construction trades, particularly in the Atlanta area, and he put key union chiefs in touch with civil rights leaders. Via worked closely with representatives of the NAACP and the Urban League, who were particularly concerned about the lily-white composition of the building trades. Despite extensive lobbying, the SRC found that integrating the trades was very difficult, as managers and unions blamed each other for the situation. Both continued to fight civil rights laws, resulting in a large body of Title VII litigation. The need for change was clear; in 1967 blacks made up only 1.6 percent of the membership of the Electrical Workers' Union and only 0.2 percent of the Plumbers. Gradually, however, pressure from court cases and federal inspectors pushed the trades to admit more blacks. By October 1972, black union leader Bayard Rustin claimed that blacks constituted 13 percent of all construction union apprentices, and the SRC can take some credit for this increase.[23]

The issue of minority workers in craft unions strained relations between organized labor and civil rights groups, two interests that the council tried to bring together. AFL-CIO president George Meany fiercely defended the federation's efforts to recruit black craft workers. "No more effective program exists to equip young blacks with the skills they need to share equally in the work of the world," he wrote in 1974. Black interest groups remained unconvinced;

the U.S. Commission on Civil Rights, for example, complained in 1973 that progress was unsatisfactory because the Nixon administration was not taking a hard enough line with recalcitrant construction unions.[24]

In the mid-1960s, the SRC decided to concentrate a "special interest" on improving black opportunities in the textile industry.[25] Most jobs in the mills were not particularly skilled, and SRC leaders reasoned that the case for employing more blacks was compelling. By the mid-1960s, textile executives were hiring more blacks, but African Americans remained grossly underrepresented in higher-paying jobs. In 1966 composite data from forty-six leading textile companies showed that blacks held just 0.7 percent of white-collar positions.[26] In January 1967, Via told a special EEOC forum that the textile industry was "uniquely qualified" as the South's "predominant industry" to employ more blacks. While noting that some breakthroughs had been made, the council activist complained that too many blacks were still confined to low-paying mill jobs: "the old pattern, to those concerned with employment fairness, continues in that Negroes are severely underrepresented in clerical, skilled, technical, professional, and managerial occupations." He asserted that much more needed to be done to ensure "the eradication of discrimination from the entire industry."[27]

With a renewed understanding of the barriers facing African Americans in the textile industry, Via met with other civil rights leaders shortly after the forum to try to tackle the problem. Five agencies, including the NAACP Legal Defense Fund and the National Urban League, joined with the SRC and launched TEAM (Textiles: Employment and Advancement for Minorities). Initiated in March 1967, TEAM was a one-year project supported by a twenty-five thousand dollar Field Foundation grant.[28] The initiative was based in the textile state of South Carolina and adopted far-reaching goals. As TEAM leader Jean Fairfax put it, the program was an interagency effort to "eliminat[e] all forms of discrimination in the textile industry." She added that "Our sights are very ambitious. Our program should be so structured that substantial employment of Negroes would result, not only in entry level jobs but in professional and managerial positions."[29]

TEAM chose to concentrate on a fourteen-county region in the western part of the state where textile mills provided 65 percent of all manufacturing employment. African Americans comprised 29 percent of the total population, yet they were severely underrepresented in the mills, holding just 8 percent of all jobs.[30] A young black lawyer with degrees from South Carolina State College and Howard University, Mordecai C. Johnson aimed to change this. As project director, Johnson operated out of a modest rented office in Greenville and was responsible for the hiring and supervision of field agents. Usually local black activists, Johnson's staff spent most of their time visiting mill executives to encourage them to hire more African Americans.[31]

TEAM agents found that they faced a variety of obstacles. While they were hiring more blacks in these years, most company executives disliked outside interference in their business and were "vague and non-committal" when representatives called. "I got the impression that none of the plant managers were willing to talk to TEAM," reported Robert Ford from Greenville County. "I had no interviews in any mills." Managers from the large Westpoint Manufacturing Company refused to speak to TEAM, asserting that "we comply with the law." Johnson described a visit to the large Deering Milliken Company as "horrible. . . . The plant manager was unavailable and the personnel director and the equal employment director were both uncommunicative and uncooperative." Many companies used "avoidance tactics," referring TEAM agents back and forth between corporate offices and local plants.[32]

Insisting that whites were better qualified, executives remained particularly opposed to placing blacks in skilled positions. Managers generally proceeded cautiously as they integrated, aware that white resistance was more likely if blacks entered lucrative posts. TEAM agents found it difficult to get blacks placed in higher-paid posts. Agent William Patrick Flack wrote from Anderson County that "there is no job shortage; but there is a shortage of up-grading jobs. This is a general picture of the entire area. Jobs, yes, but service types. . . . There is a picture of not up-grading black folks." In several locations, agents related that their main "breakthroughs" were in securing lower-level jobs in older plants with poor working conditions. "We should be careful," warned one, "not to build in a new kind of discrimination under which the black man gets the hot dirty jobs while the good jobs, say, with air conditioning go to whites." TEAM staff also found that many blacks were afraid to file charges of discrimination against powerful textile corporations. Other blacks feared reprisals from the Ku Klux Klan, and even TEAM agents complained that they were subjected to "tremendous pressure" because of their activism. Staff found themselves denied credit by local banks and harassed as they went about their daily activities.[33]

TEAM staff also found that many employers were reluctant to hire any African American women. Many white women were only able to work in the mills because they employed black domestics to look after their children. Employers were afraid to alienate these employees, who worried about losing their domestic help if black women landed mill jobs. In the 1960s, over 40 percent of southern textile workers were female, making it the biggest employer of women in basic manufacturing. By 1965, when the Civil Rights Act became effective, black women had made little progress into the cotton mills; in South Carolina, for example, the percentage of black females working in the textile industry actually declined from 1 percent in 1925 to 0.7 percent in 1965. TEAM agents found that they were able to get some black women hired, yet they still remained underutilized, both in the Palmetto State and across the region as a whole.[34]

While reports documented the problems that agents encountered, TEAM was able to secure some significant results. Most important, the project gained jobs for over five hundred African Americans in local mills. Some agents even became a source of recruitment within the black community. Johnson described Union County field worker Alice Gallman, a local nurse, as "one of the best, if not the best, aide we have. She is a master at manipulating the system." A tenacious activist, Gallman was successful at persuading several plants to hire more blacks. "In one case," noted Johnson proudly, "Mrs. Gallman was able to get a truckload of Negroes employed at Buffalo Mills," which was one of the largest mills in Union County.[35]

TEAM agents also helped to identify a new generation of black leaders and nurtured an upsurge of civil rights activism in an area of the rural South that had been largely untouched by the movement. TEAM worked with new local leaders to set up a chapter of the Black Awareness Coordinating Committee (BACC), a grassroots group with a strong interest in economic rights. The BACC became active in identifying targets in the community that were refusing to integrate. In addition to filing EEOC charges, BACC launched a selective buying campaign against Kash n' Karry, a major grocery store that refused to hire black clerks. As a result of this pressure, the outlet took on nine black clerks in a week. After receiving complaints from BACC, K-Mart also appointed several African American cashiers.[36]

In 1968 TEAM agents helped to recruit several volunteers for the SCLC's Poor People's Campaign, which aimed to persuade Congress to spend more money on combating black poverty. In addition, TEAM also encouraged blacks to use their legal rights to gain greater economic power, especially by filing EEOC charges. In the years that followed, groups of local blacks joined together to file Title VII lawsuits against several local mills. Overall, much had been achieved; Alice Gallman was even successful at helping local mothers to obtain a daycare center, facilitating women's entry into the workforce. "Whether or not TEAM stays in operation," concluded a project summary, "Greenville will never be the same again." Another report asserted that the agency had produced "continuing gains from community organization, the stimulation of groups to act on their own, and the goading of public agencies to enforce laws or to carry out their duties equitably."[37]

The TEAM project reflected broader interests within the SRC and the civil rights movement as a whole. In the late 1960s, many civil rights leaders felt that the movement needed to focus on securing economic power for African Americans. In 1968 the SRC's executive director concentrated extensively on economic issues in a keynote address, noting that advances in the political and legal spheres had still left most black southerners with what he called "a pathetically disproportionate lack of access to economic opportunity." "The black southerner" he added, "will not be a man until he can earn a decent wage."[38] In 1972 the SRC's "Program for the '70s," a broad policy document, reasserted the council's judgment that "legal victories and the civil rights laws of the past decade have not substantially changed the economic status of the poor."[39]

The following year, the SRC organized a conference on Title VII that brought together civil rights lawyers, union leaders, public agency representatives, and citizens' groups. Attendees encouraged black workers to use Title VII to tackle the discrimination that was still practiced by both companies and unions. Behind the scenes, however, Al Kehrer of the AFL-CIO Civil Rights Department complained about the gathering, feeling that it was designed to "kick the hell out of the unions." Business leaders, he fumed, should also have been invited. The bickering highlighted how the alliance between organized labor and civil rights groups became strained when the latter became openly critical of unions' racial record.[40]

In the 1970s, the SRC also became particularly concerned with publicizing southern poverty. In these years, the media consistently described the southern states as a prosperous "Sunbelt," contrasting their growth with other parts of the country that were experiencing industrial decline.[41] The SRC, however, was keen to point out that many southerners still lived in poverty. "The benefits of economic development are not reaching poor Southerners," warned the SRC's 1973 Annual Report. In the following year, the council's "The Other Twenty Percent: A Statistical Analysis of Poverty in the South" carefully documented such bold claims. Based on detailed data from the 1970 census, the well-publicized report highlighted that the South was not as prosperous as the rest of the country; with only 25 percent of the nation's population, the region contained 38 percent of the country's poor. Poverty, moreover, was concentrated among blacks, especially in rural areas. Overall, the council's research acted as an important corrective to the positive headlines that proclaimed the region as a booming "Sunbelt."[42]

Again, the council pursued action alongside research and education. As well as continuing to lobby economic and political leaders, SRC strategists launched their Black Women Employment Project, a pilot effort in which the council acted as a liaison to help qualified African American women find skilled, professional, and managerial jobs in the Atlanta area.[43] Initiated in March 1972, the program was motivated by research showing that very few African American women held higher-paying white-collar jobs. Alexis Herman, who later became secretary of labor in the Clinton administration, directed the project. Most of her work concentrated on liaison with employers, community organizations, and local colleges. In all, over one thousand college-educated black women contacted the program, and 15 percent of them were successfully placed in technical, professional, and managerial positions. "I heard about Black Women Employment Program and visited them," noted one woman who had secured her first white-collar job as a computer programmer. "They took a very personal interest in me and worked very diligently in trying to get me placed." Project leaders also claimed that they had increased the confidence of many job applicants and proven to skeptical employers that black women could perform non-traditional jobs effectively.[44]

Following the conclusion of the Atlanta project, the SRC continually argued that the South had fundamental economic problems that the Sunbelt image only concealed. In 1976 it asserted that the region was still "the nation's number one economic problem," a reference to President Franklin D. Roosevelt's famous proclamation from the 1930s.[45] To back up its assertion, the council again noted the prevalence of poverty and low wages in Dixie. Rates of unionization also remained lower than they were in other parts of the country, and southern employers' "powerful opposition" to collective bargaining had helped to depress wage rates and deprive workers of fringe benefits.[46]

The council also argued that despite the passage of the 1964 Civil Rights Act, entrenched patterns of racial segregation had proved resistant to change. Many southern whites were slow to accept that blacks could perform non-traditional jobs. Even in government jobs, where African Americans did make strides, their progress was patchy, especially outside of major metropolitan areas. In 1980 an SRC report into public employment in the rural black belt found that African Americans were still victims of discrimination. Black women were again the hardest hit. "There are today," noted the report, "sizeable rural Black Belt government workforces in which *all* permanent, full-time employees are White or male, and no Black woman holds a job (not even the clean-up job that is the traditional lot of Southern Black women)." Of 871 jobs surveyed, black women held only 12. "The effects of past or present barriers to equal employment opportunity clearly persist," it concluded.[47]

In the 1980s and 1990s, the SRC continued its long fight for equal employment opportunity. In 1985 strategists created the Southern Labor Institute (SLI) in order to "strengthen the historical commitment of the Southern Regional Council to address the problems of low wages and non-union working conditions in the South and to unite the goals of the civil rights movement with the struggle for economic justice." The main emphasis of the SLI was on research and education, and over the next fifteen years it produced a series of studies that skillfully documented the plight of the South's poor.[48]

Headed by Kenny Johnson, a former director of the National Rural Center, the SLI quickly assembled a copious body of data. Drawing on this material, in 1986 the institute released "The Climate for Workers: Where Does the South Stand?" Typically well-researched, the study showed that despite the headlines about economic growth, Dixie was still the poorest region in the country. Regional elites, asserted the SLI, had placed too much emphasis on attracting low-wage, non-union industry, resulting in few improvements for ordinary southerners. Southern blacks remained disproportionately poor; in 1986 all of the nine states with the highest proportion of black poor were in the Southeast, and in Mississippi 44 percent of all African Americans lived in poverty. This was partly because racial discrimination in employment continued to be worse in the South than in other regions. As "The Climate for Workers" noted, southern blacks were still frequently excluded from traditionally "white" jobs.[49]

The SRC attempted to build on the report by developing strategies that would create a more prosperous region. A follow-up conference attracted community heads, union leaders, civil rights activists, and local government officials with sessions focused on the need to create higher-paying jobs. The gathering, noted the SRC, "brought to the same table people who do not ordinarily meet to discuss economic issues and policies." It proved easier to document patterns of economic behavior than to change them, however, and the council struggled to get its message across to the region's political and economic elites, who remained committed to attracting low-wage industry to their states.[50]

The SLI nevertheless performed a valuable role by exposing the poor working conditions that many southerners continued to endure. In 1988 the institute issued a report on the prevalence of temporary agencies or "day labor pools."

Many African Americans and Hispanics were registered with these agencies, being hired on a daily basis for low wages with no benefits. Prospective staff showed up at the labor halls around 5:00 AM and usually ended up with around twenty dollars from a day's labor after deductions. Many felt angry about their treatment, but they also saw themselves as powerless to change it. "Labor pools? Labor fools would be more like it," remarked worker Johnny Tartt. "He [the pool owner] makes more money than you do to go out and do all the work," commented another. "They just pull all they can get out of you in a day. Technically I guess they're not breaking any laws. It's the American way—exploit the worker a little bit."[51]

The SRC report offered a vivid insight into a little-known part of southern life. The council exposed the underbelly of the Sunbelt South, showing that gleaming suburban offices were cleaned by an army of poorly paid workers bused in from crumbling inner-city neighborhoods. "To be honest, temporary service ain't nothing but a tossover from slavery," observed John Zachery, one of the few black owners of a labor pool. "It's flesh peddling. They modify it and dress it up some. But it's slavery. The difference is you pay today. Back in slavery time you told them what to do and gave them some grits and hog jowl. I'm just telling like it is." Despite SRC calls for greater regulation of the pools, they continued to be a part of daily life in southern cities.[52]

In a broader sense, the SRC did much to expose the plight of the "working poor." In a growing South, council leaders pointed out, finding work was generally not a problem, yet many jobs did not pay enough to support workers' families. As a result, many toiled long hours in two or three jobs in an effort to make ends meet. "Today's poor aren't just the ones out on the street; it's the people working hard trying to make a decent living," noted Jennifer Morris, a single mother from Arkansas. "I wish there was something that could be done to make it just a little bit easier. It seems like sometimes it's not worth it to work." Another family claimed that in order to survive they had to be "Olympic champions in bill juggling." Council studies also highlighted that well-qualified African Americans were still finding it difficult to secure positions commensurate with their training. One 1990 report spotlighted the case of Deborah Abdullah, who was in the final stages of a degree in gerontology. Employers rebuffed Abdullah when she endeavored to get a post as a nurse's aide in Atlanta. "They just said, 'We'll call you when something opens up in the laundry,'" she noted sadly. After several rejections, Abdullah moved back to her home state of Arkansas, where she secured a job paying just $4.50 an hour.[53]

In the 1990s, the SRC continued to be active in its struggle for improved rights for all southern workers. The SLI, in particular, documented that many companies were continuing to locate in the South specifically because of its low wages and weak labor laws. For the council, the growth of the poultry industry epitomized the South's continuing dependence on low-wage factories. In this burgeoning southern industry, a predominantly African American and Hispanic workforce performed monotonous tasks at a high speed, leading to alarming rates of workplace injury. In 1997 the U.S. Department of Labor found that 60 percent of poultry companies were in violation of the Fair Labor Standards Act. In an industry where they were easily replaced, most staff were afraid to speak out; as poultry worker Thomas Oates commented in 1991, "talking out there is like asking for a bullet in your head." The plight of the poultry workers spotlighted the ongoing struggle of many southerners for decent wages and benefits. As the SRC entered a new century, it was all too aware of the need to keep fighting for racial justice. "The struggle for racial equity in the South," commented executive director Wendy S. Johnson in 2000, "knows no time."[54]

Between the 1940s and the 1990s, the SRC carried out some important work in its efforts to break down employment discrimination.[55] The council may not have captured the headlines in the way that SNCC or CORE did, and on some occasions it seemed too content to document injustice rather than fighting to overcome it. While these other groups had ceased to exist by the end of the 1960s, however, the SRC continued its efforts into the 1970s and beyond. Like the NAACP, the SRC fought to overcome white resistance to the civil rights legislation of the 1960s. Since 1944 the long-lasting organization has consistently attacked employment discrimination because it has seen it as a central cause of the region's persistent poverty. For over sixty years, the SRC has fought for a South not blighted by stark economic inequality. "The South," claimed one typical SRC report, "need not, if it will only provide opportunity for all its people, be classed as 'economic problem number one.' It is quite possible that the South may become the nation's 'economic opportunity number one.'"[56]

4

"A brand new shining city"

Floyd B. McKissick and the Civil Rights Movement of the 1970s

On a crisp fall day in November 1973, North Carolina governor James Holhouser broke the ground at the new community of Soul City. Located in Warren County, Soul City was the brainchild of Floyd McKissick, an African American activist and Tar Heel native who had led CORE between 1966 and 1968. At the time, Warren County was at the heart of a range of poor counties that ran along the Virginia state line through eastern North Carolina. In 1973 the seventeen thousand residents of the majority-black county had a per capita income of just $2,739, one of the lowest in the state. The county did not contain any large towns, and most of its inhabitants worked in low-paying agricultural jobs. McKissick's idealistic goal of building a brand new city in the area that would serve to "symbolize the achievement of the disadvantaged people of America" attracted both federal and state funding, and Holhouser generously praised the far-reaching venture before an audience of visiting dignitaries. Flanked by McKissick, the Republican governor described Soul City as "far more than just another city. Soul City is a tribute to man's ability to dream new dreams and to put those dreams to work." The emerging community, he added, represented "a new milestone in our nation's constant search for better human relations."[1]

Soul City was significant because it represented the first time that a new town had been planned and built by a minority-owned developer. According to the *New York Times*, the town was "the biggest black commercial enterprise in the history of the nation."[2] An ambitious project, Soul City also represented the first effort to build a "free-standing" community rather than develop a satellite of an existing settlement. McKissick Enterprises planned a city of around fifty thousand people that would attract the poor to Warren County. While stressing that the community would be interracial, McKissick particularly hoped to lure back many African Americans who had left the area as young people, thus stemming the out-migration that had hurt Warren County for decades. In July 1972, he succeeded in securing a $14 million guarantee for Soul City bonds from Housing and Urban Development (HUD) secretary George Romney. The award was the first such guarantee given to a new town whose principal backer was a minority-owned business. By the late 1970s, the federal government had invested over $19 million in the project, with a further $8 million coming from state and local sources. In June 1979, however, HUD decided to foreclose on Soul City, citing a lack of progress, particularly in attracting industry. "The area itself just didn't work out," commented HUD official William J. White. "There was not enough of a market to draw from."[3]

The Soul City story is an important one that has remained largely untold.[4] In the last twenty years, historians have published a great deal of fine work on the civil rights era. The vast majority of these studies, however, have focused on the golden period of black activism between 1954 and 1965.[5] McKissick's efforts to build Soul City reflected a broader shift in the thinking of African American strategists. After 1965 many civil rights leaders felt that their main priority was to develop black economic power so that African Americans had the resources to take advantage of the legal rights they had recently won. Rev. Martin Luther King commented on this problem shortly before his death when he noted that it did no good for any black person to be allowed to eat in a restaurant if they could not afford to settle the check. Soul City encapsulated the economic focus of civil rights activism after 1965, reflecting McKissick's belief that a "strong black economy" would be "the spearhead of racial equality." For McKissick, Soul City symbolized the new drive for black economic self-determination. "This is the civil rights movement of the 1970s," he declared.[6]

An important figure, as a young man McKissick was instrumental in integrating the University of North Carolina, and he went on to have a long and distinguished career with CORE, the civil rights group that initiated the high-profile Freedom Rides of 1961. Despite this, historians have largely overlooked the Asheville native, particularly after he left CORE in 1968.[7] McKissick's recently catalogued papers detail his career in unprecedented detail, particularly his untiring efforts to construct a model new town. While a lack of sources has often restricted scholars' efforts to explore the period after 1965, the McKissick collection is strongest on the Soul City venture, which consumed its founder's time for well over a decade. This collection makes it possible to provide a detailed chronological account of Soul City's turbulent history and to revise existing interpretations of the project's fate.[8]

At the time, Soul City became synonymous with allegations of financial mismanagement, particularly within North Carolina where both the *Raleigh News and Observer* and state politicians led by Republican senator Jesse Helms repeatedly attacked the project. Helms dismissed Soul City as a "massive wasteful boondoggle," a far cry from McKissick's vision of the city as a "model of democracy." Although both federal and state audits cleared McKissick of any wrongdoing, they still delayed the project and attracted negative press coverage that irrevocably tarnished its image.[9]

In reality, however, Soul City was hurt by a broad variety of problems that were not fully recognized at the time. Above all, the project confronted the truly massive task of trying to build a completely new town in one of the poorest counties in the United States. The town struggled to attract new industry, failing to develop the job base that it needed to thrive. Soul City became trapped in a classic dilemma; without industry, it could not attract enough residents, but without a local labor force, it was difficult to entice industrialists, especially at a time of economic downturn. Business executives were also deterred by the name of the town, which they felt identified it as an all-black community, yet proposals to change the name divided Soul City's interracial staff. While McKissick succeeded in winning over some white leaders in the area, white residents also remained reluctant to move into a community that they saw as all-black. Despite the passage of the civil rights laws of the mid-1960s, the Soul City story highlighted the racial divisions that still existed in rural North Carolina more than a decade later.[10]

Soul City struggled to get off the ground, and it never recovered from HUD's decision to pull its funding. McKissick and his aides certainly made mistakes, and their idealism was sometimes a barrier to the town's development. Despite this, Soul City is deserving of a more sympathetic exploration than the press gave it in the wake of the *News and Observer*'s attacks. McKissick's papers clearly document that Soul City was always envisioned as a thirty-year project, a fact that press accounts often failed to spotlight.[11] In June 1979, however, HUD stopped funding the effort at a time when many of its initiatives were just beginning to take shape. Many of Soul City's problems were also caused by forces beyond its control, such as the poor state of the national economy in the 1970s, a decline in federal support for new towns as a whole, and restrictions imposed on the project by HUD.

Despite Soul City's obvious problems, it was not a complete failure. While McKissick and his staff failed to establish the sizeable community that they had envisioned, they did help to develop the infrastructure of a poor rural area. Providing concrete benefits to the community was, they insisted, ultimately more important than anything else. "Soul City was founded not as the huge money making scheme as has been depicted by the press and our Senators and Representatives," claimed a 1979 project paper, "but as a catalyst for the growth of an extremely depressed area. It is designed to help local governments and the people in the region help themselves and become productive in a society which has passed them by because of their isolated location." By the end of the 1970s, Soul City's planners had established a health clinic, recreational facilities, and a $12 million water system that served a three-county area. They had also brought some much-needed jobs to the region. A core of residents refused to abandon the settlement, and McKissick himself never fully gave up on the town, living there until his death in the spring of 1991.[12]

The son of the head bellman at the Vanderbilt Hotel in Asheville, Floyd Bixler McKissick was born on March 9, 1922. As a child he helped support the family by carting ice on a homemade wagon, delivering newspapers, and shining shoes.[13] He vividly recalled growing up in the segregated Asheville of the 1920s and 1930s. In one incident, he had wanted to sit at the front of a city trolley car so that he could watch the driver, but a "big heavy man" threatened to throw him to the rear of the car if he did not move. As a teenager McKissick was told by his scoutmaster to help direct traffic on South French Broad street, where scouts were skating through an intersection. The city police soon arrived and gruffly told McKissick that he "didn't have no business being there," hitting him when he refused to move on. The Asheville chapter of the NAACP protested against his subsequent arrest, initiating his longstanding association with the civil rights group.[14]

McKissick's service in the military during World War II was particularly important in motivating him to protest against racial segregation. During the war he served in the army as a sergeant in the European theater, receiving the Purple Heart and five battle stars. Like many returning veterans, McKissick came back to the South determined to fight for racial equality. "I think," he later reflected, "most of the fellows who had been in World War II had been around the world, and they had seen things, and they knew that they were not what America had depicted them to be. They had seen the whole world, and they were not going to live in a pattern of segregation as they had in the past." Shortly after the war, McKissick initiated a legal case to gain admission to the law school at the University of North Carolina at Chapel Hill. Represented by Thurgood Marshall, in 1951 McKissick became the first African American man to enroll at the prestigious university's law school.[15]

As a Durham-based lawyer, McKissick represented many civil rights protesters and successfully filed suits to enable all of his children to attend formerly all-white schools. He was also a leading activist in CORE, and in January 1966 he left North Carolina to head the New York–based organization. At the time, CORE was moving away from its biracial identity. Although McKissick embraced the emerging calls for "Black Power," as national director he disagreed with moves to exclude whites. In the summer of 1968, he left a disintegrating CORE to form McKissick Enterprises. The new organization reflected Mc-Kissick's belief that civil rights organizations needed to address economic issues more directly. "If a Black man has no bread in his pocket," he wrote at the time, "the solution to his problem is not integration; it's to get some bread. Real simple—that's what McKissick Enterprises is all about." The economic system, he argued, should be reformed to include blacks and other excluded people. One of the ways to do this was to build a new town for the poor.[16]

For McKissick, building a new town was a long-term ambition. He traced his interest in the idea back to his military service in World War II, when he witnessed how the Marshall Plan had helped to rebuild war-ravaged areas of Europe. "Soul City was an idea before the movement," he reflected in 1973. "Soul City actually started after World War II, in my mind. And it was first talked about when we saw the use of the Marshall Plan, and all like that." By the late 1960s, McKissick saw the building of a new community as a "constructive" way of applying black power; rather than attacking the system, blacks needed to "get involved in economics, in politics, in government, in the whole fabric of life." After forming McKissick Enterprises, he began to look for potential sites in his home state. With the help of local attorney T. T. Clayton, he settled on Satterwhite farm, a 1,810-acre site located around forty-five miles northeast of Durham. With a $200,000 loan from the Chase Manhattan Bank, together with a similar contribution from supporter Irving Fain, the firm purchased an option on the site for $390,000.[17]

Although McKissick considered several possible sites, he chose the Warren County location for many reasons. Close to both Interstate 85 and a major railroad, the site had good transportation links, and McKissick hoped that this would make it attractive to industry. Planners also liked the idea of building their new community on what had originally been a slave plantation. The site had "historical ambience," and it included Green Duke house, a sixteen-room antebellum mansion.[18]

McKissick was keen to tackle the poverty that had led many African Americans to migrate from large parts of the rural South. Warren County suffered particularly badly from this problem. The county was more than 60 percent

African American and was one of the poorest in the state. In 1960 the median family income in the county was a mere $1,958 a year, but for blacks it was even less—just $1,308. Living conditions were very poor, with around 40 percent of homes still lacking indoor plumbing. Upon graduating from high school, local blacks were said to have three alternatives—"Heaven, Hell, and Baltimore"— and invariably chose the latter option. Black out-migration showed no signs of going away. Between 1960 and 1970, for example, Warren County's population decreased by 20 percent, the greatest percentage loss of any county in the state. By 1979 the estimated per capita income in the county was $4,301 a year, well below the state average of $6,330. It was hard to imagine a more challenging environment in which to build a new town. As the *Durham Morning Herald* noted, "Warren ranks in the lowest 10 of the 100 counties in a state that ranks in the lowest 10 among the 50 states in prosperity."[19]

Following the purchase of the land, in 1969 the Soul City Foundation (SCF) was incorporated to carry out the social planning of the new town. The Soul City Company (SCC), meanwhile, was set up as a land development company. The following year, McKissick and his staff established the Warren Regional Planning Corporation (WRPC). Envisioned as "the technical and planning arm of the project," the WRPC concentrated most of its work on trying to attract industry to the site. McKissick left New York with three other staff and moved to Soul City in 1970, living and working out of a series of mobile units erected near the Green Duke house, which became the base for a Head Start program. Among those who moved with him was Gordon R. Carey, a white activist who had previously been CORE's assistant national director. Friendly with McKissick since their CORE days, Carey served as SCF director and an officer of McKissick Enterprises. The skeletal staff set about the task of attracting funding and developing the plans for their new community.[20]

Until the summer of 1972, McKissick spent most of his time working to secure federal funding, commuting back and forth regularly to Washington. He was particularly keen to submit a funding application to HUD's New Communities Program, which had been established in 1968. Under the program, HUD had authority to grant loans for the development of new communities. In December 1970, funding opportunities increased further when President Nixon signed the Housing and Urban Development Act, which liberalized regulations for community development. In particular, Title VII of the act offered direct loan and grant assistance to both public and private developers. In the early 1970s, HUD agreed to fund fifteen new communities across the United States, including several in the South. In securing a $14 million loan guarantee for Soul City, McKissick relied heavily on his friendship with Samuel Jackson, an NAACP lawyer who was HUD's assistant secretary. At the time, Jackson was the highest-ranking African American in the federal government. Increasingly confident, McKissick soon announced an increase in Soul City's projected population, which he had originally pegged at eighteen thousand. Citing favorable studies, he now claimed that the town would have fifty thousand residents by 1990. McKissick's effectiveness as a fund-raiser was further confirmed as he subsequently gained a $1.7 million grant from the Office of Economic Opportunity, together with $100,000 from the Department of Health, Education, and Welfare.[21]

From the start, Soul City's planners were idealistic, envisioning their community as a model interracial city. Soul City, claimed the WRPC, represented "people working with people to eradicate the social and economic ills so rampant in today's urban centers. It is the amalgamation of races, of social and political interests, of religious sects, of ideas and ideals."[22] The town, added the SCC, would be "a symbol to millions of blacks and other depressed groups that the American system can and does include them."[23] Soul City was to be "a brand new shining city," a settlement without prejudice, poverty, or slums. The town was planned with "welcoming signs" to indicate that it was "a place of harmony and freedom for all."[24] Promotional literature promised potential residents a "fresh start." "Here," it added, "people of all ages, races and religions work together. Play together. Learn together."[25] Planners envisioned an ambitious range of facilities, including an art museum, golf course, common parks, and a central library. A large industrial facility was to be separated from the residential area by a sixty-acre lake. Promoters also spoke of Soul City becoming a "cultural mecca" and a "major tourist attraction and resort area."[26]

McKissick's dream of building a new town in a poor part of the South fascinated and won over many. The liberal press was largely supportive. In 1972 the *New York Times* called Soul City "an imaginative concept," seeing it as a possible solution to southern poverty. Soul City, added the *Washington Post*, was "perhaps the most vital experiment yet in this country's halting struggle against the cancer of hectic urbanization."[27] In August 1974, Rev. Jesse Jackson of Operation PUSH also pledged his support. Impressed by McKissick's ability to win funding, even local white leaders overcame their initial skepticism and soon backed the African American developer. Early on, the *Raleigh News and Observer* was largely positive and called McKissick's plans "exciting" and "fascinating" but cautioned that it would be very difficult to make the Soul City "dream" come true.[28]

To some degree, the new community did succeed in attracting African Americans who had previously left the South. Many northern blacks wanted to return south and were animated by Soul City's idealistic effort to build a new refuge for returning migrants. David Carolina moved to Soul City from Newark, New Jersey, seeing the town as an escape from ghetto life. "It's a pioneer city," explained the South Carolina native, "just like the beginning of the whole doggone country." "Soul City is like a dream to me," claimed another resident. "When you say you're from here, you really have got something to brag about. You feel good." Californian Henry Chew, meanwhile, claimed that buying his $31,000 home in Soul City had made him feel like a "forty-niner" going to the frontier.[29]

Lifestyle advantages also attracted residents. A Warren County native, Johnie Johnson moved to Soul City from Newark. In 1979 she explained her reasons for returning to the South. "We wanted to get [the children] out of that congested, dirty city," she related. On visits to her mother, Johnson learned of the community that was taking shape nearby. "I used to always come up here; it had a future in it for me," she explained. "It had good recreation here for the kids. It was quiet. And it looked like it had potential."[30] Soul City certainly appealed to northern blacks who were tired of living in polluted and crime-ridden urban environments. In June 1979, the *New York Times* reported that "scores of black New Yorkers" attended meetings in the Big Apple to learn about the novel Tar Heel community. Most were enthusiastic about returning to the South. "I want to dig in the dirt again and go fishing when I feel like it," explained Elaine Alexander. "I'm tired of the noise, the crowds and the fear of walking the streets or into your own hallway." Some of those who decided to move to Soul City praised McKissick for giving them the opportunity to return south. "Thanks to Mr. McKissick and those who assisted him in the 5 year joint venture," wrote one, "220 individuals' lives have been improved."[31]

Into the mid-1970s, press coverage of Soul City remained largely positive. In October 1972, the *Charlotte Observer* reported that the new community was gradually winning over its "skeptics." In particular, local white store owners felt that the new community would bring them more business. In June 1973, the *Greensboro Daily News* was similarly upbeat, claiming that McKissick had silenced his "scoffers." The *News* pointed out that the proposed regional water system had been endorsed by all of the town councils in the three counties involved (Granville, Vance, and Warren), while voters in the towns of Henderson and Oxford had also approved bond issues for the project.[32] The *New York Times* remained enthusiastic about Soul City. In January 1974, reporter

Wayne King noted that the new development was "moving from dream stage to reality." The state had erected highway signs announcing the town's presence, while on the site roads had been cut, sewer lines laid, and construction started on ninety housing units. In December 1974, just a few months before the *Raleigh News and Observer* began a series of negative articles on the project, the *Times* held it up as a model development. "Construction is continuing apace, within budget," it noted, "there is a substantial cash reserve on hand and early resentments from some surrounding areas seem to have changed to a spirit of mutually beneficial cooperation."[33]

In March 1975, the *Raleigh News and Observer* launched a series of articles on Soul City that forever changed the relationship between McKissick and the media. In the course of an eight-day period, the paper carried seventeen negative stories on the project. The paper alleged that Soul City represented a wasteful use of federal funds, arguing that the pace of construction at the site was unsatisfactory. The *News and Observer* also attacked McKissick directly, claiming that he had received federal funding as a reward for his backing of the Republican Party in the 1972 presidential election and that he and his family were too closely involved in a "tangled web" of organizations that oversaw Soul City's development. Justifying the articles, the *News and Observer* claimed that the media had been too sympathetic to McKissick and had failed to ask hard questions about what they saw as the slow pace of development at Soul City.[34] McKissick had also lost the support of *News and Observer* editor Claude Sitton, a white journalist who had previously written positive articles on the civil rights movement for the *New York Times*. Sitton, who had worked for the *Times* between 1957 and 1964, had fallen out with McKissick, allegedly blaming him for passing on an unreliable piece of information.[35]

The stories hurt Soul City partly because McKissick and his staff struggled to respond effectively. The project in fact had no public relations staff to coordinate their answers to the allegations. In his papers, McKissick put forward a variety of arguments to make his case, but many of these were never printed in the press. McKissick defended himself by pointing out that HUD would not allow any permanent structures to be built until the financial closing occurred and the first bonds were sold. As a result, physical development could not begin until March 1974. McKissick also stressed that because the SCC was a land development company, the government did not allow them to build housing. HUD also linked housing development to the creation of jobs, preventing the construction of large subdivisions without a corresponding employment base. Answering claims that he had won funding as a reward for his backing of Nixon in 1972, McKissick accepted that his switch to the Republicans "may well have affected the timing of the HUD commitment to provide a federal guarantee to Soul City." He pointed out, however, that he had endorsed Nixon as early as the 1968 election and that he had also supported Dwight Eisenhower in 1952. A political pragmatist, he argued that blacks should support whichever party offered them the most assistance. He also asserted that it was important for African Americans to develop their political skills by becoming involved in two-party politics, and he pointed out that many of his colleagues on the project were Democrats. Admitting some "mistaken judgments," McKissick nevertheless insisted that Soul City was on track. The federal funding it had won, moreover, was benefiting the entire region. As he pointed out, 80 percent of a $6 million federal grant to develop the regional water system met the needs of Oxford, Henderson, and the unincorporated parts of Warren and Vance counties.[36]

While McKissick struggled to get these points across, the *News and Observer*'s allegations were widely reported. The paper's attacks were particularly damaging because of its high profile within the state. Many smaller Tar Heel papers ran abbreviated versions of the *News and Observer*'s stories, recycling the allegations to thousands of North Carolinians. Others simply reprinted them verbatim.[37] Taking their cue from the influential state newspaper, the whole tone of press coverage in the state quickly changed. Papers such as the *Laurinburg Exchange* and the *Mooresville Tribune* quickly attacked Soul City as an "exaggerated experiment" and "the $19 million boondoggle." Soul City, added the *Alamance News*, was "a costly blunder that is not likely to be resolved by throwing good tax dollars after bad."[38] The *News and Observer*'s allegations also hurt the project because they led directly to a federal audit. Carried out by the General Accounting Office (GAO), the audit was demanded by both Jesse Helms and North Carolina Representative L. H. Fountain in the wake of the stories. As well as casting an air of suspicion over the project, the audit also further delayed it. As an internal status report later noted, "the ensuing ordeal of the GAO audit virtually stopped all progress at Soul City for one entire year."[39]

When the GAO audit was released in December 1975, it largely cleared Soul City of the *News and Observer*'s allegations. The report found that the project had not violated any federal laws and gave it a clean bill of health. Helms, however, refused to accept the findings and seized on the GAO's discovery of some "unallowable expenditures" to confirm his judgment of Soul City as a wasteful mess that should be investigated further. Anxious to justify its stance, the *News and Observer* supported these calls. The project, however, was also exonerated by the North Carolina legislature's Fiscal Research Section, which found "no specific evidence of improper actions" in the use of state funds at the site.[40]

McKissick and his supporters claimed that they had been vindicated. Many insisted that the civil rights leader was being unfairly attacked. In February 1976, the North Carolina Association of Black Lawyers declared that the actions of Helms and the *News and Observer* were "racially inspired . . . part of a continuous effort to discredit and prevent black people from entering the economic mainstream of this state and the nation." Another supporter wrote ironically to McKissick: "I am quite certain a black in control and command of such a large endeavor [millions of dollars] is *too much power*." Characteristically belligerent, Helms refused to back down; denying any racial motivation in his efforts, he argued that Soul City should be denied funding as "a matter of fiscal responsibility."[41]

While the controversy that the *News and Observer* unleashed clearly damaged Soul City, there were many other circumstances that held back the town's development. It suffered from problems that also affected other new towns at the time, particularly the massive task of constructing new communities at a time of high inflation. In particular, its difficulties in recruiting industry were decisive, as the project's strategists themselves admitted. In addition, it was HUD's decision to foreclose on Soul City in June 1979 that ultimately ended the venture. A highly ambitious undertaking, Soul City needed time to secure real results.

Soul City's planners understood clearly that attracting industry was vital if their project was to be successful. They envisioned Soultech, a sixty thousand–square foot industrial complex, as the "backbone" of the development.[42] "The developer has made industrial development its first priority," noted a promotional brochure, "for creating job opportunities is essential to the success of the new town." McKissick spoke of attracting as many as eight thousand "basic sector" jobs to Soul City.[43] Yet planners also realized the scale of the task ahead of them. They were trying to attract industry to a predominantly rural area that had a poorly educated and largely untrained labor force. As one internal document put it, "The success of Soul City, therefore, depends on the creation of a viable economy in an area that has not, heretofore, attracted private capital on a sustained basis."[44]

Throughout the 1970s, Soul City struggled to recruit industry. McKissick frequently cited unnamed companies that he claimed were interested in moving to the site, but few of them actually materialized. In June 1973, for example, he boasted that he was on the verge of bringing several firms to Soul City, in-

cluding a new paper converting company, yet none of these plans came to frui-
tion.[45] Shortly after the completion of Soultech, McKissick's staff did succeed
in attracting Wilmetco to be Soultech's first tenants. A New York corporation,
Wilmetco made duffel bags and field packs for the military, employing around
one hundred people at the site. This company, however, closed its facility in
1978 after disputes with the government and an insurance company. By July
1979, only one firm, Fashioncraft Industries, was operating out of the giant
Soultech building, most of which was unoccupied.[46]

In its search for industry, Soul City faced intense competition. In the 1970s,
scores of southern communities were fighting to try to obtain new plants, with
many willing to offer generous economic incentives to interested firms. As
economic historian James C. Cobb has shown, in the post–World War II era
southern political and economic leaders vigorously "sold" their region to outside industrialists because they believed that manufacturing jobs would lift the
South out of poverty. Communities competed with one another to land big
firms. In the late 1970s, when the Japanese carmaker Nissan announced that it
wanted to build a plant in the region, dozens of southern communities fought
for a prize that was eventually secured by Smyrna, Tennessee. In order to persuade firms to choose them, communities had to build up relationships with
industrialists and offer them an attractive economic package. In July 1970, a
textile company agreed to build a plant in the Warren County community of
Norlina only after extensive work by both state and local officials. City officials,
for example, agreed to extend water and sewer lines outside city limits in order
to serve the plant. At the same time, noted the *Warren Record*, the state Department of Conservation and Development "worked many long hours with all
phases of this plant location."[47]

As southern communities were competing to secure outside industry, companies could afford to be choosy and were unwilling to take risks. Many demanded that communities offered them completed industrial buildings rather
than potential sites. As the SCC reported, "Over 90% of the industrial clients
currently seeking to locate in North Carolina reportedly want to look at existing buildings."[48] In this respect Soul City was at a disadvantage, as construction
on Soultech did not begin until March 1974, four years after the WRPC had
begun trying to attract industry to the site. Designed by prominent African
American architect Harvey Gantt, the imposing structure was not completed
until the fall of 1975. Soul City had many other obstacles to overcome. The
lack of housing and other amenities at the site was a concern for industrialists,
forcing Soul City's promoters to try to attract firms based on the facilities avail-

able in the surrounding area. Soul City's planners also faced delays in selling industrial land, blaming HUD's tardiness in approving the required covenants. As late as July 1979, the town also did not have its own sewage plant. "Until Soul City has adequate sewer capacity," admitted planners, "it will not be in a competitive position to attract industrial development." Throughout the 1970s, the new development also lacked natural gas service. In April 1979, Soul City staff complained that they had been trying to attract industry without the necessary infrastructure in place. "Our industrial promotion to date," noted the SCC, "has been like hunting with blank cartridges."[49]

The workforce in the Warren County area also lacked industrial experience. In 1974 a report prepared by outside consultants highlighted that any industry coming into the area would find it difficult to recruit well-qualified staff. There was a "shortage of skilled workers" in the area, and much of the workforce had "unstable . . . employment habits." Most adult residents also lacked formal educational skills, a reflection of the "questionable" quality of public education in Warren County. In fact, over 40 percent of all potential workers had not finished high school. As a result, Soul City confronted "significant problems" in attracting industry.[50]

The poor state of the national economy also hurt efforts to attract outside industry. After more than three decades of steady growth, in 1973 the U.S. economy entered a prolonged recession.[51] The economic downturn made corporations cautious, with many quickly ditching expansion plans. Several companies specifically shelved their interest in locating in Soul City because of the poor state of the economy. In 1974 the SCC reported that C. C. Granger, a utility building manufacturer, was said to be "very interested initially" but later delayed its plans "due to [the] economy." The SCC also related that the giant textile maker Burlington Industries had "tabled" its expansion plans "because of the economy." Johnston Associates International, consultants hired by the Soul City Company to try to attract outside industry, reported in 1974 that although they had met with a wide range of local and national firms, "no firm commitments" had resulted because of "the state of the economy."[52] The recession coincided with the launching of HUD's new town program, and it was clearly responsible for the difficulties experienced by many of the fledgling communities. Michael Spear, former general manager of the new community of Columbia, Maryland, later commented that "launching a new towns program in the early 1970s was like asking the Wright brothers to test their airplane in a hurricane and then concluding, when it crashed, that the invention did not work."[53]

Soul City staff also claimed that negative press coverage hurt their efforts to recruit outside industry. Given the paper's prominence within the business community, the *Wall Street Journal*'s coverage was particularly damaging. Several Soul City officials castigated the paper for an April 1979 article that asserted that the project was failing while McKissick lived "in style." In a front-page story, the *Journal* paid close attention to McKissick's lifestyle, detailing the family fleet of cars and even commenting on his "big microwave oven." The civil rights veteran was furious. "My house and my wife's automobile hardly seem to me to be national news," he fumed in a letter to the *Journal*'s editor. "Frankly, it is amusing to learn that the readers of the *Journal* are interested in our microwave oven." Other officials blamed the article for deterring outside industrialists from locating in Soul City. "By your colored and misleading writing," noted SCC partner Julian C. Madison, "you have severely damaged our vigorous efforts to attract the industry to the area that is needed to insure growth."[54]

The failure to attract industry was ultimately decisive. As the *Journal* itself noted, "Soul City's most serious problem is a shortage of jobs."[55] HUD made it clear that Soul City's success turned on its ability to secure industry. "The whole trick is getting jobs," concluded Roy Gast, the department's liaison with Soul City. "You need an engine, not just a chassis. That engine is jobs. If you fail to get those, the project isn't going to go."[56] Residents recalled that the lack of work deterred more people from moving in. Johnie Johnson later related that visitors to the town would tell her "the only thing that kept them from moving here was jobs. There was no industry, and they couldn't get jobs, and that is what kept them away."[57]

Business executives also claimed that they were reluctant to locate in Soul City because the name of the community had racial connotations. Rebuffing approaches from Soul City staff to build a plant in the new community, General Motors expressed concern about the name on three separate occasions. As early as May 1970, Hammer, Greene, and Siler, economic consultants to the project, warned McKissick that the name was "racially identifiable" and could inhibit "your immediate plans for soliciting industrial participation in the project."[58] In 1978 consultant Billy Carmichael made similar points. "Research would prove," he wrote, "that if you ask the public what 'Soul' means, a high percentage would respond that it has an association with things black i.e. soul food, soul music, etc." Seeking to find a racially neutral name, Carmichael suggested renaming the new community "Sunrise," "Genesis," or "South City."[59]

The proposal to change the name split Soul City's supporters along racial lines. Together with white consultants, Gordon Carey was a leading advocate of the move. "The evidence seems to be quite clear," he wrote in February 1978, "that from the standpoint of industrial development the name has become a negative factor."[60] Harvey Gantt, on the other hand, wanted to keep the status quo. "I am not convinced that a name change will do wonders in attracting industry," he wrote. "Anyone who is using the name 'Soul City' as a reason for not locating is merely reflecting traditional racism."[61] McKissick himself had always insisted that the name had biblical, and not racial, connotations.[62] Like Gantt he argued that changing it would amount to a surrender to white racism. In a biting memo, he dismissed the idea: "Those who have problems with the name, I submit, also have problems with Black Folks."[63]

It is questionable whether a name change would have given a significant boost to Soul City's efforts to attract more industry. As economic historian Bruce Schulman has shown, most of the companies that moved south in the 1970s and 1980s located in majority-white areas. Hoping to avoid racial conflict and believing that blacks were more prone to join unions, corporations steered clear of majority-black areas. As such, it was the racial composition of Warren County that was the real problem, something that the project had little control over. As Carmichael reported in 1978, "industry appears to have an objection to locating where the ethnic balance does not have some relationship to the national and/or regional ratios. The State feels that this is a major stumbling block to locating industry at Soul City."[64]

Throughout the 1970s and 1980s, the heavily black counties in the east and northeast of the state struggled to secure their share of the industries that were moving into North Carolina. Executives' fears that blacks would be more receptive to unionization were decisive, especially as the state attracted a great deal of investment by selling its low rate of unionization and ample supply of "willing labor."[65] Despite the state's efforts to attract industry to a wide variety of locations, new plants were most likely to locate in majority-white piedmont counties. In 1979 the mayor of the mostly black Northampton County town of Garysburg commented on the difficulties of securing outside industry even when a sound infrastructure was in place. "We've begged them to come," noted Wendell Perry. "We've got roads, we've got people to work, we've even got new sewers. We just can't get anybody to come."[66]

While McKissick won out in the fight to keep the name, the internal debate spotlighted the fact that Soul City had struggled to recruit white residents. By early 1977, builders were constructing housing subdivisions, and HUD reported that Soul City had a permanent population of fifty-five. Future residents had purchased lots, yet the town had failed to draw many whites. In February 1978, Gordon Carey charged, "Of the lots purchased in the subdivision, not one has been bought by a white homeowner except purchases by staff of our own Company."[67] Many local whites saw the development as all black, a perception encouraged by press reports. When the town was first announced, for example, the *Warren Record* headlined that Soul City would be an "All-Negro City."[68] Local whites also feared that an influx of poor blacks from northern ghettos would lead to a decline in local property values and would allow blacks to control the political life of the county. "A lot of folks went around saying the county was going to be ruined," recalled *Warren Record* editor Bignall Jones, "that the white folks were going to have to leave." Many whites also resented that the Soul City project had publicized Warren County's poverty.[69]

The Warren County area also had a sizeable Ku Klux Klan presence, and some local whites strongly resisted the town's development. When plans for the community were first announced, the white farmer who had sold the original site to McKissick was threatened by the Klan and had to leave the area until passions subsided. In 1973 a local white contractor working on the site noted sarcastically that he had supported Soul City "all along." "I think all the niggers should move in there and we could put a fence around it and let 'em stay there," he added. At the same time, however, many whites also doubted that the town would succeed and felt that there was little need to oppose it openly.[70]

Few local whites, however, were willing to move to the community. As was often the case in the rural South, integration proceeded at a slow pace in Warren County.[71] By the end of the 1960s, the county's schools had still not integrated, despite the best efforts of the NAACP. In July 1970, the state Department of Public Instruction reported that the county had a lower proportion of African American pupils enrolled in integrated schools than any other in the entire state. Whites in the area were also unused to blacks holding positions of authority; despite its black majority, whites dominated politics, and in the late 1960s no African American had held political office since the end of Reconstruction. Whites were unused to living and working with blacks as equals in the way that Soul City's supporters envisioned.[72]

By the summer of 1979, builders had completed the first subdivision at Soul City. Named Green Duke Village, it consisted of seventy-seven single-family homes on quarter- to half-acre lots.[73] Even internal literature steered clear of specifying exactly how many whites lived in the new homes, although the SCC insisted that some white families had taken up residence. As the company pointed out, negative press coverage did little to help. In an April 1979 article, for example, the *Wall Street Journal* described Soul City as a "new black town," angering residents. "As a matter of fact," wrote homeowner Janice R. Crump, "black people in this country historically have not engaged in building institutions which are racially exclusive." The *Journal* itself claimed that only four white families lived in Soul City.[74] Project supporters conceived of Soul City as "a Black-built, multi-racial town," yet many white observers assumed that because the town was black-built, it was for blacks. Project publicity stressed again and again that Soul City was open to all, yet it proved impossible to change entrenched white perceptions. In June 1979, the report that HUD used to justify its decision to cut off funding to Soul City pointed out that most whites still saw the development as "black": "The average potential white buyer sees Soul City as a negative connotation. . . . He conceives of it as a community built by Blacks for Blacks and is concerned that he would be living in an alien atmosphere."[75]

Despite the problems in securing industry and recruiting white residents, other parts of the Soul City project were more successful. In October 1976, the three-county water supply system was finished, benefiting a wide area. By February 1977, Soul City had a new public swimming pool and tennis courts, the only facilities of their type in the entire county. Operating on a pre-paid basis, a new health clinic served around fifty patients a day. Funded largely by a $1.1 million grant from the Office of Economic Opportunity, the HealthCo clinic made an important contribution to an area that lacked sufficient health care facilities. Before it was built, just twelve general practitioners had covered the forty-eight thousand residents of Vance and Warren Counties.[76]

The problems that Soul City faced were not unique; many new towns experienced similar difficulties. By May 1979, HUD had shut down or started foreclosure procedures on seven of its fifteen new developments, not including Soul City. The federal agency estimated that it had lost around $200 million as a result.[77] As the *Washington Post* reported, the entire new town program had fallen into "economic and political disarray," with rapid development often being constrained by excessive "red ink."[78] In 1973 a study by the Center for Urban and Regional Studies at the University of North Carolina concluded that the task of building new towns was truly "enormous." Inadequate financial backing, zoning problems, opposition from local officials, and difficulties in acquiring sufficient land held back many new communities. It was also very hard for emerging settlements to attract a balanced mix of housing and employment, with many satellite communities failing to create an independent job base. "Fully balanced new towns," noted the study, "that is, those providing job

opportunities, as well as housing and recreation facilities, are few in number."
Given these difficulties, by the late 1970s there was little public support for
further new town development.[79]

In pulling its funding for Soul City in June 1979, HUD cited a number
of problems with the development, although the failure to attract industry
was clearly decisive. The move to cut funding was also undoubtedly a reflection of declining levels of federal support for the new town program. In addition, McKissick's backing of the Republican party did him few favors once the
Democrats regained control of the White House under Jimmy Carter.[80]

Much of the press viewed HUD's decision as confirmation that Soul City
was a dismal failure. The *Richmond News Leader* called the project a "total
loss." "Who would want a jerry-built skeleton of an embryo town stuck in
the middle of nowhere?" it asked.[81] In contrast, McKissick and his supporters
argued that the HUD decision was premature because they had not been given
enough time to prove that their ideas could work. They asserted that they had
improved the value of the land and got it ready to receive industry just as HUD
had abandoned them.[82]

African Americans and liberal whites rallied behind McKissick. The North
Carolina Black Leadership Caucus protested the decision to HUD secretary
Patricia Roberts Harris. Soul City, they insisted, was "successful" and had "posi-
tively impacted on the quality of life for the majority of residents in the Vance,
Granville, and Warren Counties' region." As such, it would be a "travesty of
justice" if the project were to be shut down. In August 1979, more than one
hundred members of the caucus attended a picnic in Soul City to affirm their
support. Many backers of the new city saw HUD's decision as an example of
racial bias against minority projects. "The destruction of Soul City" claimed
the United Church of Christ's Commission for Racial Justice, "is yet another
example of the Carter Administration's flagrant demonstration of insensitivity
and disdain for Black people and Black economic development." McKissick
was pleased with the wide range of support he received, although he spent
much of the summer of 1979, a critical time for the project, recuperating from
a serious automobile wreck.[83]

Soul City's supporters were adamant in insisting that the project had not
been a complete failure. In March 1982, Durham minister Rev. Jerry E. Harper
Sr. defended the venture, citing the creation of the water system and a fire department, as well as new recreational facilities and industrial buildings. UNC–
Chapel Hill law professor Daniel Pollitt, a long-term supporter of the effort
who had served as an SCF Director, made similar points. In a letter to President

Jimmy Carter, Pollitt asserted that the journalists who looked for "sensational exposé" on Soul City had neglected its positive legacy. "The critics," he explained, "overlook and ignore the achievements: a three county water system; a sewerage disposal system serving a large area; the first health care delivery system in rural Warren County serving 250 patients each week; recreation and community facilities, and new jobs."[84]

McKissick himself repeatedly asserted that the project should be judged on its social merits. He claimed that Soul City had helped to stem out-migration, had taught African Americans how to use the political process, and had allowed black children to see black planners, architects, and engineers "for the first time." He was pleased that he had worked effectively with local officials to launch the water system, which he believed had helped promote interracial cooperation, one of the community's major goals. He was particularly proud of HealthCo. "We brought badly needed health services to this region," he wrote. "This was the first request of the citizens of this area to McKissick Enterprises."[85]

Soul City did play some part in stemming the out-migration that had plagued Warren County for decades. Between 1970 and 1979, Warren County's African American population actually increased by 20 percent. The county's experience was part of a broader trend; in the 1970s, for the first decade since Reconstruction, more blacks came to North Carolina than moved away. Over the course of the decade, North Carolina's African American population increased by 16.8 percent, slightly more than the growth in the white population. The change was caused by a variety of factors including the breakdown of Jim Crow segregation and increased employment opportunities. The Soul City project clearly made a contribution to this influx, especially as it publicized the idea of moving south to many northern blacks.[86]

Soul City had also helped to win funds for an economically depressed area. Planners claimed that 80 percent of the money they had won, or more than $17.9 million, went into projects that benefited the eighty-four thousand people who lived in Warren, Vance, and Granville counties. Grants for the construction of new water and sewer systems accounted for most of this amount, although Soul City officials also helped Warren County to secure a $1 million award for the construction of a new high school.[87]

Following HUD's decision, McKissick tried to fight on. In August 1979, he filed a lawsuit against the department in an effort to block a shutdown of the project, but ten months later he reached a settlement allowing the federal government to assume control of the vast majority of the site. In return the SCC kept eighty-eight acres, including the Soultech building. The settlement also protected the property of the residents and allowed them to maintain a parks and recreation association. Although the large sign at the main entrance to the new community remained, residents' addresses reverted to rural routes. In the years that followed, some firms did come into Soul City, although the town was never home to the large employers that its supporters had hoped for. By 1988 a chicken hatchery, a small textile firm, and a packaging company all operated facilities in Soul City, although many of their workers came from outlying communities. Incentives offered by the county had helped to secure these investments. "Soul City is not dead, we're not dead," claimed one of the two hundred residents still remaining. "The county is still trying to bring business in here. But it's hard."[88] In 1995 residents unsuccessfully tried to block the construction of a three hundred–bed prison just outside Soul City, worried that it would deter growth. Eight years later, they noted that the state facility had created employment, yet it had also ensured that many local people now associated Soul City with the prison. In 2000 residents endured another disappointment as CVS Pharmacy failed to locate a planned distribution center in Soul City, although a company that manufactured janitorial supplies subsequently moved into the Soultech building.[89]

The two hundred remaining residents were also anxious to dispute judgments of their community as a failure. Like Jane Ball-Groom, a New Yorker who had moved south in the 1970s, many still believed that Soul City was a special place. On learning of HUD's decision to foreclose, she rejected the idea of moving back to the Big Apple. "I thought to myself 'Why can't this be home?'" she later explained. "And that's what it turned out to be." By the mid-1990s, Ball-Groom had become president of Soul City's Park and Recreation Department, which also acted as the town's homeowners association. "We still have a community," she asserted defiantly. Others argued that Soul City continued to offer a good quality of life. "I love it here," commented resident Lucinda Goode in 1995. "I love the open space."[90]

McKissick himself epitomized residents' determination not to turn their back on the Soul City dream. Throughout the 1980s, he stubbornly stayed on in his Soul City home, commuting to his legal practice in Oxford. "Let's say I'm sorry that the government withdrew its support," he reflected in 1987. "I'm not disappointed. I'm the eternal optimist. I believe that Soul City will go and that we will have a city where it is now." In June 1990, McKissick was appointed a district court judge, a promotion that capped a distinguished legal career. As befitting a life spent breaking down racial barriers, the civil rights activist was the first African American judge in the ninth district.[91]

Despite its obvious problems, Soul City was clearly not the unmitigated failure that much of the press claimed at the time. Over the course of time, a new generation of the state's journalists came to recognize the project's positive contributions. In 1995 *Raleigh News and Observer* reporter Deidra Jackson journeyed to the community and noted that the project had left behind some important "legacies," including an assisted-living center named in McKissick's honor, a preschool/day care center, "a comprehensive bicounty health clinic," and "a full-fledged recreational facility." In 2003 *Durham Morning Herald* writer Jason Alston also wrote a generally positive account of McKissick's brave venture. Soul City, claimed Alston, was "the birthplace of a bold effort to improve the quality of life for the economically depressed rural regions of north-eastern North Carolina." By the early twenty-first century, local newspapers had hired more black journalists, and they treated Soul City more favorably than their white counterparts had in the 1970s.[92]

For more than a decade, McKissick devoted his life to Soul City, his unceasing energy driving the project forward. Many of the problems that afflicted the venture, such as the downturn in the economy and declining federal support for the new town movement, were also beyond his control. At the same time, however, McKissick should not be absolved of all responsibility for Soul City's problems. To some extent, his idealism hurt the project. The very features that attracted McKissick to Warren County—its remoteness and poverty—meant that he always faced an uphill battle to develop an economically viable community. As such, Soul City's social goals ultimately clashed with its economic ones.[93]

It would have taken an extraordinary amount of funding and time for McKissick to achieve his goals, which envisioned building a town of fifty thousand people in a location where even the county seat was a sleepy crossroads containing fewer than one thousand people. As such, McKissick's dream was highly ambitious. He had originally toyed with the idea of basing a community around small farming cooperatives, and this more limited proposal would have stood a greater chance of success. It was more in keeping with the existing economic base of the area, but McKissick sought an ambitious solution to the problems of the urban ghettos and later expanded his ideas.[94]

Historians have generally viewed the period after 1965 as a bleak one for supporters of the civil rights movement. While there were gains in integrating schools and workplaces, white support for civil rights fell away, creating a hostile political climate. By 1966 polls indicated that 70 percent of whites believed that blacks were pushing too fast for equality, and two years later three out of four felt that blacks were receiving the same treatment as whites in their own communities.[95] Following the collapse of Jim Crow segregation, some civil rights organizations also lost a clear sense of direction. Like CORE, SNCC fell apart, while the SCLC and NAACP struggled to secure positive media attention. A key problem facing all these groups was that they no longer had a clear-cut enemy to focus attention on. It was relatively easy to organize a march to desegregate public facilities, but after 1965 the problems that remained—employment discrimination, poverty, slum housing—were much harder to dramatize. Once African Americans had achieved legal equality, it also became much more difficult for them to mobilize white support. Many whites felt that it was wrong for blacks to be denied individual rights such as the vote, but they rejected group solutions to tackle black poverty. In addition, whites often opposed moves toward housing integration, feeling that this was a private domain that should be protected against government intrusion.[96]

In many ways, the Soul City story highlighted the difficult climate that confronted civil rights groups in the 1970s. Reflecting broader resistance to equal housing, whites failed to respond to McKissick's call to live in a model, integrated community.[97] Soul City also showed just how difficult it was to change fundamental patterns of economic inequality. When it came to tackling the poverty of North Carolina black belt counties, there would be no quick fixes. Despite the influx of some industry, since the 1970s these counties have consistently failed to secure their fair share of the state's economic growth. Although North Carolina has become "the superstar of the Sunbelt," it has also had consistently high poverty rates. Ironically, some of its poorest counties are located little more than an hour away from the booming Triangle area. In the last decade, scores of small Tar Heel communities have been further hit by the decline of the textile industry, the backbone of the state's economy for most of the twentieth century.[98]

The Soul City story also reminds us that important civil rights activism took place after 1965. It shows how movement veterans such as McKissick and Carey kept fighting to address the thorny problem of economic inequality. Like the workers who brought Title VII litigation, Soul City's supporters knew that they were unlikely to secure quick victories, but they also felt that it was important to keep up the struggle for racial justice. McKissick himself repeatedly put economic concerns at the forefront of his agenda after 1965. "There's nothing," he blasted in 1978, "that cannot be put into an economic equation."

For the former CORE chief, Soul City was a bold effort to show that the fight for civil rights was an ongoing one. As *New York Times* journalist Wayne King reported in 1974, for McKissick the pioneer community was "a culmination of the civil rights struggle—an integrated, livable community that will not only bring blacks and whites together on an equal footing, but that will also demonstrate the black man's capacity to take on and achieve vast projects such as new communities." Despite all the setbacks, he fought to realize his idea until the end. "I don't intend to leave Soul City; I intend to stay and help it grow," he commented a few years before his death. "I will never leave, period, because I believe in the concept. I see it taking root, and the new-town concept is a valid concept notwithstanding what anyone says." True to his word, McKissick stayed on in Soul City until his death from lung cancer in April 1991. He was buried in a small family plot, in the shadow of the Green Duke House.[99]

"They don't care nothing for Blacks"

The *Sledge* Case and the Long Struggle
for Civil Rights at J. P. Stevens

In the 1970s, the unassuming textile town of Roanoke Rapids, North Carolina, regularly made national headlines. The small settlement in the northeastern part of the state was dominated by the giant J. P. Stevens textile firm, which employed close to four thousand people in eight separate mills.[1] Starting in 1963, the Textile Workers Union of America selected Stevens as the target for a major organizing effort. Bitterly resisting the TWUA's drive, Stevens gained national notoriety as a labor law violator. As the site of the company's most significant production center in the South, Roanoke Rapids became the key battleground in this battle. It was at a Stevens mill in Roanoke Rapids that Crystal Lee Sutton stood on a dusty work bench and held up a handmade sign that read "UNION," an act of defiance that was later immortalized in the movie *Norma Rae*. It was also in Roanoke Rapids that representatives from J. P. Stevens and the Amalgamated Clothing and Textile Workers Union (ACTWU) gathered in October 1980 for crucial talks to bring the Stevens campaign to a conclusion. The resulting agreement brought an end to a brutal fight that had lasted for over seventeen years.[2]

In addition to the union campaign, Roanoke Rapids was also the setting for *Sledge v. J. P. Stevens*, a landmark Title VII case. In the fall of 1970, thirteen black employees charged Stevens with discrimination in hiring and promotion, initiating what the U.S. Court of Appeals called "an across-the-board assault upon the employment practices of the J. P. Stevens and Company."[3] The case later expanded to involve nearly three thousand plaintiffs, and it stayed before the courts for nineteen years. *Sledge* was significant for its role in pioneering the use of statistical evidence to prove class-wide discrimination. Despite this, the case has not received the attention from scholars that the union campaign has, even though it was one of the first large class actions brought under Title VII. *Sledge* was also a training ground for Richard T. Seymour, the young lawyer who was the plaintiffs' lead counsel. In the wake of *Sledge*, the Washington-based attorney went on to bring high-profile employment discrimination cases against Home Depot, United Parcel Service, and Boeing. "The class action procedure," noted Seymour in 2002, "has for thirty-seven years been, and remains, the most important means for achieving the goal of equal opportunity promised by Title VII."[4]

While Title VII litigation proved crucial in forcing employers to redress employment discrimination, it had severe limitations. Many big class actions became mired in complex legal proceedings, and thousands of aggrieved workers ended up retiring before cases were resolved. *Sledge* itself reveals both the important role played by Title VII litigation and its drawbacks. The case prodded Stevens to improve its treatment of African American workers, but the wheels of justice turned slowly. Although the courts consistently ruled against Stevens, its intransigence meant that the plaintiffs had to fight long and hard to secure justice. Top company officials approached *Sledge* just as they did the union dispute, appealing unfavorable decisions and forcing their workers to wait many years in order to secure piecemeal gains.

Sledge reminds us that many blacks had to keep fighting for their rights long after 1965. The passage of equal rights legislation in the mid-1960s has often been considered the high-point of the civil rights movement but it left much undone. In particular, legal equality did not mean that blacks had economic equality, as in a wide range of industries they still struggled to get jobs or were only hired in low-paying positions. Further activism was needed to break down employment discrimination, especially in the southern states, where legalized racial segregation had helped to codify the best positions as "white."[5]

Sledge graphically spotlighted just how much remained to be done before blacks could get a fair deal at the nation's second-largest textile firm. Until at least 1969, all clerical, supervisory, and weaving jobs were completely reserved for whites, and hiring was dependent on the whims of supervisors who had close social and familial links with white employees. It took many years to even begin to break down deep-seated discrimination at J. P. Stevens. Both the *Sledge* case and the union campaign ultimately forced the textile giant to treat its employees better, but the battle was a long and torturous one. The 1964 Civil Rights Act was a starting place in this struggle rather than and an end in itself, and the meaning of the act was still being contested well into the 1980s.[6]

After 1965 civil rights lawyers paid considerable attention to the textile industry because it was the region's largest employer. As NAACP lawyer Julius Chambers recalled, textile cases were crucial because the industry was the "lifeblood" of many southern communities.[7] From a twenty-first century perspective, it is easy to forget how textiles dominated the southern economy just thirty years ago; in 1973, for instance, it employed nearly seven hundred thousand workers in eight states, almost twice as many as any other industry. If blacks were to improve their economic position, they needed more jobs in the hundreds of textile mills that dotted the region.[8] Right across the textile belt, however, African Americans were barred from holding production jobs in the industry. In South Carolina, the Segregation Act of 1915 made it illegal for anyone "engaged in the business of cotton textile manufacturing . . . to allow . . . operatives . . . of different races to labor and work together within the same room." The law even specified that black and white textile workers could not look out of the same window. As late as 1964, less than 5 percent of mill workers in South Carolina were African American. In other southern states, social customs ensured that the minuscule number of African American textile workers toiled in separate areas from whites.[9]

While some African American men could secure menial mill jobs, African American women were largely barred from the southern textile plants. This ban reflected a broader cultural reluctance to hire black women for "public work"; tobacco was the only southern industry to employ significant numbers of black females, and here they were confined to dirty jobs stemming and sorting the raw product. Worried that they might lose their domestic help, white industrial workers fought to keep black women out of the plants.[10]

By the mid-1960s, little had changed to break down traditional discriminatory practices in the southern textile industry. In 1966 an EEOC investigation found that black textile workers were clustered in a limited range of low-paying jobs. As a result, between 1964 and 1980 virtually every large southern textile company was involved in Title VII litigation. The companies that were sued included household names such as Burlington Industries, Cannon Mills, Dan River Mills, and Cone Mills.[11] Apart from *Sledge*, Stevens was involved in separate class actions at its plants in Abbeville, South Carolina, and Stanley, North Carolina.[12]

In the Title VII cases brought against textile employers, black men, who had always been employed in menial, non-production jobs, complained chiefly about the difficulties of upgrading to better positions. In contrast, black women complained about how hard it was to just get hired at all. Once employed, however, they were able to secure assignments largely similar to white women, partly because white men monopolized the best-paying jobs in the industry.[13]

Sledge illustrated these broader patterns of discrimination. Throughout the case, female plaintiffs charged the company with hiring discrimination, but their male counterparts concentrated on the difficulty of securing promotions. As Seymour explained in his trial remarks, "One of the curious things about textile cases, including this one, seems to be that there is a very different treatment accorded to black females than to black males. We believe that black females find it more difficult to get hired and once hired, we think that their initial assignments tend to be much more like those of white females than the initial assignments of black males are like those of white males."[14]

Until the mid-1960s, hiring patterns at Stevens' Roanoke Rapids plants followed the industry norm; African Americans made up less than 5 percent of the workforce, and they were confined to dirty, non-production positions. After buying the mills from the Simmons Company in 1956, Stevens hired local managers who saw segregation as normal. As late as 1962, the company's personnel manager told an interviewer from the American Friends Service Committee that blacks were "not qualified" to run most textile jobs.[15] Although a small number of African American men worked in the mills, they were never allowed to run the machines. "I worked for Simmons when they had the plant," recalled Sammy Alston, a Halifax County resident who came from a large farming family. "There weren't no black peoples doing no production job; only thing they was doing were like hauling this cotton, and run these hand trucks and keeping the yard clean." Blacks who worked for Stevens in the 1960s related that little had changed. Bennett Taylor, a soft-spoken man who started at the mills in 1965, explained that "blacks then was getting hired but they was getting hired in a job that that was the only place that they could go, it was a dirty job that a white person didn't want to do."[16]

The textile town of Roanoke Rapids was a predominantly white community in an area of the state that was heavily black and poor. In the early 1970s, the town's population was 26 percent African American, but the surrounding county was around 50 percent black.[17] In *Sledge*, company officials argued that they had traditionally hired only a few blacks because they had not applied for textile jobs. Executives painted a picture of a largely content black community that had chosen to stay in the countryside and work on the land. As veteran company manager Edwin Akers put it, the "industrial town" of Roanoke Rapids was located in a "predominantly agricultural" area. "During earlier years of operation," he explained, "while we had Negroes in our plants, they did not come in large numbers seeking employment and competing with whites for these jobs." Personnel director James Miller concurred. "In past years," he testified in 1972, "blacks have not sought the jobs particularly in textile mills, they've not come after the jobs, that they've not been applying to us, whereas whites were." Like many whites, Akers and Miller believed that blacks had accepted segregation as a way of life.[18]

In reality, however, opportunities for blacks in the town's textile plants were very limited. Whites jealously guarded the best jobs in the mills and conspired to ensure that they were qualified to fill them. J. P. Stevens' managers had close links with the white community, links that *Sledge* cleverly exposed. During the trial in 1972, company officials admitted that the all-white high school ran textile-training classes as part of their curriculum and even used equipment supplied by Stevens. Akers explained that the high school had been home to a "textile department" operated by Professor Will Nelson, a former dean of the textile school at North Carolina State University. The relationship provided the company with a steady stream of young whites who left high school and went straight into the mills. "Many of our employees who are white got their training in the schools," he noted, "and this kind of background which gave them greater skills for the technical operations of our plant; the textile department in our high school had a course in textile design, it had looms and other machines in the high school so that people could learn to operate these machines while still in school. . . . Many of our employees grew up in Roanoke Rapids, went to these schools and therefore had a better opportunity to perform well on these jobs." Under cross-examination, an awkward Akers admitted that the black schools had not been provided any of these facilities and were indeed "separate but unequal."[19]

Whites used both formal and informal mechanisms to keep control of the best jobs. Into the 1970s, the company's application form asked applicants whether they had any immediate family members working in Roanoke Rapids, a move that officials defended on the grounds that they needed to ascertain whether a potential employee was a "stable person." In reality, however, the form allowed company officials to identify the relatives or friends of existing employees and give them preference. White workers and supervisors also attended the same social clubs and churches, and many lived in the neat mill houses that clustered near the plants. Promotion opportunities were restricted to workers in the same department, effectively excluding employees in the all-black non-production departments. In addition, job opportunities were never posted, ensuring that employees outside of the immediate area were unlikely to know about them. Stevens was able to continue these practices largely unchallenged. As the dominant employer in town, few residents were willing to criticize the firm. Even the *Roanoke Rapids Daily Herald* provided a mouthpiece for the company, faithfully supporting its opposition to organized labor and promoting the activities of workers who opposed the union.[20]

African Americans saw Roanoke Rapids as a deeply racist and conservative community. Their oral testimony directly contradicts white assertions that blacks had accommodated themselves to the social order and were not interested in holding the best jobs in the mills. A lifelong NAACP activist, Joe Moody related that when blacks tried to secure non-traditional jobs at Stevens' plants, company officials "always had some kind of excuse." After investigating the company's hiring patterns, he came to the conclusion that "lot of sections of people . . . got on at J. P. Stephenson because of who they know."[21] Bennett Taylor had similar memories, relating that blacks could only "get on" at the plant if they had a contact with one of the white supervisors. "When I first went to work there," he asserted, "back then, bear in mind now a lot of times the only way that black workers got to work in that plant you had to know somebody that already worked in there." Bearing this out, Taylor was only hired because one of his former classmates put in a good word with his boss. Taylor also explained that supervisors retained enormous authority before *Sledge* began to bring the firm to accountability. "They allowed their supervisors to do whatever and however they wanted to to the employees back then," he reflected sadly.[22]

Those who did challenge Stevens often paid a heavy price. The company that became famous for discharging union members also disliked any criticism of its racial practices. In the late 1950s, Stevens worker Jettie Purnell made efforts to breach the color line and claimed he was "blackballed" as a result. Wiry and energetic, he bitterly recalled how blacks had been restricted to a small range of non-production jobs and had had to watch as whites were promoted over them even when they had less seniority. "Let's go back to the fifties when I worked there," he related in a 1996 interview. "At first all the black did was scrub floors, worked out there in the opening cotton, you know inhaling cotton, wasn't no blacks in the mills, didn't have any black women. . . . The only thing they would hire you for was to clean, work out in the yard, cleaning up the yards. The mill company controlled everything then, the hospital, the country club. . . . This town has been something else, man; the textile mills was here before the town." Purnell felt that only outside pressure could force the company to change. "The mill," he charged, "seemed like as long as we was in semi-slavery, they was pleased with it."[23]

Most African Americans felt that a lawsuit was the only way to improve their opportunities at the area's largest employer. Former plaintiffs emphasized that they brought the suit to gain better promotional opportunities and to tackle the favoritism that company officials showed to whites. "I had been there like ten years," explained Sammy Alston. "They would bring people in there right off the street, white. I was qualified for a job making fifty more cents an hour, a dollar an hour, they wouldn't move me up. They'd put them right over the top of me. You couldn't get no promotions. . . . They wouldn't hire the black people because they just didn't want them to get ahead." Experienced African American men described repeated rebuffs while whites rose easily up the line. "I have been refused a position," wrote plaintiff Jasper Daniel, "but outsiders are brought in and given positions."[24]

Sledge showed that many blacks desperately needed textile jobs. In the 1970s, increased mechanization allowed southern farmers to lay off thousands of black laborers. Across the region as a whole, the number of blacks working in agriculture was halved between 1950 and 1959, and the fall continued in the 1960s and 1970s.[25] While textile jobs were not lucrative, they were a more reliable source of income than farming. Scores of African Americans tried to get hired at Stevens every day, making repeated trips to the cramped personnel office. Here they sat and watched as whites were invariably hired more easily than blacks. "I applied in '74 and I would check every Tuesday and Thursday for a good four month and always the same bull," wrote Denise Johnson. "I know for sure that they wouldn't call me so finally I just stopped going." "I felt it was because of my color," wrote another unsuccessful applicant, "because whites were hired, and I told them I would accept whatever they had and still was not hired." A local woman in her twenties, Lucy Sledge fronted the case after Stevens refused to recall her following a layoff. Applying to get reemployed, she noticed that whites got positions much more easily than blacks. "Every white that went in got hired," she charged. "Every black that went in didn't." She later recalled that so many blacks were waiting to get jobs that they often resorted to lining up on the porch outside the office.[26]

African Americans also complained that when they were fortunate enough to secure jobs at Stevens, they were made to work harder than their white counterparts. The official complaint in *Sledge* alleged that blacks were given "more difficult work" than whites, and many plaintiffs told the court of how they had struggled to deal with heavy workloads. "I was gradually given more looms until they reached 18 or 19 in all," explained Victoria Nicholson, who started work in the late 1960s. "My job was to keep these machines running as much as possible in my 8 hour shift. I had no lunch breaks. I had to eat whenever I got all my machines running or eat on the job. . . . I was doing all I could to keep all these machines running with bad warps, machines being worked on, no lunch breaks and running from one end of my job to the other. I was fed up with all of this so I walked out."[27] Sammy Alston charged that Stevens used the integration of the mills to "get more" production, an allegation heard in other places. It had some validity. As textile manufacturers faced increasing foreign competition, they looked for any way they could to increase labor productivity and were able to capitalize on blacks' desperation for industrial work.[28]

By the late 1960s, aggrieved African Americans wanted to bring a class action against Stevens. Joe Moody recalled that blacks became increasingly frustrated with the textile giant after 1965. A muscular man in his forties, Moody worked at Albemarle Paper Company, the other main employer in town. A fearless activist, he was the lead plaintiff in *Moody v. Albemarle Paper* (1966), an important Title VII case.[29] Moody became especially interested in filing charges against Stevens after it took his wife more than five years to secure an entry-level position with the firm. Although Mable Moody was finally taken on in 1967, she was only given a position on the undesirable graveyard shift and watched as newly hired whites were placed on straight days. "My main problem," she explained later, "was that there was some in after I asked for first shift. Some on first shift that came after I went there."[30]

In the late 1960s, many blacks complained to Moody that Stevens was not hiring blacks or was refusing to promote them fairly when it did. In the summer of 1969, Moody persuaded several brave activists to file EEOC charges against the giant firm. Later in the year, he contacted Richard T. Seymour about the complaints. A recent graduate from Harvard Law School, Seymour was working with the Washington Research Project, a non-profit group that sponsored fair employment litigation. Immediately interested in the case, Seymour visited Moody at his Roanoke Rapids home and recruited him to help build a broad class action. "The lawsuit started in my living room, right here, where we got together right here," recalled Moody. "I followed the case on up to Raleigh. . . . Richard T. Seymour, he just had come out of law school, and then he came up here and myself at my house and we met with some of the group straight after then. Then I done a lot of investigation for him all over Halifax County and Northampton County . . . and he give me a list of names because he was trying to reach the peoples was involved and worked in J. P. Stephenson at that time."[31]

In October 1970, thirteen plaintiffs charged the company with a wide range of discriminatory practices. "For many years," they asserted, "the defendant has discriminated in hiring, initial assignments, promotions, and the terms and conditions of employment against black employees and applicants because of their race."[32] Because of their broad claims, the district court certified the class to include all black workers at the plants on and after October 2, 1967, as well as unsuccessful black applicants since that date who charged that they had been turned away because of their race. Under North Carolina's statute of limitation, the company's liability was restricted to the three years before the filing of the case. At the time of the trial in November 1972, the class was identified as 1,618 present and former employees in addition to 1,268 applicants. Partly as a response to the demands of *Sledge*, in the early 1970s Seymour set up his own law practice and devoted much of his time to working on the challenging case.[33]

The case revealed that Stevens had only begun to hire more blacks after the passage of the 1964 Civil Rights Act and that this law was just the starting point in the long struggle for equality. "When the 1964 Civil Rights Bill was passed in 1964," recalled Moody, "all companies had a year to comply with the law, and at that time Stephenson didn't feel, he didn't feel that he should comply with the law." Using company documents that they obtained through pleadings, the plaintiffs documented their charges of hiring discrimination in statistical terms, showing that whites had a much better chance of being taken on than blacks. Although African Americans consistently made up the majority of applicants, whites still got more jobs. In 1971, for example, 74.5 percent of white male applicants were hired, compared to 41.9 percent of black males. Among women, whites were almost three times as likely to be hired as blacks (56.4 percent compared to 20.3 percent). Similar disparities were present in data samples from 1969, 1970, and 1972.[34]

Data produced at the trial also showed that although Stevens had hired more blacks since 1965, they remained disproportionately grouped in the lower-paying jobs. From 1967 to 1972, the number of African American employees in the plants rose from 533 to 1,271, while the number of white workers fell slightly (from 2,809 to 2,499). As the company admitted, however, it was hiring more blacks partly because many whites were leaving textiles and taking jobs in higher-paying industries.[35] Whites still monopolized the best positions, and this was reflected in pay disparities. In 1972 black males in the Roanoke Rapids plants earned $2.33 an hour while white men made $2.67.[36] Seymour's team also proved that blacks were not paid less because they were less qualified, as company officials suggested. An analysis of employees hired between 1960 and October 1, 1972, showed that a black male with previous textile experience earned $2.38 an hour while a white man with the same qualifications received $2.81. A similar differential was present when employees had not worked in the industry before.[37]

The well-paying weaving jobs proved particularly difficult to secure. At the time of the trial, weavers earned $2.74 an hour, almost twice as much as the lowest-paid entry-level workers, but the job could still be performed by applicants with no textile experience. Whites were able to secure the lion's share of weaving positions through their contacts with supervisors and were reluctant to relinquish them. From 1969 to 1972, around one-third of white new hires got jobs as weavers, but only 1 percent of blacks secured these posts. In May 1969, all of the weavers in two of the company's main mills were white.[38] Whites also stopped blacks from becoming fixers, relatively high-paid workers who repaired looms or kept them in good working order. In November 1972, Stevens employed 180 fixers, and just two of them were black.[39]

It proved difficult for blacks to get higher-paying jobs because company officials clung to beliefs that whites were better qualified and more efficient. Even in the 1970s, Edwin Akers insisted that blacks were not as capable as their white counterparts. "The Negroes in these weaving jobs have not had as much experience in many cases as some of the whites," he claimed in 1972.[40] Company officials also worried that their white employees would leave if more blacks were hired.[41] As Joe Moody alleged, whites clearly felt threatened by a black influx into the mills. "You had a lot of the whites resisted," he explained, "same thing with the Albemarle Paper Company Case, resisted, because they felt like we was going to take their job, we were taking these jobs away from them."[42]

White-collar and supervisory jobs also remained off-limits to African Americans. At the time of the trial, Stevens had 165 overseers, and all of them were white. In November 1972, the company also had over two hundred white clerical employees but had only just hired its first two black clerical workers, clearly a response to the pressure created by *Sledge*. James Miller explained this pattern by again insisting that whites "were better qualified for the jobs than the blacks were." Many blacks had tried hard to break into office jobs. Among those turned away were a number of persons with college qualifications or previous office experience. Some applicants had made twenty trips to the personnel office to seek white-collar positions.[43]

When Judge Franklin T. Dupree issued his decision in the case in December 1975, the statistical evidence amassed by the plaintiffs proved to be decisive. A native North Carolinian, Dupree understood the issues well. Although the judge dismissed most of the individual claims on the grounds that they could not be proven, he found the evidence of collective wrongdoing to be overwhelming. Stevens, he ruled, had discriminated against blacks as a class with respect to hiring, initial job assignments, transfers, promotions, layoffs, and recalls. Hiring and promotion were decided entirely by the "subjective opinions" of the company's all-white supervisors. "Stevens' policy of heavy reliance upon subjective considerations in hiring and promotion," he explained, "and its policy of relying exclusively upon an informal 'grapevine' network among departmental overseers in making interdepartment promotions, in effect gives the officials making these decisions the power to discriminate. This finding is strengthened by the fact that all officials making these decisions are white, and all such officials have always been white." Dupree later admitted that he had been swayed by the plaintiffs' statistical evidence. "In the problem of racial discrimination," he asserted, "statistics often tell much and courts listen."[44]

Dupree required that Stevens use racial quotas in order to redress its wrongs. In particular, in each calendar quarter the company was required to offer the same percentage of positions to both white and black applicants. The company was also mandated to show for two years that the average pay rate for new black and white employees was the same, and it had to establish an employee training program in which half of the trainees were black. In addition, company officials were obliged to make "special efforts" to recruit African Americans into clerical, supervisory, and weaving jobs. They were not allowed to place whites in supervisory positions until blacks constituted one-third of all supervisors.[45] Class members were also entitled to back pay relief, although they had to file claims so that the court could determine their individual payments. This requirement drew protests from both Seymour and from EEOC lawyers, who argued that it would discourage valid claims. As EEOC general counsel Abner W. Sibal put it, "The only purpose the claim filing requirement will serve in this case is to eliminate the claims of class members who are either confused or afraid."[46]

Arguing that the relief required by Dupree was "drastic and draconian," Stevens immediately appealed the decision. The company's objections centered on the use of quotas, which they viewed as "discrimination on the basis of race." In a notice to its employees, the company declared that its actions in hiring and promoting should be determined by "ability and merit" rather than "race and color." Company attorney Whiteford Blakeney vigorously resisted the plaintiffs' efforts to speed up the pace of integration by imposing quotas; managers had to retain the right to manage, he insisted, and imposing numerical targets represented "insanity in short order." Managers feared that their plants would be overwhelmed by an influx of blacks, causing whites to flee the industry.[47]

As the basis for their appeal, company officials also pointed out that they were already hiring more blacks, and they took heart in the fact that the individual claims had not been proven. If discrimination had not taken place on an individual basis, they asserted, then Dupree was wrong to conclude that it could occur in general. Retained by Stevens in both its labor relations and civil rights cases, Blakeney scoffed at Seymour's reliance on collective data, insisting that his adversary had presented "nothing" except statistics that could be interpreted in many different ways. Executives also continued to see blacks as less qualified for textile jobs. As Blakeney related in 1976, "If the company operated, as they tell me, strictly on efficiency, they wouldn't be moving the blacks as fast as they are moving them now."[48]

Stevens' conduct in *Sledge* paralleled how it reacted to the union campaign. In both cases, company officials jealously defended their right to manage and appealed unfavorable rulings. During its long fight with the union, the company accumulated what National Labor Relations Board trial examiner Marvin Roth called "an extraordinary history of unfair labor practice litigation before this Board and the courts." Between 1965 and 1976, Stevens was cited for violating the National Labor Relations Act in fifteen different cases, paying out around $1.3 million in back pay to approximately three hundred workers.[49] The firm's resistance to outside interference reflected the strong control exerted by top managers such as Robert T. Stevens and James D. Finley. Both men came from military backgrounds and felt that civil rights and union groups were unfairly targeting their firm. They vigorously defended the direct relationship between employer and employee and disliked intrusion from unwanted third parties. In its annual reports, Stevens grouped civil rights and labor litigation together and defended itself against any accusation of wrongdoing in both areas. Such litigation, noted the firm's 1972 report, was "normal in the course of business" for a company with over forty thousand workers. Shareholders were also repeatedly assured that the company's financial position would not be "materially affected" by the cost of lawsuits.[50]

The union campaign also helped to mobilize blacks to support *Sledge*. Some plaintiffs, such as James Boone and Bennett Taylor, were keen TWUA members who saw the union as a means of tackling racial discrimination. The union attracted a considerable amount of support from blacks, and this helped it to eventually prevail over Stevens. In 1959 and 1965, the TWUA had lost representation elections at the mills, but in 1974, with considerably more blacks in the plants, they were able to win a narrow victory. Paul Swaity, who helped run the 1974 campaign, recalled that, "The first meetings were almost totally all black people, who would come out to meetings." In 1976 the TWUA also intervened as a plaintiff in the case and criticized the company's efforts to "delay relief" to the affected class.[51]

The union's popularity among blacks did make it difficult to recruit whites, a problem that organizers also confronted in other locations.[52] In Roanoke Rapids supervisors used their contacts with the white community to their advantage, telling their friends and relatives to oppose the union. On the eve of the 1974 election, company propaganda also warned whites that blacks could "dominate" the union and "control it in this Plant." Some whites steered clear of the TWUA on racial grounds, worried that it would only accelerate the advancement of blacks that *Sledge* was threatening.[53] Wilson Lambert commented in 1977 that he was opposed to the union because it supported "nigger rights." "It seems to be," he added, "that the ones you get at the union hall are colored." Kermit Smith also associated the TWUA with black rights: "I believe because the union is about eighty-five per cent black people, that they have been promised—or maybe they tend to believe more what they're promised, I don't know what it is—but they have been promised a lot of things that the Union cannot possibly deliver." Both the *Sledge* case and the union threatened white workers' control over the best jobs. "The whites resented the union," remembered Jettie Purnell, "because they was told that union would elevate black above them, and they believed that." Aware of the need for some white support, in 1976 the union tried to reshape the seniority system in a way that was fair to both blacks and whites, but Stevens successfully rebuffed these proposals.[54]

A large and complex case, *Sledge* remained on appeal until October 1978, when the fourth circuit court in Richmond agreed that Stevens had violated the 1964 Civil Rights Act. The court, however, failed to grant all of the relief sought by the plaintiffs and struck down the "rigid" racial quotas that had been ordered by Dupree. Justifying its move, the court argued that other injunctive relief should be given the opportunity to work before strict affirmative action remedies were applied. Taking note of the company's concerns, it also accepted that quotas could cause "disruption" to "the operation of the defendant's business."[55]

Following this, the parties engaged in lengthy negotiations in order to draft an amended consent decree.[56] After eighteen months of proceedings, both sides approved a heavily revised document. In it, Stevens was required to take a number of concrete steps to help black workers, including appointing a special complaints officer who was empowered to act upon charges of racial discrimination. Although quotas were ruled out, company officials were also required to institute a job bidding and posting system.[57] Under the amended agreement, Stevens had to report its progress to the court, and the plaintiffs' lawyers were empowered to bring proceedings if they felt that the company was not in compliance.[58]

These provisions undoubtedly pushed executives to offer blacks a wider range of jobs. Between 1972 and 1981, for example, the proportion of blacks at the bottom of the pay scale fell from 34.8 percent to 21.7 percent.[59] By the early 1980s, company officials also pointed out that around 50 percent of their new hires were black, a clear increase from the pre-*Sledge* period. By this time, African Americans were working their way into well-paid production positions in much larger numbers. Some noticeable breakthroughs occurred; in October 1980, for example, the company hired its first black technician, and by February 1981 it had fifteen black salaried workers. Until the case was filed, no blacks had ever held salaried posts. Blacks were also taking part in training programs in healthy numbers. In the second half of 1984, for instance, forty blacks and twenty-seven whites were being taught to operate highly skilled jobs.[60]

Despite these improvements, much remained to be done. Carefully monitoring the company's progress, Richard Seymour was quick to point out that black men continued to be paid less than their white counterparts. In December 1981, for example, the attorney complained that there were "still strong patterns of racial disparities in pay rates of male employees, indicating that black males are assigned to substantially lower-paying jobs than those to which white males are assigned." White men in the mills earned an average of $5.50 an hour but blacks made only $4.97. The company was also slow to implement its job bidding and posting system, even though this was required by both the consent decree and the union contract.[61]

In correspondence with their lawyers, plaintiffs charged that J. P. Stevens was still guilty of racial discrimination. "They don't care nothing for Blacks at J. P. Stevens and Co.," wrote Hattie F. Lewis in February 1981. "They are Prejudice." "I would like to thank some one," added David Burnette, "because it time for somebody to do something about J. P. Stevens and start helping the Black." Others still reported being turned away by company officials while whites were hired. "The people who got jobs was white and I wonder why," fumed Larry Cornelius Dowton. "Is my skin the wrong color or is it no place for a black man trying to live and make it in a white man world[?]"[62]

The company's officials certainly refused to accept that they were guilty of discriminating against blacks. Throughout the 1980s, the firm's lawyers continued to fight the case in the courts. In February 1989, Dupree returned to court to hear company arguments that he should vacate his findings of liability in the light of recent Supreme Court decisions that had limited the scope of employment class actions. In particular, in *Watson v. Fort Worth Bank and Trust* (1988), Justice Sandra Day O'Connor ruled that a Title VII plaintiff must prove that a defendant had acted with "discriminatory intent or motive" in order to secure relief. After *Watson*, just proving the discriminatory impact of employment policies, as the plaintiffs had done in *Sledge*, was no longer sufficient to secure a finding against a corporation. Dupree, however, stood by his original ruling. In an eloquent judgement, he referred again to the statistical evidence in the case: "At trial plaintiffs offered statistical evidence which showed unmistakably that the percentages of white applicants hired by the defendant far exceeded the percentages of black applicants hired; that the hourly rates of pay of whites were substantially greater than that of blacks; and that these disparities persisted despite the fact that black applicants were shown to possess qualifications such as education and experience equal to and in many cases superior to those of white applicants." After carefully reviewing the company's arguments, the experienced judge added that "the defendant has pointed to nothing . . . that would preclude such a finding if the trial were conducted today on the same evidence."[63]

While Dupree's ruling stood, it was overshadowed by the decline of the southern textile industry. By the late 1980s, the industry had fallen on hard times and was no longer hiring large numbers of new employees. Hit by rising competition from cheap imports, Stevens employed 23,400 people in 1987, down from 44,100 a decade earlier.[64] In 1988 the company disappeared as a corporate entity when it was bought by West Point Pepperell and divided up into three separate firms. Pepperell's lawyers tried to argue that *Sledge* liability did not apply to them, but Dupree refused to let the firm off the hook so easily. The new company, he declared, retained access to the "records and managerial personnel" necessary to defend itself in the case. This ruling ensured that the firm was finally forced to accept the judgment of the court, although by this time many plaintiffs had left the mills.[65]

By the 1990s, Roanoke Rapids had become a struggling mill town. Although some mills still ran, others had closed, and few new industries had come into the area to replace them. In the fall of 2000, West Point Stevens, the successor to West Point Pepperell, shut a major towel-making plant in Roanoke Rapids, severely damaging the area's economy. By this time, many class members had retired, lost their jobs, or moved to other towns in search of work. Those who stayed in the industry emphasized that they still confronted racism. Veteran worker James Boone declared in 1996 that "it has improved a little bit, but it's not improved the way I think that we should be at this point, in the nineties. Minorities still have a hard time being promoted to higher-paying jobs, minorities are still fighting to climb the ladder. . . . We took the jobs that the whites didn't want to do . . . and right now we're still taking the jobs that they don't want to do."[66]

While racism continued to exist, former plaintiffs also stressed that *Sledge* had forced Stevens to treat its black employees more fairly. Sammy Alston declared in 1996 that "nothing wouldn't have changed if we hadn't filed. J. P. Stevens, he was really, he was a lawbreaker. He was a hard man to deal with, that company were, I'm telling you." Boone himself acknowledged that the measures forced on Stevens by Dupree represented "the only way that minorities and women can get part of the pie in order to deal in the arena of big business or small business." Former plaintiffs also praised Seymour's persistence, claiming that he had worked tirelessly on the case for two decades. In 1996 white union representative Clyde Bush agreed with these assessments. He claimed that *Sledge* had "helped change," adding that southern textile firms would "never" have integrated unless pressed into it by Title VII cases.[67]

Between 1965 and 1980, other lawsuits raised similar issues to *Sledge*. In particular, the *Sledge* case highlighted how gender shaped the character of Title VII litigation in the South's largest industry. Across the region, African American women banded together and sued firms that refused to employ them. In *Lea v. Cone Mills* (1966), a group of black women forced managers of a mill in Hillsborough, North Carolina, to hire black females for the first time. Filed in 1972 and 1973, the cases of *Lewis v. Bloomsburg Mills* and *Lewis v. J. P. Stevens* both focused on black womens' complaints of hiring discrimination. As in *Sledge*, plaintiffs in these cases described how they were unable to land textile jobs as easily as their white counterparts.[68]

In other textile cases, black women joined forces with black men to attack a broader range of discriminatory practices. In *Adams v. Dan River Mills* (1969), *Hicks v. Cannon Mills* (1970), and *Ellison v. Rock Hill Printing and Finishing Company* (1972), black workers at mills in Danville, Virginia, Kannapolis, North Carolina, and Rock Hill, South Carolina, came together to bring class actions that opened up a broad range of production jobs. In *Ellison*, the company agreed to change the seniority system to allow black workers to bid on "white" jobs. "You just had a labor job up until this suit got in the way," recalled former *Ellison* plaintiff Jake Boger in 1996. "We were awarded some jobs then, after that, but before then you just actually did what somebody else told you to do." Many Title VII plaintiffs also won payouts to compensate them for discrimination; the consent decree in *Hicks*, for instance, granted $1.65 million to 3,700 black workers. Taken as a whole, Title VII lawsuits clearly forced companies in a range of industries to hire more blacks and to treat them more fairly once they entered the work force.[69] As LDF attorney Jack Greenberg declared in 1971, the civil class action was "the only truly effective vehicle for affirmative relief under Title VII."[70]

Sledge also reveals much about the divisive nature of affirmative action. Affirmative remedies became commonplace following the Supreme Court's 1971 ruling in *Griggs v. Duke Power*, which also originated in North Carolina. In *Griggs*, the court held that the 1964 Civil Rights Act was designed to ensure that the consequences of hiring practices should not have a "disparate impact" upon blacks.[71] Following *Griggs*, discrimination was now to be tested by effect rather than by intent, and Dupree's ruling in *Sledge* drew on this shift in thinking. After *Griggs*, courts repeatedly handed down affirmative remedies, and by 1972 federal quotas covered three hundred thousand companies. A groundswell of popular opinion, however, rejected the idea of affirmative action, and by 1988 some 80 percent of whites opposed the idea that African Americans should receive preference in college admissions and jobs (compared to 50 percent of blacks). This broad polarization was all too evident in *Sledge*; former plaintiffs asserted that only strict remedies could force change, but company officials and many white workers argued that racial quotas represented "reverse discrimination."[72]

Sledge was an important part of the civil rights struggle in eastern North Carolina. In the late 1950s and early 1960s, national civil rights groups largely bypassed the eastern part of the Tar Heel state, a poor, agricultural area where whites retained strict economic and political control over blacks. Local African Americans were forced to demand change themselves, and many did so only after they were protected by national equal rights laws. In many heavily black eastern counties, little had changed with the passage of equal rights legislation, and only ongoing black activism pushed intransigent whites to give ground.[73]

Several communities in the eastern part of the state witnessed upsurges in civil rights conflict after 1965. In Warren County, Floyd McKissick's efforts to build Soul City directly challenged white control of local political and economic life.[74] In 1969–70, the eastern North Carolina towns of Henderson, Warrenton, and Elizabethtown all witnessed rioting and disturbances related to school integration. The protests were marked by blacks' willingness to use violence when threatened by whites.[75] The same themes were evident in Wilmington and in Ayden, a small Pitt County community where blacks seized on a racial killing as their opportunity to protest against broader discrimination. "The harassment of blacks in eastern North Carolina is as bad or worse than Mississippi," commented SCLC leader Ralph Abernathy in 1971. "It's the same old story: police brutality, poor housing, lack of employment and the educational system." As Timothy Tyson's pioneering work shows, scholars have much to learn about black protest after the mid-1960s, especially in eastern North Carolina.[76]

In the 1990s, Roanoke Rapids was home to many veterans of the town's labor and civil rights battles. They lived on in a quiet community, their efforts little known outside of the immediate area. Despite all the setbacks, aging activists remained proud of how they had pushed an intransigent and defiant opponent to treat its employees better. Without this outside pressure, they insisted, the company would have continued to keep the best jobs in its mills for what Jettie Purnell called "the good old boys." "Nobody's going to give you nothing unless you demand it or take it," asserted the black leader as he sat in the town's main union hall, "you see they wouldn't have give up nothing if it hadn't been for the civil rights movement."[77]

6

"We were trying to get equal employment"

The *Myers* Case and the Battle to Integrate Gilman Paper Company

In September 1972, twenty-eight African American workers at Gilman Paper Company in St. Marys, Georgia, filed a detailed complaint of discrimination with the Equal Employment Opportunity Commission. Ever since the mill had been built in 1941, black employees had been confined to a small range of menial jobs, and little had changed following the passage of the 1964 Civil Rights Act. With the help of Fletcher Farrington, a local attorney from the NAACP Legal Defense Fund, they mailed a petition to the commission's head-quarters in Washington, D.C. By filing the complaint, the group of male workers initiated *Myers et al. v. Gilman Paper Company*, a legal case that would take a decade to resolve. The "long and complicated" case would eventually expand to involve more than two hundred and fifty plaintiffs and would become a landmark in determining unions' liability for practicing discrimination. Throughout the litigation process, the black employees were sustained by their firsthand knowledge of discrimination. "The basis of this complaint," explained plaintiff George Jones in 1974, "was they take these new whites and put them in these higher paying job capacities and had us in a deadend job."[1]

The plaintiffs' determination eventually paid off, as the U.S. District Court for the Southern District of Georgia ruled decisively in their favor in both 1975 and 1981. "The job differences of which the plaintiffs complain," concluded the court in 1981, "are the result of an intention to discriminate because of race, and as such, are violative of Title VII of the Civil Rights Act of 1964."[2] African American workers pushed the company and unions to negotiate a fairer senior-ity system and to implement a consent decree that gave them much-improved promotional rights. By 1982, when the case was resolved, the class had also won $430,000 in back pay from the company and the unions, compensation for some of the money they had lost because of decades of racial discrimination.[3]

The *Myers* case is typical of the litigation that plaintiffs brought under Title VII to tackle job discrimination. As the St. Marys story illustrates, national civil rights laws provided a framework for African Americans who were battling to achieve their rights, but ongoing local activism was necessary in order to realize them. The Gilman story reminds us that a great deal of social protest occurred after 1965; African Americans kept fighting for their rights, and they also inspired new protest movements by other groups. In fact, a considerable amount of activism occurred in what Jacquelyn Hall has dubbed the "much-maligned 1970s."[4]

Black activism at St. Marys occurred in two phases. Prior to 1970, African American workers tried to use internal mechanisms to address their complaints. Working primarily through their segregated local union, they repeatedly petitioned whites for a fairer share of jobs, but these appeals failed to produce substantive action. Over the course of the 1970s, the balance of power gradually shifted as increasingly militant African Americans used litigation to force changes in white behavior. They slowly began to gain access to a greater range of jobs, and both Gilman and the unions were forced to give ground. Whites were pushed to accommodate themselves to a new, more equal relationship with African Americans. It was in the 1970s, and not the 1960s, that the black workers at Gilman made real progress in integrating jobs. Their segregated union was not abolished until August 1970, and the seniority system did not change until August 1972, ushering in a new era for both races at the plant.[5]

Myers was a significant case because it involved the key issue of whether unions and companies had together negotiated seniority systems in order to discriminate against blacks. The issue was at the heart of a great deal of Title VII litigation, especially in heavily unionized industries such as steel, rubber, and paper.[6] Recognizing that it was in trouble, in 1974 Gilman negotiated a consent agreement with the plaintiffs, altering the seniority system and giving them much-improved promotional rights. The company also paid the plaintiffs $300,000 in back pay. The unions at the site, however, continued to contest the case, forcing a trial to be held in 1980. The plaintiffs won the case hands down, the court ruling after the trial that "the seniority system used by Gilman and the unions had its genesis in racial discrimination and . . . had been maintained for a discriminatory purpose."[7] Following the judgment, the union's attorneys had little choice but to make concessions. In 1982 the United Paperworkers International Union (UPIU) agreed to grant $130,000 in back pay to the plaintiffs, plus $138,000 in attorneys' fees. The International Brotherhood of Electrical Workers (IBEW), which represented a small group of skilled workers at the plant, agreed to disburse an additional $20,000.[8] The money was distributed between the 201 plaintiffs that the court had ruled were entitled to receive it. As the court noted, the payment was "the largest ever in a Title VII class action against a union in the paper industry." At the time, it was also one of the largest monetary judgments ever awarded against any labor union.[9]

The hostile position that unions took to *Myers* throws light on the attitude of organized labor to the civil rights movement. Alan Draper has skillfully exposed how the black struggle created a "conflict of interests" within the houses of labor. The national leadership, he argues, was largely supportive of civil rights because it hoped that black enfranchisement would energize the Democratic Party and "create a class-based party system" in the region. White union members in the South, in contrast, consistently defended the economic benefits that they received from the Jim Crow system. Much of the scholarship on organized labor's response to the civil rights issue has focused on the period between 1954 and 1965, although recent work by scholars such as Thomas Sugrue and Nancy MacLean has emphasized the importance of grassroots activism in the adoption of affirmative action programs. The Gilman story reinforces this emerging literature, showing that pressure from below was crucial in pushing the company and unions to adopt affirmative remedies.[10]

The *Myers* plaintiffs were certainly brave. When the suit was filed, St. Marys, located in the far southeastern corner of Georgia, had a population of just 5,200. Gilman Paper Company employed 1,800 residents, practically all of the town's breadwinners. As *Harper's Magazine* noted in 1972, St. Marys was a "company town," a community controlled by the "awesome" presence of Gilman Paper Company. Mill manager George W. Brumley boasted that at least 75 percent of the economy of Camden County was dependent on the mill. The sprawling plant was by far the biggest employer in the area, and employees commuted from neighboring counties in both Georgia and Florida to work its well-paying jobs. Gilman also exerted considerable political influence over the region and controlled the local *Camden County Tribune*.[11]

African Americans made up 40 percent of the town's population, but they did not hold their fair share of jobs at Gilman. One of the reasons for bringing the *Myers* suit was to tackle hiring discrimination; at the time the complaint was filed, the mill employed 377 African Americans, less than a quarter of the total workforce. Almost all of these workers were men. Those who did work at the plant had endured years of being passed over for the best jobs. After decades of waiting, they were ready to take Gilman and the unions on.[12]

A New Hampshire corporation, Gilman Paper Company began operations in St. Marys in the summer of 1941. The building of the mill was part of a broader expansion, as paper companies were lured south by the region's fast-growing pine trees. In the 1930s, refinements in the sulfate process for making kraft paper also aided the growth of the southern paper industry. In 1950 Gilman added a new division to the St. Marys plant, manufacturing bags from the paper produced at the mill.[13]

In the first days of the mill's operation there were no unions representing employees. In this period, the company promoted its employees automatically within lines of progression based on a rate structure. As a result, African Americans were able to secure a few of the better-paying jobs. In the summer of 1941, Anthony Jackson was assigned to work as a crane operator, while Isaiah McGee became a helper in the recovery room.[14] After a few months of operation, however, the company voluntarily recognized the United Papermakers and Paperworkers (UPP) and the International Brotherhood of Pulp, Sulphite, and Paper Mill Workers as bargaining agents for their production employees. The UPP represented workers in the paper machine department, while the IBPSPMW covered the other production areas including the wood yard and pulp mill. In addition, the IBEW and International Association of Machinists (IAM) were also allowed by Gilman to represent small groups of mechanical and electrical workers. The paper industry was one of the most heavily unionized in the country, and it was not unusual for firms to voluntarily recognize labor organizations.[15]

In the southern paper industry, it was common for local unions to be racially segregated, as labor leaders argued that they had to follow local customs in order to organize effectively. "If you said that you was going to have black and whites in the same union," recalled IBPSPMW organizer Russell Hall, "then the whites wouldn't have joined." At Gilman, whites clearly wanted segregated unions. The UPP and IBPSPMW locals were chartered in the fall of 1941, but a separate black IBPSPMW local was not organized until May 1942, the white unions having already secured control of the best jobs.[16] Whites tried to argue that black workers had wanted a separate union, but the plaintiffs rejected this claim, terming the black local "a creation of the Company and white Unions." The local, explained the court in its decision, "was given jurisdiction only over those jobs which were menial, low paying and which held little or no promise or promotion. In short, the black Local 616 was given the dead-end jobs while the white locals retained jurisdiction over the more desirable and higher paying jobs."[17]

The arrival of the union clearly helped to codify segregation in the mill.

Black employees were now told that their union lacked jurisdiction over the better "white jobs," and any workers holding these positions were sent back to "black" ones. Thomas McGauley, for example, spoke to union officials about working as a carpenter but was told that "the job was not under the jurisdiction of Local #616." For his part, Anthony Jackson was soon evicted from the crane and moved to a lower-paid position under the black local's jurisdiction. "Because of the union, I lost the job," he recalled sadly. As an additional barrier, job vacancies were not posted in the plant, ensuring that they were often filled before African Americans were even aware of them.[18]

The seniority system also discriminated against blacks. Under the labor agreement, seniority in one line of progression could not be transferred to another.[19] Any employee wishing to change lines of progression had to give up all their seniority for promotional purposes and start at the bottom of the new line. As black lines of progression were much more limited than white lines, this system worked to further restrict black opportunities. As the court put it, "For a white employee, seniority on the job could be used to advance into jobs with more opportunity and higher pay. To most black employees, however, seniority meant nothing. A black employee often reached the pinnacle of his one-job 'line of progression' on the first day he started work. . . . Because transfers into white lines of progression were made impossible by the jurisdictional seniority system, black workers were irretrievably mired in undesirable jobs, no matter how much seniority they accumulated." Although union leaders argued that black workers had their own lines of progression, many African Americans felt that true lines of progression only existed for whites.[20]

While the arrival of the union helped to confine blacks to the worst jobs, the company was also at fault. Gilman officials, however, sought to shift blame, insisting that they were simply following local customs in segregating their workforce. During the trial, industrial relations manager John Love asserted that jobs were segregated "because of the custom—the industrial custom and the social custom of that time." He added, "We would have had difficulty getting along with the unions had we not made the assignments as we did." Throughout the 1960s and 1970s, the company and union had a very good relationship, and this helped to ensure that they worked together to uphold the status quo.[21]

African American workers vividly recalled how blacks were barred from the better-paying jobs before *Myers*. A lively, energetic man, Leroy Hamilton started at Gilman in 1953. "I was working in the yard service," he explained. "During the time when I went to Gilman, blacks had a certain place that they could work. They wasn't no millwrights, no helpers, no electricians. All we could do was common labor, for blacks until they started integration. . . . All the heavy work, that's all we did." Gerald Roberts, who was hired as a yard worker in 1962, added that "Mostly the blacks did . . . clean-up work, anything as a helper."[22]

Prior to the passage of civil rights legislation, African American workers did try to challenge their exclusion from the best jobs. Some asked their supervisors for promotions, but officials reacted angrily to these requests. In a typical incident, "painter helper" Harvey Jordan wanted to become a painter. In court documents, he described the reaction of his supervisor to his appeal: "Guy Austin, late 1950s, I asked him if there was any possible chance of my getting into either the painters or carpenters. He cursed and said 'if you want to work, you stay where you are.'" Jeff W. Brewton hoped to secure a welding position but was angrily told by a company official "that no nigger could transfer to welding." He dropped the matter because he feared that he would lose his job if he persisted.[23]

White workers also fought to keep blacks out of the better-paying jobs. Anthony Jackson recalled one incident in which a white local union leader told him that "he never was going on a job where a 'nigger' relieved him or he had to relieve a 'nigger,' and he ain't never thought nary 'nigger' should get paid as much as he got paid." Reviewing the case, Judge Anthony A. Alaimo concluded that "The record is replete with a litany of discriminatory actions taken by the company and the unions alike."[24]

Supervisors rigidly enforced a color line that clearly marked all jobs as "white" or "black." African Americans got nowhere when they tried to cross this barrier. "I spoke to Mr. George Haverty," related Nathaniel Joseph, "about being a scale clerk, he told me that they don't have any black scale clerk, that was a white man job."[25] Company officials and union leaders proved adept at passing black employees back and forth. The experience of George E. Jones was typical: "Spoke to company official Gerald Bass, supervisor, and asked why can't we get the job as shipping clerk [since] we are responsible for training them? He replied it is not the company; it is your local union. Spoke to president of Local 958 Robert Woods on same question; he replied, Local 616 employees can't merge into Local 958 jurisdiction. Result: None." Many black employees felt frustrated about the situation. "I spoke with relatives, fellow union members and friends, on numerous occasions," explained Earnest Baker. "Almost everyone I knew then and now works for the Company and we all wanted the same thing—to be able to work in the better-paying, white jobs."[26]

Apart from individual approaches to company officials, blacks also tried to use their local union to challenge discrimination. As labor leaders pointed out, by having their own union blacks got automatic representation at the negotiating table and at union conventions. Recognizing the voice it gave them, close to 100 percent of African American employees belonged to Local 616. The union also protected black workers from being unfairly dismissed, and this helped them to challenge the company and white locals.[27]

From the outset, however, the inequality of the black local was clear when it tried to challenge discriminatory job assignments. As late as the mid-1960s, the officers from Local 616 were still having separate meetings with the company and were not allowed to sit at the table with the white unions in order to argue their demands. In the 1960s, Leroy Hamilton served as an officer in the black local and explained that the union's efforts to integrate jobs got nowhere. "We was overpowered," he recalled, "just a little handful of us, wasn't nothing we could do but swallow it, but take it. And if you started talking about it in negotiations, the plant manager would tell you, 'This is the company policy, and we're not going to change it.' He was doing that to satisfy the whites; they was together, and the company leaned over backwards to satisfy them. We just was there and that was it to do all the nasty, dirty work for them on the lowest pay in the mill, and our contract book didn't cover nothing but our union, so we couldn't get what they was doing." As former officeholder Thomas McGauley admitted, "Opening up the lines of progression, we were not effective at all in that."[28]

Even when black union leaders attended regional conferences, their power was severely circumscribed. A former president of Local 616, Madison Jenkins explained that he attended regional union conferences shortly after World War II, but the African American delegates were not allowed to lodge at "the white hotels" in Savannah or Mobile. Instead, they "stayed with black families who also prepared meals for us." At the gatherings themselves, whites failed to show solidarity with their African American coworkers. "At each meeting," explained Jenkins, "when the time came to conduct business, the whites would leave the room or have us to leave the room. They would conduct their business then come back in the room where we were."[29]

Despite its limited power, black workers did not give up on their separate union. In August 1963, the local submitted an extensive list of demands. They called on the company and the other unions to put the past behind them and "assist us by helping to plan for a better future." Drawing inspiration from the civil rights movement, the African American employees pressed the company to eliminate all forms of "discrimination, segregation, separation or exclusion." Blacks should get access to every job in the mill, including lucrative maintenance positions. The company and unions, however, rebuffed these demands.[30]

The local also pressed for the integration of all facilities in the mill, and here they were more successful. Following lengthy discussions with black union leaders, in November 1963 the company agreed to "remove all signs which indicate separate facilities for colored and white employees." Although white workers were told that these changes would begin immediately, in practice company officials held back from fully integrating all facilities.[31] While the signs came down, for example, the mill's cafeteria retained two separate dining areas. Following continued pressure from the black local, the company agreed that African Americans could use either area, but it was left to brave blacks to request service in the "white" section.[32]

In the early 1960s, the black local also tried to get white union leaders to abolish segregated locals. In April 1963, the local even set up a committee that was designed to bring about the "emerging of the two unions."[33] In June 1963, the two main leaders of the black local also presented a list of demands to IBPSPMW president John P. Burke. "We intend," they noted, "to inter two non-discriminatory clauses into our next contract. . . . We would like to hear from you on this matter as soon as possible." Noting that their approaches to the white locals had gotten nowhere, the African American leaders asked Burke to assist them, but he never responded.[34]

Through the 1960s, many segregated locals continued to exist despite pledges from union leaders to abolish them. In 1969 UPP president emeritus Paul L. Phillips expressed concern about the problem to the union's executive board. "There seems to be a strong feeling . . . that no one either from the local or from the Regional Staff has made or is making any serious effort to bring about the abolition of these segregated locals," he noted.[35] At Gilman the black local stayed in existence until the fall of 1970, more than six years after the passage of the Civil Rights Act. A former president of the main white local, Don Wilkes remembered that the international union was slow to demand that the locals should merge together. When the unions did finally unite, whites forced blacks to surrender their charter. Worried that whites would not stand up for them, some black members resisted this move unless they secured guaranteed representation within the merged union.[36]

In the late 1960s, many whites in the plant remained strongly opposed to integration.[37] As Wilkes admitted, some whites were "old down South rednecks who were not going to go along with any type of integration." Thomas Mc-

Gauley remembered that as black workers started to push for more rights, the situation in the mill became "explosive." Undeterred, the black activist would not back down. "Basically I would tell them, if things had been right in the beginning, they wouldn't have brought on this situation," he recalled. "And they'd say, 'Well I ain't responsible for what my daddy or uncle or people before me did.' I said, 'Well, it's correction time now.'"[38]

In March 1970, the tense racial climate was graphically illustrated when black employee Amos Rawls used the toilet facility in the basement of the mill's machine shop, where whites worked in large numbers. Despite the official integration of mill facilities, the toilet was still seen as a "white" facility. While he was in the commode, someone on the other side of the partial partition poured a quantity of caustic chemicals down onto Rawls. As a result, the black worker received first and second degree burns to his head and scrotum. In the wake of the incident, African Americans complained that Gilman had done little to ascertain who was responsible. In 1974 an arbitrator, commenting on the incident, asserted that "the Company manifested what can only be described as an almost total indifference to a shocking event, amounting in the legal sense to condonation."[39]

On the job, most blacks still toiled in the lower-paying, laboring positions. Between 1965 and 1970, only nineteen African American workers were transferred from black jobs to white jobs.[40] Many African American workers came to feel that they needed to exert outside pressure on the company and the unions in order to secure real results. In 1969 and 1970, several activists filed charges with the EEOC, outlining the allegations that led to *Myers*.[41]

By this time, Elmo Myers had emerged as a leader among the group. A large, determined man, Myers was well suited to be a chief plaintiff. As an owner of beachfront property in Fernandina Beach, Florida, he was freer of the company's economic ties than many other workers. He was also more educated, having attended college before starting at Gilman in 1967. For several years, he had been active in the black local union, sharpening his organizing skills in the process. Prior to working at the mill, Myers had also served in the military and had captained a shrimp boat for a local seafood firm. Filing the suit was a public act of protest against the area's largest and most powerful employer, but Myers coped with pressure well. The plaintiffs did feel exposure from the case; when it was filed, the *Camden County Tribune* published the names of all twenty-eight complainants on its front page, helping disaffected whites target these individuals for verbal abuse.[42]

By 1970 Myers had helped to organize a group that he termed the Black

Association of Millworkers (BAM). The creation of BAM signaled the growing confidence and determination of Gilman's African American employees. It also indicated that some of them had been influenced by the rising popularity of Black Power, and BAM had much in common with the Black Student Unions that were emerging at predominantly white colleges around this time. While studying at Fort Valley State University, Myers had been influenced by the rise of Black Power. Although its ideology was broad, Black Power was characterized by a belief that blacks could best address their problems through their own institutions.[43] Drawing on these ideas, in May 1970 BAM presented a petition to IBPSPMW representative Don Walker that called for the union to embrace affirmative action and provide automatic representation for blacks on its international executive board. In response, Walker was critical of BAM, calling its demands "completely unrealistic" and arguing that black workers should seek to resolve their complaints through normal union channels. Myers was not satisfied with this response.[44]

Aware of growing restlessness among black workers, in the summer of 1972 the unions and Gilman sat down and negotiated "supplemental labor agreements" in an effort to belatedly bring their contract into compliance with Title VII. The agreements changed the seniority system to provide for the retention of plant seniority by blacks who changed lines. In addition, Gilman agreed to post all job vacancies and restructured some lines of progression to help black employees. Despite these changes, many blacks doubted the willingness of the company and the union to treat blacks fairly. They knew that the new, merged union was dominated by the white majority and would be unlikely to help blacks get promoted. Only a few days after the implementation of the supplemental agreements, Myers and twenty-seven other blacks instituted a class action against both the company and unions.[45]

Myers initiated the lawsuit by getting in touch with LDF attorney Fletcher Farrington. A group of six workers, including several NAACP members, then traveled to Savannah for a meeting at Farrington's office. "We wasn't trying to get a lawsuit," explained Myers in 1974. "We were trying to get equal employment for employees—more particularly black employees in the mill . . . and to bring those unions that we felt like were not in compliance with the Civil Rights Bill. We did a lot of things, you know, we met with the company, with management. We met with union officials. We discussed this thing for a long, long length of time." Other plaintiffs also viewed the suit as the only way to bring about a fundamental improvement in their job opportunities. "That was the main issue," recalled Gerald Roberts, one of the original plaintiffs, "trying

to get the blacks to move in the line of progression and to hold what we considered as meaningful jobs." Roberts pointed out that most whites who held
higher-paying posts had received extensive on-the-job training, and he could
not see why blacks should not have the same opportunity. "The whites who
was hired, they had to be trained on the job. . . . We were saying, 'Give us the
chance and we could have done the same thing.'"[46]

In their original complaint, the group asserted that the company and the
unions were colluding to violate the provisions of the Civil Rights Act.[47] The
list of specific grievances was wide-ranging; blacks were locked out of white-
collar jobs, they were still required to train whites to fill positions "more desirable" than those they held themselves, and they were not being hired as easily
as whites were. Most important, the plaintiffs charged that Gilman had yet to
institute a "non-discriminatory" seniority system.[48]

Recognizing that the company was in trouble, Gilman's lawyers entered into
lengthy negotiations with the plaintiffs. In 1974 the issues between the two
sides were settled when the court approved a consent decree that included substantial back pay payments to the class. Under the decree, Gilman also agreed
to increase its efforts to promote blacks into "white" jobs and to report the results of its actions to the court. The decree went further than the supplemental
agreements; it provided, for example, that if an affected class member was the
most senior bidder for a vacancy but was not qualified to perform the job, the
post would be kept open, subject to certain conditions, until the class member
became able to do it. In the meantime, other employees would fill the job
temporarily. Arguing that they were being discriminated against, many whites
detested this provision.[49]

The consent decree did not settle the case because the unions objected to it.
They disliked the fact that parts of the decree were allowed to "supersede and
replace" provisions in the labor agreement, feeling that this undermined the
authority of the contract. In their objections, the unions also argued that the
supplemental agreements were sufficient to meet Title VII's requirements. Fur-
thermore, local union representatives asserted that they had tried to change the
seniority provisions in 1970 in order to bring the mill's system into conformity
with Title VII. The union argued that it had struck in order to try to secure
these changes but that the company had refused to give ground.[50] The records
of the 1970 strike, however, fail to make any mention of the union's efforts to
change the seniority system, showing instead that workers walked out to secure
improvements to the pension plan and a wage increase. As mill manager G.
W. Brumley commented at the time, "the major point of disagreement is on

improvements in the retirement program." The union's papers confirm that seniority was not an issue in the dispute. Black workers supported the walkout, but they were also unaware that seniority was a concern. "The issue number one in that strike was pensions," recalled Myers.[51]

Following extensive investigation, in January 1975 the court found that there had been ongoing Title VII violations at the plant and approved the consent decree. Judge Alaimo also ruled that the unions and the company were "equally responsible" for the discrimination that had occurred between 1965 and 1972, meaning that they were each "liable for 50 percent of the economic loss suffered by each individual class member."[52] Formed in 1972 when the UPP and IBP-SPMW merged, the UPIU continued to fight the case and asked the district court to stay further back pay proceedings. In the wake of the Supreme Court's decision in *International Brotherhood of Teamsters v. U.S.* (1977), in which the court ruled that "bona fide" seniority systems did not violate Title VII even when they "perpetuate[d] the effects of an employer's discrimination," the union argued that the seniority arrangements at Gilman had not been designed to discriminate against blacks.[53]

Resisting any settlement, the union's southern leadership fought the case into the 1980s. They saw it as a point of principle, as they did not want to concede that unions should compensate blacks for discrimination. Gilman, they pointed out, had ultimate responsibility for hiring and firing. The union tried to argue that it was a racially progressive organization that had "been at the forefront of the movement for racial equality, limited for a time by the realities of the southern tradition which it was compelled to accept." In public they pointed out that both the UPP and IBPSPMW had always welcomed black members and had passed several nondiscrimination resolutions at their national conventions in the 1950s and 1960s.[54] Privately, however, union leaders frequently complained about the case. "We had no choice," wrote UPIU southern director Jesse W. Whiddon in 1977, "but to operate under a Court Decree which has been appealed." Even in 1982, the union was still trying to oppose a back pay settlement. "Believe me," wrote UPIU representative Ben Wooten to Whiddon, "if I knew how to get this behind us without back pay from the union I would do it in a minute. We will continue to do all that we can in that effort."[55]

Despite this recalcitrance, Title VII litigation did push the union to do more to help its black members. The *Myers* judgement was an important cause of this change. The January 1975 ruling was particularly devastating for the union, establishing that they could be as liable for past discrimination as corporations were.[56] Later in the same year, UPIU president Joseph P. Tonelli declared that all local unions should negotiate "supplemental agreements" to allow African American workers to use their plant seniority to reach their "rightful place," or the place that they would have occupied if discrimination had not occurred. Aware that such agreements would be unpopular with many whites, Tonelli reiterated to his staff that "your union pursued this course of action because the law and the courts mandate that we do so. . . . We are forced by the developments in the field of civil rights to make substantial and radical changes in our seniority, progression lines, promotion and lay-off practices." Seeking to minimize opposition, the union leader also assured his representatives that he understood "the difficulty in persuading people to give up the familiar and the contract rights which they now enjoy."[57] By 1975 the UPIU had also set up a Human Rights Department that was authorized to "investigate and act" on discrimination charges. Until that time, the union had no internal machinery to deal with civil rights complaints, and the new department was clearly designed to "resolve discrimination claims" before they reached the courts.[58]

Back in St. Marys, the court settlement ushered in a new era. Change happened slowly, but gradually blacks were able to make progress into the better-paying jobs. Between April 1977 and April 1978, eleven blacks were promoted to formerly "white" positions. Although this was a small proportion of the mill's overall workforce, it represented a significant breakthrough.[59] African American employees saw *Myers* as the cause of many positive changes. "After the lawsuit," wrote Wilbert O. Sibley, "I recived a chance to become a scale clerk and I made it a *good one*. . . . With my ability I am a store clerk. All I need[ed] is a chance." Gerald Roberts recalled that job opportunities "started to improve" after the consent decree. "The decree that the Judge, that we was awarded, there was a lot of things in it that helped us a lot—line of progression was one of the main ones. If an opening was to come, the affected class . . . we was allowed first preference on that particular job. And there was quite a few that took advantage of that and helped their position." In 1978 Thomas McGauley became the first African American to secure a position in the maintenance department. Initial opposition from whites gradually subsided, and McGauley became an established part of the maintenance crew, paving the way for others to follow him. Job opportunities, he related, "improved considerably" after the decree.[60]

By 1981, when the case was in its final stages, many of the plaintiffs had secured the jobs that they had always wanted. Arthur Dawson Sr. finally became a truck driver, while Elvridge Lawrence landed a better-paying position in the pulp mill. Elmo Myers secured a post as a scale clerk. Like many plaintiffs, he wanted to get a lighter, cleaner job. The new era helped younger workers the most, however, and elderly blacks were less likely to move up. Many died or retired before more opportunities opened up.[61]

Many whites disliked the way that blacks used the decree to gain better jobs. In April 1975, UPIU representative Benjamin Wyle noted that there was anger on the ground because whites felt that the committee charged with implementing the consent decree was interfering "with the Union's authority." The union continued to regard its right to bargain with Gilman as sacrosanct and felt that the *Myers* plaintiffs were undermining this prerogative.[62] By the late-1970s, Gilman had appointed Lemon Dawson as its first African American supervisor, another move that was resented by some whites. In 1982 white worker Jesse Sam Jones filed a reverse discrimination suit against the company after being fired by Dawson. The company, however, claimed that Jones' attitude to Dawson was one of "insubordination and disrespect," and white witness Clay Kemp testified that Dawson had treated African American and white employees equally. As a result, Jones failed to get his job back.[63]

Nevertheless, by the early 1980s there were signs that the racial climate at the mill was improving. New local union president Jerry Ridenhour explained in 1983 that he was working hard to stamp out racist language in the mill, where a "marine corps vocabulary" had traditionally existed.[64] By this time, Leroy Hamilton had become chief shop steward in the merged local union and was respected by both races. "I'm over about 18 Shop Stewards and I cover the whole place," Hamilton proudly noted in 1983. "When I first started representing the Union, we had an all black union. After we merged I held my same job. It must be about five whites to one black. And they voted for me. They said, 'We want Leroy Hamilton to represent us. He did a good job for the blacks and we want him.'"[65]

After an initial period of resistance, some whites came to tolerate or even welcome blacks as coworkers. Thomas McGauley recalled that for the first few weeks that he was a maintenance worker, the company would not give him time off to build a "buggy" to carry his tools in. When a new employee came into maintenance, it was customary for supervisors to allow them to build their buggy on company time and for their coworkers to help them. Without a buggy, McGauley had to carry his heavy tools in a bucket. "Then one day," McGauley recalled, "one of the old fellas, couple of the older fellas, white fellas, after about six weeks, he said, 'We're going to get your buggy built,' and they went upstairs and told the supervisor that I was part of the local like everybody else, and they wanted me to have time to build a tool buggy like everybody else. That was the end of that."[66]

Title VII cases rarely offered easy victories, and the *Myers* plaintiffs had to fight for a decade to break down white opposition to integration. Working together, however, the plaintiffs had pushed the company and unions to treat black employees much more fairly. In the 1980s and 1990s, a new generation of African American employees had opportunities that their parents could only dream of, and many of them managed to secure top positions in the mill. Given the union's hostility, the plaintiffs had also won a point of principle by securing a substantial payment from the UPIU. The consent decree represented a significant breakthrough, especially as it operated until all of the affected class members had retired. Until the late 1980s, when he was killed in a car wreck, Elmo Myers chaired the committee responsible for implementing the decree's provisions. After Myers' death, Gerald Roberts took over his duties.[67]

What occurred in St. Marys was replicated in scores of small towns across the South. Assisted by the NAACP Legal Defense Fund, African American workers brought hundreds of lawsuits to enforce the nondiscrimination provisions of the 1964 Civil Rights Act. These cases gradually created more job opportunities in key southern industries such as textiles, paper, chemicals, steel, and rubber. As LDF attorney James E. Ferguson II recalled, "Once the Act was passed, nothing much happened. It was only the filing of lawsuits to implement the change . . . to implement Title VII, that made the difference there. . . . So I think that it did not make just a difference, I mean it made all the difference to bring those lawsuits."[68] For the black activists Ferguson helped, the civil rights acts of the mid-1960s represented not an ending but a beginning, a platform from which to begin the process of gaining equality.[69]

Litigation was not confined to employment. Refuting suggestions that the civil rights movement was dying, in 1979 LDF director Adrian W. DeWind wrote the *New York Times* that "LDF is counsel in hundreds of civil rights cases involving employment, schools, housing, prisoner rights and capital punishment, in which it has been almost always successful." Another influential LDF attorney, Julius Chambers, felt that the group's suits were crucial in breaking down lingering resistance to the law, especially in rural areas: "with the Title VII of 1964 you also had a public accommodations section and many restaurants and movie houses were . . . segregated. . . . We had school cases along with it, we had some housing cases. . . . There was a kind of community-wide effort to challenge discrimination in all phases of the lives of people." In his most famous case, Chambers represented the plaintiffs in *Swann v. Charlotte-Mecklenburg*

County Board of Education. In 1971 the landmark case was decided when the Supreme Court gave its approval for busing to be used to promote racially desegregated schools. The verdict paved the way for several racial crises in the early 1970s, making Chambers highly unpopular with many whites.[70]

In the course of his work, Chambers watched as whites and blacks adjusted to a new form of race relations. As in St. Marys, both groups had to get used to interacting with one another. These changes left a lasting impression on the native North Carolinian, who had graduated from a segregated high school in Mount Gilead. "To watch people move from a rigidly segregated to a somewhat integrated work force and then community was quite an interesting experience," he commented in 1996.[71]

The union's posture in the *Myers* case is a reminder of the large gap that often existed between organized labor's national policies and actual practices on the ground. While the case was making its way through the courts, the national AFL-CIO continued to be supportive of civil rights organizations, giving donations to the NAACP and SRC and helping to fund the construction of the Martin Luther King Jr. Center for Social Change in Atlanta. Despite this, local autonomy ensured that many affiliates opposed equal rights. In addition, labor leaders often failed to back up their verbal pledges. The UPIU's leadership certainly only amended discriminatory contracts when it was forced to do so by cases such as *Myers.* The union's decentralized structure also meant that southern representatives such as Whiddon and Wyle retained a great deal of independence.[72]

While Title VII litigation has helped African Americans to gain access to better-paying jobs, since the 1970s many southern industries have declined, laying off thousands of workers in the process. In the steel and textile industries, it was bitterly ironic that African Americans gained access to lucrative positions just before firms began to close their doors. African Americans have been disproportionately hurt by plant shutdowns, especially as they continue to face opposition when they look for new jobs.[73]

Paper companies resisted large-scale downsizing until the late 1990s, when overcapacity caused firms to close some plants. In addition, increased volatility in the industry led to corporate takeovers and mergers, with foreign firms increasingly moving into the U.S. market.[74] Gilman Paper Company was not immune to these trends; in 1998 Corporacion Durango, a Mexican paper making operation, purchased the family firm. Unable to modernize the aging facility, four years later Durango closed the St. Marys mill. The shutdown accelerated the area's reliance on tourism, and by the early twenty-first century many residential and tourist developments had been built on the prime coastal property near the old paper mill that stood as a disused relic. This new service economy provided jobs for laid-off mill employees, but they came with lower wages and fewer benefits. While the pollution from the paper mill was no longer around, neither were the well-paying positions that it had offered to area residents. When the plant closed, the average worker was paid close to twenty dollars an hour.[75]

In 2002 when the plant closed, African Americans held jobs right across the mill and occupied several positions of local union leadership. They made up 35 percent of the workforce, up from 20 percent in the early 1970s. Workers at Gilman had come a long way, and the outcome of the case helped former plaintiffs look back on their lives with some satisfaction. Although the struggle to integrate jobs had not been easy, they insisted that litigation had been needed to make the mandate of the law a reality in their small corner of Georgia. As Thomas McGauley explained in 1998, "There were no changes until, really, the suit was filed. . . . That was always my comment about the lawsuit; I said if the company had moved and tried to do anything, the lawsuit never would have been necessary."[76]

"They over there and we over here"

The Fight for Civil Rights in Port St. Joe, Florida, 1938–1997

In 1938 construction was completed on a paper mill located on a reef in the Gulf of Mexico off Florida's panhandle coast. The opening of St. Joe Paper Company is a reflection of the expansion that the American paper industry made into the South in the 1930s. The decade saw the establishment of many major paper mills in the region, including several International Paper Company facilities and the large Union Bag mill in Savannah, Georgia. Much of this growth took place in northern Florida. Headed by the building of a sprawling IP plant in Panama City, paper factories arose throughout northern Florida, stretching from Pensacola in the west to Jacksonville in the east.[1]

Although the paper industry has formed an important part of Florida's economy since World War II, little attention has been paid to the social or labor history of paper mill communities. Florida as a whole has not figured prominently in the recent expansion of southern labor history, and where studies of workers have been carried out they have usually concentrated on the southern part of the state. Despite the growing amount of scholarship being published on southern workers, the paper industry as a whole has also been largely neglected.[2]

Port St. Joe, a small, isolated town located along Florida's panhandle, was a paper mill community in an area of the South that is only beginning to receive historical attention.[3] The town witnessed a major civil rights lawsuit in the 1970s and 1980s as black workers struggled to overcome racial discrimination at the mill. *Winfield v. St. Joe Paper Company* was one of the largest and longest cases to occur in the southern paper industry. The suit was based on charges filed with the EEOC in 1970, yet it was not until 1988 that a consent decree settled the Title VII claims, giving $3.8 million for lawyers' fees and cash awards to the workers. In addition, the agreement granted blacks greater rights to promote into formerly "white" jobs. Even then, proceedings continued into the 1990s as the plaintiffs alleged that the company had violated the consent decree. As the UPIU's executive board put it, *Winfield* represented "the most protracted, involved, time-consuming, costly and hard fought of all UPIU cases." The case was not fully settled until 1997 when the U.S. Court of Appeals finally rejected the plaintiffs' request for further relief.[4]

As in St. Marys and Roanoke Rapids, former plaintiffs felt proud that their case had been upheld, but they were also disappointed that it took so long. By the time *Winfield* was settled, the mill was not running because of production problems, and it closed for good a few years later. A long and dramatic tale, the Port St. Joe story highlights the bitter irony of African Americans gaining access to better-paying jobs just as the South's staple manufacturing industries began to decline. In the early years of the twenty-first century, the black neighborhood in Port St. Joe remained depressed and forgotten. Although the region was developing as a tourist destination, many former paper workers were unemployed or worked in low-paying service sector jobs. Their story illustrates why African Americans have found it so difficult to translate legal equality into economic equality.[5]

The Port St. Joe case epitomized the long struggle for racial change that occurred after Title VII of the Civil Rights Act came into effect. In the two decades after 1965, Title VII litigation occurred right across the region.[6] These suits illustrate that the act, which has often been viewed as the climax of the civil rights movement, actually sparked a new round of protest in many southern communities.[7] Historians are only beginning to explore efforts to integrate southern industries, and much remains to be learned about the ongoing activism of black workers.[8]

Job discrimination was particularly prevalent in the steel and paper industries. As was the case in the steel mills, black workers in the southern paper plants were locked into the least desirable jobs by segregated lines of progression and separate unions. White workers and supervisors clearly derived considerable benefits from this system of racial segregation, and they fiercely opposed efforts to integrate the industry. Under increasing pressure from federal agencies, paper companies did move to promote some blacks after 1965, but progress was slow and uneven. In July 1967, a survey by the American Paper Institute (API) found that blacks held only 1.6 percent of all paper machine positions. As the API admitted, these results were "not very good." Between 1965 and 1980, almost every major southern paper mill experienced at least one Title VII case. According to Kent Spriggs, the plaintiffs' attorney in *Winfield*, the paper industry quickly became "the most litigated industry in the South."[9]

Although lawsuits were common across the paper industry, larger chain companies integrated more quickly and decisively than smaller firms. Big players such as International Paper and Scott Paper made more progress because executives implemented national non-discrimination policies. In addition, the federal government closely watched large employers, whereas less-prominent companies fell through the cracks. In the late 1960s and 1970s, several lengthy court cases involved little-known paper companies in the rural South. An experienced attorney, Spriggs later reflected that St. Joe Paper Company was "at the back of the train of progress in the paper industry, there's no doubt about that." Fifteen years after the Civil Rights Act, little had changed at St. Joe. The company typified just how difficult it was to integrate jobs at smaller mills.[10]

Colorful entrepreneur Ed Ball owned St. Joe Paper Company, and the firm's resistance to civil rights laws was a reflection of his intransigence and idiosyncrasy. One of the most powerful men in Florida, Ball controlled a vast business empire from his estate in Tallahassee. Short and gnome-like, the industrialist had augmented his fortune by marrying into the DuPont family. For over forty years he managed the paper firm and two other local employers—the St. Joseph Telephone and Telegraph Company and the Apalachicola Northern Railroad. In addition, the businessman was one of the Sunshine State's biggest landowners. For Ball, as writers Kathryn Ziewitz and June Wiaz remind us, lawsuits were part of business; the tycoon even professed to enjoy fighting prolonged legal battles because they kept him "sharp and on target." Very conservative, Ball was a fanatical anticommunist who worried that unions and civil rights groups were taking over the country. Despite this, Ball was not closely involved in *Winfield*, at least publicly. Instead, he delegated control of the mill to personnel manager John Howard, who also detested federal involvement in the firm's business.[11]

Ball's attitudes had wider consequences for Port St. Joe. Employing nearly one thousand workers in a settlement of less than four thousand people, most Port St. Joe residents felt that, as R. C. Larry commented, "St. Joe Paper Company is the town. Whatever they say goes. They run the town." Segregation at St. Joe Paper Company, then, mirrored that in the town of Port St. Joe. Throughout the 1970s and 1980s, the town was residentially segregated, with all blacks living in a neighborhood known as North Port St. Joe, which was located adjacent to the paper mill, literally on the "wrong side" of the railroad tracks that divided North Port St. Joe from the white neighborhoods to the east. The black community lacked political and economic power; there were no elected black officials, and blacks were restricted to menial jobs at the telephone company and the railroad. In 1972 blacks and whites engaged in brutal fights when the public schools were finally integrated. The Klan was active in the area, and blacks remained afraid to even visit the neighboring town of White City, a segregationist stronghold. In Port St. Joe itself, whites controlled the small and tidy business district, and blacks complained that they were not accepted as customers in the stores until the 1980s.[12]

In the mill, the pace of racial change was also very slow. Issued in June 1979, federal district judge William H. Stafford's opinion in *Winfield* was a damning indictment of the company. "The black employees of St. Joe Paper Company," he noted, "have been the victims of institutionalized discrimination both before and subsequent to the effective date of Title VII." The experienced judge concluded that "In the paper mill discrimination in initial job assignments and segregation of [lines of progression] continued largely unabated following passage of Title VII. . . . The evidence shows, in fact, that . . . even as late as 1976 the overwhelming majority of initial job assignments for black workers were in traditionally black jobs."[13]

Written in 1985 by Judge Maurice M. Paul, the district court's decision in the case confirmed that illegal practices had continued long after 1965. Finding that the company discriminated in its hiring practices, initial job assignments, and transfers, Paul ruled that the lines of progression had been designed with a discriminatory intent. Between 1968 and 1971, only two blacks were assigned to "historically white" jobs. "Plaintiffs' proof on this issue," concluded Paul, "is so strong as to leave room for no other inference but that the Company's initial job assignment practices were based primarily upon racial identity of hirees."[14]

The decisions were validation for Spriggs, the white Legal Defense Fund attorney who had represented the plaintiffs since the early 1970s. A native of New York who had been inspired by the civil rights movement, Spriggs worked hard to show that the company had violated Title VII. Spriggs assembled witnesses such as veteran employee M. D. Yon, who was able to read through union contracts from the 1960s and mark "B" by jobs that had only been given to blacks. Further testimony confirmed that these positions were much lower-paying than their "white" counterparts.[15]

The segregation that prevailed at the mill in the 1970s was a legacy of historic practices that few whites were willing to change. In case testimony, black witnesses explored the roots of these practices, describing how they had been restricted to laboring jobs while whites operated machines. Ellis Dunning, who started at the mill when it opened in 1938, explained how the company began operations with "white operators and colored labor," a segregation maintained by supervisors and white workers who vigorously defended machine work as "white." African American employees complained that they were forbidden to even touch machines unless they were cleaning them. Alphons Mason, who had been working at the mill since 1939, summed up the feelings of many African American employees when he declared in 1977 that "There were two job in St. Joe Paper Company, white job and a black job."[16]

Black jobs were also more dangerous and dirty than those performed by whites. Broke beaters toiled underneath the paper machines, which were operated solely by whites. The African American laborers picked up reject paper that the machines discarded and put it in a big container that took it back to the machine. A broke beater for over twenty years, Adrian Franklin Gantt remembered that black and white employees worked in clearly defined areas. "We had separate jobs," he asserted, "broke beater was a separate job. The whites worked upstairs and we worked downstairs. . . . Broke beater was the start-up point for the blacks and the ending point in those days." Gantt related that black workers had to pick up the hot paper from the machine and move quickly to ensure that it would not burn their hands: "That paper was real hot, we didn't have no gloves. . . . When it falled, it would be hot. . . . You had to run."[17]

African Americans who came to work at the paper mill described how they soon learned the reality of job segregation. A tall, lean man, Robert Bryant applied at St. Joe in 1953 after working as an operator for a construction company. "When I first came to this kind of work," he recalled,

> I worked for Florida Asphalt and Paving Company, and I was a heavy equipment operator—that's what I was, I was a professional one. I wind up out there because they had all of that stuff out there. The first day I walked in there, he looked at me, "What do you want, boy?" I said, "I'm looking for a job." "What can you do?" I said, "I'm a heavy equipment operator." "Don't no Niggers run nothing like that here." And that was it. He said, "Can you roll salt-cake." I said, "I don't know, what is rolling salt-cake?" He said, "You'll find out." . . . I found out it was putting it in a wheelbarrow and go about one hundred yards over yonder and dump it, just what I do for exercise out there in the yard. [There] really wasn't no mind to it, but it was hard labor work.[18]

Even after Title VII became law, African American employees complained that they were unable to determine their own job assignments and had to obey orders from any white worker. Hired in 1967, woodyard laborer R. C. Larry recalled that "Every white man out there was your bossman, I mean every man out there." White workers and supervisors, claimed another employee, treated blacks not as coworkers but as "children."[19]

Until the 1970s, many African Americans worked in a department that St.

Joe termed *General Mills*. Black workers, however, knew it as the "Bull Gang" because of the physical nature of the work. Many southern paper mills had bull gangs, and they consisted of jobs that were always assigned to African American men. A bull gang's miscellaneous yard jobs involved a great deal of labor and cleaning. Hired in 1970, Otis Walker toiled for several years on the St. Joe bull gang, and he gave a vivid description of what it involved. "Everybody knew it as Bull Gang," he later recalled from his Apalachicola home, "because all the work was physical, we had no machines to do the work. Working in hazardous areas, of course digging ditches, cleaning out cascades, cleaning out liquor tanks." Led by black "pushers" who relayed the orders given by white supervisors, the bull gang was considered by Walker to be "a form of slavery." The bull gang certainly existed to perform jobs throughout the mill that white workers did not want to do, such as cleaning machinery and unloading chemicals. "The Bull Gang have caught the blues at St. Joe Paper Company," added Walker, "and we, oh shucks, we've just had to work sixteen hours straight, and I'm talking about not just on the clock, man, I'm talking about physical labor, working. We've had situations where we had to sandbag, build dams. 'They can do it, they're black, they can handle it.' That was the attitude of the supervisor."[20]

African American workers at St. Joe were certainly not short of grievances, but one of their main complaints was that they had to train whites to work in higher-paying jobs but could not secure these positions themselves. Colbert Bryant testified in 1979 that it had taken him twenty years to secure his first promotion but that he had trained many whites for lucrative jobs. "All these fellows is going around me, these white boys," Bryant testified, "I could learn them the job, but I couldn't ever get it myself." Cleveland Bailey, who worked at the mill for over thirty years, became animated when he related how inexperienced whites were regularly promoted over blacks. "What I never could understand," he recalled from his North Port St. Joe home, "how could they hire a man—yes sir I should have understood it—off the streets, and you got blacks working on the job, and he pretty well knows that job. Why they wouldn't allow him the opportunity, a lot of blacks the opportunity, to learn the job? They could hire white and bring them in there, and then he had to learn the job. Well, because I know, the color of their skin, that's what made it all work in."[21]

While many paper mills maintained segregated facilities after 1964, there were few plants where segregation persisted for as long as it did at St. Joe. African American employees at the Florida mill had vivid memories of the segregated facilities. "They had all kind of segregation there," recalled M. D. Yon.

"They had, when you go in to punch the clock, the white punched in on one side of the fence and the blacks on the other. They had bathrooms on one side of the fence for blacks and whites on the other side of the fence." Again, little changed after the passage of the historic Civil Rights Act. Judge Stafford concluded that facilities in the mill had stayed segregated until 1978. Up to 1972, the company still had signs on most amenities, while others were maintained "by direct instructions to employees from supervisory personnel." After this the signs were removed but "*de facto* segregation" persisted for another six years.[22]

The 1977 trial produced some remarkable testimony by black workers as they described how facilities were still segregated more than a decade after the Civil Rights Act. Lawrence Martin calmly explained that white and black workers were continuing to use separate bathrooms. "This side here," he testified as he pointed at pictures of the commodes, "make no mistake, is for the whites and this side is for the blacks. Both of them are in the same building, but they've got a partition between there." Little had changed since the 1950s, when Martin had started out at the plant. M. D. Yon similarly described how the locker and shower rooms still operated on a segregated basis and that a white person had "never" taken a shower in the black side in the twenty-five years that he had worked at the company. There were even, as the court later noted, "some parts of the mill into which no black had entered."[23]

Testimonies also showed that company officials tried to use the small number of black workers who held relatively high-paying jobs to help them maintain de facto segregation. Experienced beater operator Capers Allen, for example, described how he was told by his foreman to instruct all newly hired black workers to use the "colored" bathroom. When Allen left the mill in 1974, he claimed that there were "still two bathrooms" and that he had never been told to teach workers that they could use either one. Allen also claimed that blacks often had to use "the ditch" because they were not permitted enough time to go to their distant toilet facilities.[24]

Replicating the way that the two races failed to mix outside the mill, every aspect of their working lives was segregated. The court concluded that until 1972 "the Company's entrance hallways, time clock, areas and clocks, first aid rooms, shower and locker rooms, and restrooms in the lime kiln and broke beater areas were actively segregated by race." Robert Bryant found the separation of first aid facilities particularly nonsensical. "I mean our first aid, one room in the whole first aid . . . but you had to go through a door with 'black' wrote up on it, not black but 'colored,'" he pondered. "I never understood that to this day." Even the code on workers' time cards were racially identifiable; blacks' numbers started with a three while those of whites began with a one.[25]

African Americans also complained that white facilities were invariably better-equipped than the black facilities. Adrian Franklin Gantt described the bathrooms as truly separate and unequal. "They were separated," he recalled vividly. "White had one and we had one. They had one with about four or five stools in it, we had one with one stool over in our end, one stool. One stool, one basin, and one latrine. And the water-fountain, we had a little old white cup, leading off from the cooler, and it was about ten feet from the cooler." A further indignity was that the "colored" water was never as cold as that provided for whites.[26] The white workers' clock alley contained a phone, yet blacks were not provided with one. During bad weather, whites also took shelter in a shack from which blacks were forbidden.[27]

Despite federal laws against segregation, St. Joe Paper Company had continued the practice. In the interim, some black workers engaged in covert protests. Jason Lewis and Robert Wilson tore down a "colored" sign on the bathrooms in 1972. Draughton Bass testified that when he worked the night shift, he used to drink out of the "white" fountain when the mill was quiet. "I had to slip in there at night when I was working graveyard and get water," he recalled. "At night there wouldn't be nobody in there and you could go in and drink without anything said." If discovered, however, blacks who used white facilities faced threats not just from white employees but from company officials as well.[28]

One of the few avenues of change available to blacks was their union, yet until 1968 the locals at the mill were themselves segregated. The largest union in the pulp and paper industry, the IBPSPMW chartered segregated local unions across the South and was slow to accept the need to desegregate. As late as 1965, the IBPSPMW still had thirty-five all-black locals across Dixie.[29]

In the paper industry, most segregated locals were set up in the 1930s and 1940s, a time when the southern paper industry grew at a phenomenal rate. They reflected the IBPSPMW's reluctance to challenge the pervasive climate of segregation. As labor historian Robert H. Zieger has shown, the IBPSPMW tried to organize in the South "along the path of least resistance," deferring to southern whites' desires for separation. White employees usually organized first and refused to allow blacks to join, encouraging them to form their own unions. As in Port St. Joe, the black locals were granted the same number but with an "A" attached. Although union leaders claimed that the black locals had "equal rights and privileges," in reality they were subservient to their white counterparts, which were numerically larger and controlled the high-paying jobs. In most mills, skilled white workers often belonged to additional locals chartered by the UPP or the IBEW. Outnumbered by several white locals, black unions found it very difficult to effectively challenge discrimination, especially as they were often not allowed to present their proposals directly to the company but were forced to appeal through white union leaders.[30]

At St. Joe the separate black local reflected white preference. Blacks disputed white claims that both races had supported the establishment of segregated unions. A number of black workers who worked at the mill in the 1930s and 1940s testified that when Local 379 was originally organized in 1938, African Americans tried to join but were barred from meetings and had their dues returned to them. Unwilling to work without union protection, blacks organized Local 379A and requested a separate charter in 1946. As black worker Howard Garland remembered, "We had one union and the white give the blacks their money back and later on we got—the blacks got them a charter."[31]

Segregated black locals usually lacked bargaining power. Between 1947 and 1951, St. Joe's black local did not even participate in contract negotiations. Its financial secretary, John Lewis, testified that he never saw a copy of the contract in those years. Lewis remembered that on one occasion he received a letter inviting him to take part in the negotiations, but no one ever came by to pick up the black representatives as they waited at the arranged time to attend. That was "as close as we got to the negotiations." Local 379A also lacked an independent grievance procedure in these early years. If blacks had a grievance, they had to present it Local 379. "All we had to do was tell our president," he related. "Now, he would go to the white president and they would do what could be done."[32]

By the early 1950s, representatives from the black local did attend contract negotiations, but their role was strictly circumscribed. They could go in and present their proposals, but they were not allowed to negotiate or argue. Herman Williams, who served as president and vice president of Local 379A between 1956 and 1959, explained that during the talks, "All we did was ask." After their presentation, they were "excused" while whites stayed in the room. When the deliberations were over, white representatives reported the results. "Whenever the union and the company reached a decision," recalled black officer Howard Garland, "the president of the white local would notify the president of the black local and the black president would call a meeting and tell us what the union done for them." As Williams put it, "We always had to get our main answer from the other—the white local."[33]

As the civil rights movement gathered pace, the black local at St. Joe also remained largely dependent on the white local to process grievances. Williams testified that the foreman usually denied black requests, and only when blacks secured the help of white union officials did they become effective: "We go to our foreman . . . and he would come back and say it's either this or that, take it or leave it, unless we could get some thing that the white union would take up for us, then we would get some help and probably get a little consideration." Even then, the grievance procedure often failed blacks. When one group filed a complaint about white workers being hired over blacks regardless of seniority, their efforts were silenced.[34]

Even when black officers took part in the negotiations they had to endure further indignities. In the 1950s and early 1960s, all contract talks took place at the company's main office, which was located on the white side of the tracks in Port St. Joe. Garland bravely told the court that black delegates had to leave the building when they needed to use the bathroom: "It was a place there, but we wasn't allowed to use that. We had to go across to the woods." On another occasion, the black delegates "went over to Mr. Thompson's filling station and used the restroom there."[35]

Although their power was limited, black union leaders across the South did attempt to open up more jobs for their members. At International Paper Company in Moss Point, Mississippi, for example, Herman Robinson, a former officer in the black local, remembered clearly how he and his fellow officers had repeatedly tried to fight discrimination: "We did all we could in order to try to talk the company into doing the right, the fair thing, but it went on deaf ears. . . . We tried to get over into the white jobs but they said those jobs were strictly for the white union." Across the region, other leaders of black locals worked to fight racial prejudice but usually found that white opposition thwarted them.[36]

Similarly, the black local at St. Joe tried to merge the lines of progression and provide better promotional opportunities for African Americans. Herman Williams purposefully used the negotiations to press for more racial justice; at the first opportunity he asked for "a raise and for mill seniority. We were wanting to get a line of progression . . . go right up in the mill like the whites was doing. But they never would grant it to us. We didn't get it." Williams believed that establishing a line of progression was "one of the most basic things we would try to work on, but we could never get anything did about it."[37]

Many former officers of the black local described how the company and white unions refused to engage in a serious debate whenever blacks demanded better job opportunities. Alfonso Lewis took part in several contract negotiations as the local's recording secretary in the early 1960s. "We had a chance to speak," he acknowledged, "but it was just to speak and be heard. And there was no cross talk about it or, you know, we don't—we didn't bargain. We just spoke and presented what we had to say."[38]

One of the most effective weapons wielded by the company and the white unions was fear. Even in the 1960s, Local 379A treasurer Alton Fennell was hesitant to push too hard in negotiations: "well, at that time, frankly putting it, I was afraid." "We wasn't so afraid of the Union," he continued, "but was afraid of what the Company might do." Other black workers worried about being "hard-timed on the job by the foreman" if they filed grievances.[39]

These fears are central to understanding why black workers turned to the courts to fight discrimination. Many increasingly thought that the separate union could never be effective because union representatives might lose their jobs if they "pushed too hard." Blacks reasoned that they needed an outside agency to help them. "That union would never do nothing," blasted plaintiff Lamar Speights, "the men worked out there, they're scared they might lose their jobs. You need somebody out of the mill."[40]

Aware of the passage of the 1964 Civil Rights Act, black workers determined to use the law to protest long-term discrimination. In 1968 a group led by Thaddeus Russ and Sam Bryant contacted Theodore Bowyers, an LDF attorney who was based in Panama City. Bowyers had become somewhat renowned for helping Florida workers file charges with the EEOC. In the back of a local store, Bowyers directed the group to sign a "charge of discrimination" to be sent to the new federal agency. This document was the genesis of the eventual lawsuit.[41]

The filing of EEOC charges did not mean, however, that workers abandoned efforts to tackle discrimination through the union. In 1968 the black and white locals joined together. Across the South, similar mergers were taking place as federal agencies put pressure on the paper unions to abolish segregated locals. After the creation of an integrated union, many black workers turned to the grievance procedure to process their complaints of racial discrimination. In 1970 Willie James Jenkins filed a grievance because his supervisor told him that his work area "look[ed] like a Negro whorehouse." In April 1975, a group of black woodyard workers complained that "We are grieved—Woodyard supervision is discriminating against employees with regard to race, creed and color." A couple of years later, Otis Walker also charged that the woodyard superintendent was using offensive language. These complaints highlight a growing mood of militancy among black workers and a reluctance to tolerate racial abuse from their supervisors.[42]

St. Joe Paper Company refused to address these complaints, in most cases simply denying that any wrongdoing had occurred. After they failed to secure results through the grievance procedure, then, black workers took up their case with the EEOC. Willie James Jenkins filed charges containing the same complaint as his grievance. But he also addressed many other areas, explaining that his ability to protest through the grievance procedure was limited because he could easily be terminated. "The affiant has complained to the Union, but without success," noted his 1972 charge. "He fears he will lose his job if he makes an issue of the practice."[43]

Leaders of the merged union played an important role in encouraging blacks to file EEOC charges. In particular, the union took up black workers' demands for a nondiscriminatory seniority system. Although they had been reluctant to support civil rights, by the mid 1970s UPIU chiefs recognized that all of their contracts had to conform to the court's rulings in *Local 189* and *Myers*. In 1975 the union at St. Joe tried to change the contract so that black workers could use their mill seniority. Company officials rejected this proposal, along with other nondiscriminatory provisions.[44]

UPIU international representative Donald Langham and local union president Charles Davis, both whites, flew to the EEOC in Miami to press their case. A young Mobile native, Langham testified that he had filed charges against a company that had "failed to negotiate in good faith" over implementing a nondiscriminatory contract. On November 24, 1975, the charges were filed in the name of Local 379.[45]

Hoping to resolve the case, EEOC representative Jimmy Mack arrived in Port St. Joe in the summer of 1976 to negotiate a settlement that would avoid litigation. He traveled around the town trying to persuade African American workers to sign waivers in return for a cash settlement. In the process, he even visited some workers in pool halls and bars. Mack's motives are unclear, although EEOC representatives did have a huge workload and were under pressure to clear up complaints quickly. While many employees agreed to take cash payouts, Langham advised them against it, arguing that the terms offered a way for the company to escape fundamental changes. Before a packed meeting on July 29, 1976, the fiery union leader encouraged black workers "to please not sign now because it would only mean a few dollars to each individual and would release the company, by signing a waiver, of all liabilities." Four St. Joe workers—Sam Bryant, James Winfield, Willie Jenkins and Clyde E. Garland—took Langham's advice, traveled to Tallahassee shortly after the union meeting, and met with Kent Spriggs. By late 1976, the young LDF lawyer had filed the original *Winfield* lawsuit. Two years later, the federal court upheld the plaintiffs' claim that the EEOC settlement had been fraudulent, clearing the way for the class to be expanded considerably.[46]

The four workers who filed the lawsuit emphasized that their motives were to end discrimination at the mill and provide black workers with much better opportunities. "We went to see Mr. Spriggs," explained Garland, "because we all had been discriminated against . . . [and] we got together to come and see what we could do about it. . . . What we wanted to accomplish was to see that most of the black peoples that was working at the mill would have the same opportunity as the white person had. This was the main purpose." In addition, the plaintiffs emphasized their attempts to file grievances through the merged union and the lack of results.[47]

Although filed in 1976, *Winfield* elicited few responses from St. Joe Paper Company. Racial discrimination continued to be rife at the mill long after the case began. Before a nonjury trial held in 1984, plaintiffs aired a variety of complaints. Slim and animated, Kent Spriggs told the court that black workers were disciplined unequally, receiving a disproportionate amount of reprimands and terminations. The main grievance, however, still concerned job assignment. Not until 1972 was the first black hired on the paper machine, and even after this most blacks could not land these positions. Many also continued to work as broke beaters, a position that whites shunned. As Spriggs put it, there was "a continuing pattern of discrimination in initial job assignment."[48]

To substantiate his claims, Spriggs employed Dr. David W. Rasmussen, an economics professor from Florida State University, to analyze company data. When asked if "massive discrimination" continued at St. Joe, Rasmussen replied, "Yes. I certainly would reach that conclusion." The academic explained that historic perceptions of "black" and "white" work had proved very difficult to overcome. "From '74 forward blacks have systematically been assigned to jobs that were historically black," he concluded. "Blacks generally are assigned to black jobs in the 1974 to '81 period, even though they may be integrated, in the sense that some blacks are in those jobs. The data is very clear on this point." Rasmussen also testified that black jobs continued to draw lower wages than their white counterparts, adding that pay differentials were something that "jumped out at me."[49]

As in other paper mills, African Americans who did break into "white" jobs faced opposition from white workers and supervisors. The first African American to apply for a job at St. Joe's bleach plant, David J. Lewis, described how he failed to become permanent because a white operator refused to help him.

Lewis believed that if he had been white, he would have succeeded. African Americans who gained positions on the paper machine in the 1970s faced similar problems, complaining that they were taken off jobs because whites failed to train them or sabotaged their efforts.[50]

R. C. Larry was the first black hired on the paper machine, and his experiences vividly highlight white resistance to blacks working in this central production area. Larry had been hired as a woodyard laborer in 1967, but within five years he moved to the paper machine. A lively, talkative man, he clearly recalled the hostility he encountered. "I was the first black on the paper machine," he explained in 1997. "It was hell up there, you talk about people giving you a hard time. Man, they made you do everything, wouldn't hardly show you nothing. You had to learn on your own. It was dangerous up there too, talking about dangerous. . . . You couldn't do nothing to satisfy them, you couldn't do nothing to suit them. . . . They were making it hard for me because I was the first one, first black that ever went on the paper machine." Larry admitted that the harassment affected his performance. "If you get under a lot of pressure," he acknowledged, "you can't think right, because you scared you going to make a mistake. That's what they were doing to me on the paper machine."[51]

Tragically, Larry's experience on the paper machine ended when a drunk white coworker failed to stop the machine, severing Larry's entire arm. The incident highlighted the dangerous nature of paper mill work, something that all workers were aware of. The disabled employee remained philosophical about the ordeal. "See I was working with a man when I got my arm cut off, man out there drunk," he explained. "It isn't supposed to happen, but it did. . . . You can't put it back on, it ain't going to grow back . . . . It was just a human error. If you drunk, you don't know what's going on, it was on a Saturday morning. . . . This man was on there, he just had the machine running too fast, and instead of him cutting it off, he went the other way. . . . It's one of those things, you just have to live with it."[52]

As late as 1984, many African Americans were still hired in the woodyard, a traditionally black area. The testimony of Howard Garland Jr. captured just how little had changed over the years. Garland was the son of one of the *Winfield* plaintiffs, and his experience was little different from that of his father. "The white workers were assigned on the woodyard to work and to operate the cranes, the front end loaders," he explained. "During that time I think the crane operator was making around 4 dollar per hour. And we were only making 2.27 per hour." Although he was hired in 1967, Garland testified that he had never applied for one of the jobs that the whites held "because that was a no no."

He added that "When you was black you went to the wood yard. You already knew your qualifications and you knew what you were there to do. We knew you were not going to operate the crane, you know you are not going to operate the front end loader. You were going to do whatever the supervisor tell you to do, other than be an operator. That was completely out of the question."[53]

Another central area of discrimination was the application of disciplinary rules. African American workers claimed that they were reprimanded and fired more commonly than white workers, and the company's records supported their case. Between 1967 and 1977, blacks made up around 22 percent of the mill's hourly workforce, yet they received 41 percent of the reprimands. African Americans who testified in the 1980s were still afraid of losing their jobs, an anxiety that never went away at St. Joe. It was responsible for holding blacks in a tenuous position at the mill.[54]

African American workers also described how foremen put more pressure on their black employees and "rode" them. Many complained that supervisors and white operators continued to use racist slurs. Mark Anthony Williams testified in 1984 that supervisors "still call you a boy or nigger." Some even claimed that the only way to secure a good working relationship with a supervisor was to adopt a deferential attitude and deliberately understate qualifications. Racial roles had changed little in Port St. Joe.[55]

Although initially settled in 1988 by a consent decree that granted black workers greater promotional rights, legal maneuvering in *Winfield v. St. Joe Paper Company* continued well into the 1990s. Plaintiffs contended that the company had violated the provisions of this decree because many of the black transfers that did take place "were aborted by a new round of racist behavior." In the historically white electrical department, for example, black workers were harassed by company officials and not trained properly. Not until 1997 was the case finally resolved when the United States Court of Appeals rejected the plaintiffs' appeal for further relief by insisting that the original decree went far enough to help them.[56]

Looking back on the case, the reaction of former plaintiffs was mixed. Many saw the lawsuit as a watershed, believing it had finally forced the company to make some improvements. According to Adrian Franklin Gantt, "They didn't do nothing until the lawsuit, until they filed a lawsuit." Other were angry, however, thinking that the company had escaped largely unpunished. Otis Walker expressed that "we lost years of wages because of discrimination. . . . We were just totally shafted by the company and, as far as I'm concerned, the judicial system. . . . Man, it was terrible, it was terrible down there."[57]

The protracted battle to integrate St. Joe Paper Company was a significant episode in the long civil rights struggle that rocked the southern paper industry. While the degree of corporate resistance to change was unusual, the fact that workers had to resort to litigation to open up more jobs was not. Within Florida itself, activists also filed important Title VII cases against both Hudson Pulp and Paper Company in Palatka and St. Regis Paper Company in Jacksonville.[58]

Both *Myers* and *Winfield* remind us of how unions at the local level often functioned to protect the interests of the white majority. Many historians have argued that unions were vehicles for racial change, but segregated unions in the paper industry, while giving black workers the opportunity to protest against discrimination, faced insurmountable obstacles.[59] Indeed, across the South black paper workers found that their segregated locals lacked bargaining power and were easily manipulated by the larger white unions. As Leroy Hamilton from Gilman Paper Company put it, "We didn't have too much of a voice, they outvote us." In both St. Marys and Port St. Joe, black workers did try to redress discrimination through their separate unions, but they never had the clout to make whites listen.[60]

Led by former union leaders, African American workers in both towns eventually turned to the courts to fight discrimination. They initiated protracted legal battles that secured some positive results, although in both towns many blacks were laid off when the mills eventually closed down. At Gilman, however, blacks were able to enjoy a longer period of access to better jobs before the plant shut.[61]

Of course, the union did belatedly assist the *Winfield* plaintiffs, whereas in *Myers* they opposed them throughout. A closer look reveals similarities between the cases, however. In both situations, the union was trying to limit its liability for back pay. Crucially, *Winfield* also occurred after the UPIU's 1975 decision to amend contracts in order to protect its legal position, whereas *Myers* took place before the UPIU's leaders reluctantly accepted the need for this shift. To a large extent, in fact, *Myers* forced the union to take a softer stance. The company's harder line in *Winfield* also made it easier for the union to back the black workers, who certainly had a compelling case.

The *Winfield* case graphically demonstrated that Title VII litigation was no easy panacea when deep-rooted employment discrimination was being tackled. While the Civil Rights Act proved very important in providing black workers with a mechanism to protest against discrimination, Title VII was clearly more effective as a weapon of protest than as a weapon of change. Moreover,

if companies chose to resist change, litigation could become protracted, unsatisfactory, and messy. And success in the mill hardly addressed larger patterns
of segregation in Port St. Joe. As was the case in the mill, African Americans
complained that de facto segregation continued throughout the town well into
the 1990s. Residentially, the town was still strictly segregated by railroad tracks,
white and black communities still lived separately, and this division seemed
unlikely to change. When asked in 1997 what Port St. Joe was like in the 1950s
and 1960s, retired black worker Cleveland Bailey exclaimed that the town was
"Just like it is now. They over there and we over here."[62]

8

"Meany doesn't sign my check"

The AFL-CIO and the Louisville Busing Crisis of 1975

In the fall of 1975, a little-known busing crisis rocked Louisville, Kentucky, tearing apart the fabric of a community that had previously been known for its moderate and peaceful race relations. Leading the opposition to so-called forced busing was United Labor Against Busing (ULAB), a coalition of local unions that included the International Union of Electrical Workers (IUE), the United Automobile Workers (UAW), the International Association of Machinists, and the Sheet Metal Workers. ULAB activists were openly disdainful of American Federation of Labor–Congress of Industrial Organizations president George Meany, who had committed the giant federation to support busing. As the 1975–76 school year got under way, local union leaders organized a work stoppage to protest busing, forcing the closure of two local Ford plants. Over the next few weeks, union members flooded onto the streets to take part in violent street protests that led to frequent confrontations with the Kentucky National Guard. In late October, ULAB also organized a mass march in Washington, with more than fifty buses and numerous private cars heading for the nation's capital. Through the fall and winter of 1975–76, ULAB members openly defied AFL-CIO national policy, creating a crisis that caused the federation considerable embarrassment and undermined its efforts to portray itself as a progressive advocate of black rights.[1]

This was not the first time the AFL-CIO's civil rights policies had been opposed by grassroots members. After the 1954 *Brown v. Board of Education* decision, the newly created AFL-CIO faced similar problems. While the federation's leaders applauded the Supreme Court decision and urged the South to comply, many union members flocked to segregationist groups such as the white citizens' councils. The actions of these workers highlighted the power of "whiteness" among union members and showed how difficult it was to build an interracial labor movement in the region.[2]

To date, however, most work by historians on the relationship between race and labor has dealt with the period from the 1840s through the 1950s.[3] Both labor historians and civil rights scholars are only just beginning to turn their attention to the period after 1965, and it is important to add to this emerging field.[4] Ongoing white opposition ensured that a lot of the real progress in integrating schools only occurred after the mid-1960s.[5] After the *Swann* decision, mandatory busing plans were adopted by more than one hundred southern school districts, including Little Rock, Jacksonville, Nashville, Tampa, Dallas, Norfolk, and Louisville. Across the region, whites were suddenly forced to deal with the prospect of immediate integration, and many reacted violently. While busing has been written about in some detail, the crisis in Louisville has been largely overlooked, despite the fact that the Kentucky city had the twelfth largest school system in the nation.[6]

Dividing Americans along race and class lines, busing was one of the most controversial issues of the 1970s. In one 1972 poll, only 13 percent of whites supported busing for desegregation purposes compared to 56 percent of blacks. By 1978 a Gallup poll showed that just 5 percent of whites endorsed the tactic.[7] "Busing for school desegregation," noted political scientists Richard A. Pride and J. David Woodard in 1985, "was, and remains, the most visible and controversial issue of race in America."[8] The tactic often pitted blue-collar whites against middle-class liberals, the former arguing that they were being forced to bear the costs of integration while more affluent whites sent their children to private schools. These tensions were especially evident in Boston, scene of a high-profile busing conflict in 1974–75. In the Massachusetts city, a strong anti-busing movement drew upon what historian Ronald P. Formisano has called "the interplay of race and class, in admixture with ethnicity and place."[9]

In Louisville race and class also fused together, and the protesters' actions were not merely a reflection of "whiteness." While union members openly used the language of racism to oppose *Brown*, by the 1970s most relied on a broader variety of arguments. Many now accepted that some degree of integration was inevitable, but they argued that working-class whites should not be unfairly victimized in the process. Protesters aimed as much of their hatred at distant labor leaders and politicians who supported busing as they did at blacks. Busing split the labor movement along class lines, as middle-class leaders who supported the tactic clashed with a blue-collar membership that was largely opposed to it. Despite this, the impact of busing on the labor movement has yet to be examined in detail.[10]

The Louisville crisis was deeply embarrassing for labor leaders who had forged close ties with civil rights organizations at the national level. While the UAW's

Louisville local was supporting the ULAB protests, its leaders were pledging $600,000 to fund the building of the Martin Luther King Jr. Center for Social Change in Atlanta.[11] In 1976 labor donations helped to rescue the NAACP from dire financial problems after the association lost a landmark boycotting case in Mississippi.[12] Through the 1970s, the federation also gave money to both the SRC and the SCLC, groups that believed in busing. These ties reflected the federation's principled opposition to racism, although donations were also designed to persuade civil rights organizations to tone down their exposure of discrimination within labor unions. In the 1970s, rising unemployment led black leaders to become more concerned with economic issues, causing them to join with organized labor in endorsing full employment legislation. Full employment, proclaimed Coretta Scott King in 1977, was "the most critical need in America today."[13] The AFL-CIO's civil rights office celebrated the close links it had forged with black interest groups. "Never before," it asserted in 1978, "has the civil rights and labor communities been so together on common goals and objectives."[14]

AFL-CIO policy makers gave clear support to busing. Following *Swann*, the federation took a public stand on the issue at its executive council meeting in February 1972. "We wholeheartedly support busing of children when it will improve the educational opportunities of the children," it declared. This policy was reaffirmed in 1973 and 1975. In October 1975, at the height of the Louisville conflict, the Kentucky State AFL-CIO submitted a resolution to the national executive council that called for "reconsideration" of organized labor's endorsement of busing. Although the resolution was unanimously defeated, George Meany disliked the effort by a state federation to challenge national directives. He warned his Kentucky subordinates that it was "emphatically against AFL-CIO policy for the Kentucky State AFL-CIO or any local central body to lend any aid or support whatever to those who seek to ignore or to pervert the policy of the AFL-CIO established in 1972 and reaffirmed as recently as October 3." The gruff-voiced, cigar-smoking Meany had been at the helm of the AFL-CIO since its creation, and he was not used to having his word questioned.[15]

Meany reacted angrily to the Louisville protests. In the process, he unwittingly contributed to the crisis by failing to take the grievances of the Louisville workers seriously. Rather than listening to them, AFL-CIO officials consistently argued that extremists and political opportunists were exploiting the workers. Underestimating the strength of grassroots feeling, they asserted that workers could be brought around to support the federation's position, arguments that only made the ULAB activists more outspoken and rebellious. Meany himself never visited Louisville to talk to members but instead criticized their actions from Washington, fueling perceptions that he was a bureaucratic and distant labor leader who had little understanding of his members' concerns. In the wake of the Watergate scandal and the Vietnam War, the faith of many Americans in federal institutions was at a very low level. In Louisville and elsewhere, the anti-busing movement drew on strong feelings of resistance to federal control.[16]

In many ways, Louisville was an unlikely setting for a major busing crisis. For many years, the bustling city on the Ohio river had held a reputation for racial progressivism. Able to vote since the 1870s, Louisville's blacks elected their own aldermen and state representatives on a regular basis. Shortly after World War II, black activism also helped to integrate the city's libraries and public hospitals. In 1956 the Louisville Board of Education turned its back on "massive resistance" and adopted a comprehensive integration plan that was widely praised by the liberal press. In 1965 and 1968, Kentucky also passed important civil rights and fair housing laws. Both the NAACP and the state AFL-CIO endorsed the 1965 act, and with subsequent amendment it came to be regarded as one of the strongest civil rights laws in the country. "Louisville," noted the New York Times in 1975, "has long been known for a tradition of moderation and tolerance that grows out of its border state mentality and river town cosmopolitanism."[17]

A closer look reveals that Louisville was not as advanced as its white leaders liked to claim. For years African American residents had argued that civic boosters used Louisville's progressive reputation to thwart fundamental changes in race relations. As NAACP activist Lyman Johnson put it, "white leaders would say, 'Look how good we are to you. Now, don't bug us too much.'"[18] In 1967 angry whites pelted open-housing marchers with rocks, eggs, and firecrackers, a disturbance that Newsweek called "the year's ugliest racial confrontation."[19] The riot revealed that many whites were deeply opposed to housing integration. Despite the passage of the 1968 Fair Housing Act, Louisville's neighborhoods actually became more segregated. In November 1974, a survey by the Council on Metropolitan Performance found that housing segregation in Louisville was more severe than in seventy-nine other major U.S. cities. Between 1960 and 1970, residential segregation increased significantly as whites fled the city, often being replaced by blacks. In the space of a decade, the number of white Louisvillians declined from 320,564 to 274,511 while the number of African American residents increased from 70,075 to 86,040. By 1970 over 95 percent of the black population of Jefferson County lived in just six of the county's fifty-five census tracts, a small cluster of districts in central and western Louisville.[20]

School enrollment reflected the rising levels of residential segregation. As a 1972 report by the Kentucky Commission on Human Rights concluded, "Louisville once again is running a segregated system and it's getting worse, fast." All but 850 of Louisville's 12,500 black elementary school children were attending historically black schools, and the situation was little better for junior high or high school students. By 1975 the student population of Louisville's public schools was 54 percent black, compared to 4 percent in Jefferson County. Documenting increasing amounts of segregation in meticulous detail, the commission, which had been set up by the state's Civil Rights Act, argued that the Louisville school system had failed to integrate for a variety of reasons. The most important of these were a lack of political will and an increasing reliance on racially divisive neighborhood schools. Despite officials' initial willingness to comply with *Brown*, by 1972 Louisville's record of school integration was worse than that of ten other southern cities, including Atlanta, Birmingham, Little Rock, and Charlotte.[21]

Arguing that black children could only achieve a quality education within an integrated system, in 1971 the commission joined with other civil rights groups and asked the federal courts to do more to tackle "racial isolation" within Louisville's schools. Black activists such as Lyman Johnson were determined to challenge city officials to live up to their claims of being racially progressive. After four years of legal proceedings, in July 1975 federal judge James F. Gordon ordered the full desegregation of local schools. Louisville became the first metropolitan area in the country to carry out the court-ordered busing of children between the central city and suburban school districts in order to achieve racial balance.[22] Under the plan, white pupils would be bused for two years of their twelve-year educational careers and blacks for eight or nine years. In all, 11,300 blacks were to ride buses from Louisville to the suburbs, while the same number of whites would take them in the opposite direction. Busing would continue until each school had a black enrollment of at least 12 percent but no more than 40 percent.[23]

Many whites vehemently opposed the plan. As the 1975–76 school year began, Concerned Parents, a new grassroots group, coordinated a boycott that was observed by around half of all white children. In early September, up to fifteen thousand protesters also attended rallies organized by the fledgling organization.[24] On September 5, violence erupted in the working-class suburb of Valley Station. Several police officers were injured, one losing an eye after being hit by a missile that had been thrown from the crowd. At one high school, a mob of 2,500 came close to overwhelming the local police, while at another protesters broke into the grounds and vandalized thirty yellow buses, the hated symbol of forced busing.[25] After two days of busing, the authorities had made more than four hundred arrests in connection with the desegregation plan. Citing reports of "injuries and serious damage to property," on September 6 Governor Julian Carroll called in nine hundred National Guard troops in an effort to restore calm.[26]

After the troops arrived, Louisville mayor Harvey I. Sloane invoked a controversial state law that was designed to curb civil disturbances and led to many arrests. Despite this, protests continued, and armed troops were placed on buses to protect both pupils and drivers.[27] In October, tensions remained so high that President Gerald Ford cancelled a scheduled trip to Louisville because advisers warned him that the antibusing protests posed a security threat. As a strong opponent of busing, Ford also felt that his appearance might spark what the *New York Times* termed "a new wave of unrest."[28] In the months that followed, police had to use tear gas on several occasions in order to disperse marchers.[29]

In late October, Mayor Sloane described the grave nature of the crisis to a senate committee. "Massive, cross-community busing is creating serious problems in Louisville," he explained. "Our community has been polarized, and the fabric of relationships that makes a community strong has been torn apart. Parents who send their children to school in defiance of boycotts are shunned by relatives, friends and neighbors. Businesses that don't display anti-busing signs lose customers. School bus drivers have been threatened. Police officers assigned to control demonstrations have been assaulted." Although the number of students boycotting the system had dropped, around 10 percent of parents were still keeping their children at home. Suspensions of students had risen 40 percent, with many staying out of classes in order to participate in the protests. Several of the largest factories had been forced to cut back production as workers participated in regular marches. While admitting that "racial intolerance" was certainly present in his city, Sloane insisted that many whites opposed busing because it was too disruptive and costly. In addition, they insisted that it would not improve the schools for either race. Sloane added that court-ordered busing had occurred rapidly, with local leaders given only a few weeks to implement Judge Gordon's order. In contrast, in the late 1950s the Board of Education's integration plan had taken many months to draft.[30]

Opinion polls taken at the time highlight the depth of community opposition to busing. Harris polls conducted in Louisville in the spring of 1976, when the worst of the violence had died down, found that 91 percent of white respondents still opposed busing. In addition, 20 percent of whites indicated that they intended to take part in future protests. Although tensions did gradually subside, more than two years after the start of the plan police were still confronting scattered antibusing demonstrations.[31]

From the start, union members were active in the antibusing movement. To some degree this was a reflection of the central role that organized labor played in many residents' lives. In the 1970s, Louisville was a significant industrial center and had a strong local labor movement. Several major corporations had plants in the city, including General Electric, Ford Motor Company, and International Harvester. These firms had been attracted to Louisville by its location on the Ohio river and its proximity to markets in both the northern and southern states. The biggest local firm was GE, which employed around sixteen thousand people at its sprawling Appliance Park site. More than fourteen thousand of these workers belonged to IUE Local 761, the largest local union in the entire state.[32]

Just before the school year was set to begin, many IUE members joined a Concerned Parents' march to the Jefferson County courthouse. "You see here that Local 761 is being heard and seen," declared executive board member James A. Luckett. "We want to challenge other unions, today, from the steps of this courthouse, to go along with Local 761 to show your opposition to busing." As the *Louisville Courier-Journal* noted, more than one thousand marchers carried signs that declared "Stop Busing: Local 761." At the march Luckett declared that the eighteen members of Local 761's executive board would be taking a public stand on September 4, the opening day of school. "The executive board is not going to work, and we're not going to be paid," he said. The protest went ahead against the wishes of the IUE's head office, which had urged the Louisville workers "to set an example of obedience to the law and the U.S. Constitution." Local union president Kenneth Cassady, however, asserted that national leaders had misunderstood the local's position. "Our opposition has nothing to do with race," he explained. "We are opposed to busing because it will lower the quality of education." Cassady added that he was "sorry at this time that our people are represented by officers at the international union who cannot understand the issues."[33]

When the school year began, other Louisville unions followed Local 761's example. On September 4, thousands of union members gave up a day's pay and stayed off their jobs. Two Ford factories were forced to close after more than half the workforce failed to show up. Other plants remained open but reported absenteeism rates of between 40 and 60 percent.[34] Despite staying off the job, few workers were punished by their employers. Although Ford belatedly issued a few ringleaders with warnings for unauthorized absences, workers responded by sabotaging equipment in the truck plant. Afraid of upsetting consumers, corporate leaders were silent.[35]

With the business community unwilling to take a stand, disturbances continued. Many subsequent protests were centered in Valley Station and other working-class suburbs where union members lived in large numbers. "Louisville labor unions," noted the *Saturday Review* in a subsequent analysis of the crisis, "took the leadership of the anti-busing movement. Thousands of white rank-and-filers at such plants as General Electric, Ford, and International Harvester joined in the demonstrations and raised money. . . . Almost every sizable union in the area joined in."[36]

ULAB helped to organize several other antibusing marches, including a mass gathering on September 27 that the group termed "the largest demonstration ever held in the State of Kentucky." According to press accounts, around eight thousand activists marched through downtown Louisville and shouted derisive remarks outside the headquarters of the *Louisville Courier-Journal* and *Louisville Times*, whose editors supported the busing program. At this march, the IUE's "Stop Busing" signs also reappeared.[37] Feeling that it needed to make a stand on the national stage, on the last weekend in October ULAB also organized an antibusing rally in the nation's capital. The *Louisville Times* estimated that over two thousand union members took buses to Washington, D.C., while several hundred traveled by car. Taking place during the congressional recess for Veteran's Day, however, the marchers had little impact on the politicians they were seeking to reach.[38]

The AFL-CIO's civil rights department closely documented the involvement of its members in the antibusing movement. In early September, department director William E. Pollard wrote that "several local unions" were "giving leadership" to the September 4 stoppage. When a protest march occurred on the same day as the work stoppage, Pollard estimated that "union members were out in sizeable numbers." His assessment was supported by the *Louisville Times*, which reported that "many of the marchers were members of unions who'd taken the day off from work." Pollard was especially concerned by the actions of Kentucky AFL-CIO president Joseph Warren, who had signed an antibusing advertisement in the local press.[39]

AFL-CIO leaders sought to limit the impact of the protests. In a letter to the Kentucky AFL-CIO, Meany insisted that busing was a "phony issue" exploited by politicians and conservative organizations who were opposed to "the right of every child to have equal access to a quality education." He pointed out that over 40 percent of American schoolchildren rode buses to school each day, and only 3 percent did so because of court orders. In Louisville, added Meany, an "emotional response" had been "fanned into hysteria" by the Klan and "other extremists" who were using the issue for political gain. Appealing for calm, the federation's leader argued that union members should try to "minimize friction" and "make the busing system work" in order to bring about the highest quality of education. In addition, Meany worked to try to stop other union members from becoming involved in the antibusing movement.[40]

In Louisville Meany's efforts backfired badly. Rather than calming the situation, workers reacted angrily to his assertions, with many feeling that their legitimate concerns were being brushed off. Jim Luckett told the local press that Meany could not halt the ULAB's march on Washington. "His views are not going to stop us; _____ him," he blasted. "And you can quote me. Meany's going to see it our way or else he doesn't speak for the rank and file union man." Cassady also cut the eighty-year-old union leader little slack. "Meany should have retired years ago; the national union leaders don't know what is going on in Louisville," he fumed.[41] On November 13, 1975, a group of 175 union members denounced Meany and invited him to Louisville "to see what's going on in the schools." "I wish he would just come down here and sit with us a few weeks," claimed ULAB vice chairman Louis Sexton. "I tried to cool it once, too. . . . But he'd be doing the same thing we are if he could see what is happening here." "Meany," added Luckett, "wants you to work eight hours . . . and put your child in school for eleven hours. The old boy is off in the head." ULAB members took particular exception to Meany's comments that the Klan was encouraging their activities. As IAM member James Lloyd put it, "it is the lowest you can get to say that I am affiliated with the Ku Klux Klan."[42]

The director of the AFL-CIO's southern civil rights office, E. T. ("Al") Kehrer, was assigned to travel to Louisville to pacify union members. Kehrer, who was white, was a Yale graduate who had formerly worked for the International Ladies Garment Workers Union. In early November, the Atlanta-based official journeyed north to Kentucky's largest city. During a brief visit he found that local union leaders had no respect for AFL-CIO policy and were even threatening to disaffiliate from the federation. "Repeatedly they told me 'Meany doesn't sign my check,'" he noted. Kehrer also reported that several local unions had made financial contributions to antibusing groups. Some national union officials had tried to block these donations because they violated the 1959 Landrum-Griffin Act, which imposed stiff standards of financial disclosure upon labor unions.[43]

Realizing that public announcement of the AFL-CIO's policies would be counterproductive, Kehrer instead worked behind the scenes to try to gain more understanding for the federation's position. Like Meany he insisted that school administrators, politicians, and right-wing elements were "inflaming" the issue for their own purposes, arguments that failed to defuse tensions.[44] In fact, school board officials accepted Gordon's ruling and local politicians did not try to exploit the issue as they had in Boston. The Louisville media also urged calm, running a campaign with the slogan, "Nobody wins when you lose your cool." Above all, civic officials were anxious not to jeopardize Louisville's carefully cultivated image as a racially moderate city. Protests continued despite these efforts to contain them, especially as many working people felt betrayed by their middle-class leaders. As one parent wrote, "editorial writers with children in private schools couldn't care less about children being bused, could they?"[45]

Although Kehrer claimed some success in defusing antibusing sentiment, he realized that he was swimming against the tide. The leaders of ULAB remained particularly defiant, with Jack Shore threatening Kehrer that he would "[try] to develop a national anti-busing union group." Shore and Cassady also told the *Courier-Journal* that they had refused to meet with Kehrer, who they viewed as Meany's minion. "If George Meany wanted to meet with me on busing, I'd turn him down," boasted Cassady.[46]

Despite Kehrer's efforts, many local union leaders took increasingly public positions in the antibusing movement. Rather than acting as private individuals, they used their unions as organizing tools. In a series of advertisements in the local press, at least nine local unions went on record to emphatically express their hatred of busing.[47] Openly defying the policies of their international unions, they asserted that busing was undemocratic and did not reflect the wishes of most parents. As Local 3931 of the United Steelworkers put it, "forced busing has been put into Federal Law by the courts against the will of the majority of the people of these United States of America." Pipefitters Local 552 concurred, urging all of its "members and friends to Oppose Forced Busing" and join Concerned Parents.[48]

Like many opponents of busing, the Louisville workers insisted that they were not racists but were simply trying to secure the best education for their children. "We do not oppose integration," claimed refinery workers local #84, "but feel that quality education can be achieved by other means."[49] The white activists argued that busing was not the best way to achieve this goal, as it caused strife and suffering for the children involved. As Cassady put it, "the children are the ones hurt by forced busing." Youngsters, he explained, were "worn out" after riding a bus for up to three hours a day. Busing also wasted resources that the public schools desperately needed. "It is our opinion," declared an advertisement by the Graphic Arts Union, "that the estimated 3.5 million dollars to be spent for forced busing would be more wisely used to upgrade the existing educational system, which is currently ranked 49th in the nation."[50]

Angry and defiant, many union members felt that both politicians and appointed judges were ignoring their wishes and that protesting was the only way to be heard. As local UAW leader Bill Williamson put it, his union was supporting a school boycott because "it looks like that's the only thing they'll pay attention to." Like antibusing groups elsewhere, ULAB members felt that busing was particularly hurting working people. The politicians who endorsed the tactic, wrote Cassady, were "working hardships on the parents who work for a living." Antibusing activists were quick to point out that politicians' children often attended private schools and were unaffected by Gordon's order. "How about busing all of them damn legislators' kids to Louisville?" quipped one protester.[51]

Aware that federal judges and national politicians supported busing, the protesters also drew upon strong antigovernment rhetoric. "It's not race," explained IUE member Charles Weber. "It's them saying you have to do something. It's the have to. If they can force this, they can force anything. They can tell me to work for Ford or sell my house." Busing came to be seen by white union workers as a line in the sand, a chance to fight back against a government that was steadily eroding the individual's rights. "The success of busing," wrote one protester, "simply reinforces the continued growth of the power of the federal government and the continued weakening of the rights of its individual citizens." Some even compared their government to the "communistic" system in Russia and joked that Judge Gordon should be sent to the Soviet Union.[52]

Busing in Louisville exposed class tensions as much as it did racism. In the fall of 1975, Mayor Sloane conducted a seventy-mile walking tour across the city and found that opposition to Gordon's edict was strongest among blue-collar families in the burgeoning suburbs. "For working-class white families," he explained, "busing is only the last straw in a series of government-imposed programs that they see threatening their individual freedom and way of life. Some of the most vocal opponents of busing are those families who have moved out of the inner city to seek what they see as a better life—better housing, better schools, better jobs, better opportunity for their children. Now, in Louisville, their children are being bused back into the very neighborhoods they left behind." Affluent whites were more able to avoid busing and therefore did not feel so strongly about it. "For wealthier families," explained Sloane, "who can afford to send their children to private schools, busing is really someone else's problem." Two Duke University sociologists, who found that opposition to busing in Louisville was strongest among the "upper working class" rather than those with the least education, confirmed these results. Industrial workers with high school educations had migrated to the suburbs and did not want their children sent back to the city.[53]

Union members also aimed their anger at Democratic politicians who supported busing, the same politicians whom union leaders had told them to vote for. Kenneth Cassady claimed that busing was "used" by policy makers "to create racial unrest when there should be no problem between the races." Federal representatives, he added, were "afraid to do the job they were elected to do." In November 1975, tensions were heightened further when the Democratic Party held a national issues convention in Louisville. Angry union members, many of them armed with baseball bats, massed outside and were kept away from the building by more than two hundred riot police. The crowd grew particularly restive when Senator George McGovern termed busing "one inescapable remedy of the Constitution for a proven case of segregation." Convention officials had tried to stop McGovern from speaking in Louisville, but the former presidential candidate had overruled them.[54]

While antibusing leaders were careful to avoid racist outbursts, the controversy did lead to a revival of the Ku Klux Klan in the Louisville area. On September 6, a Klan meeting drew a crowd of around one thousand, but divisions riddled the group and its growth was short lived. On September 11, a second rally attracted just one hundred people.[55] While racism was certainly present among the antibusing protesters, only a tiny minority expressed their views in openly racial terms. During the September 4 march, for example, a few protesters hurled epithets at passing blacks, actions that were quickly publicized by local journalists. ULAB sought to distinguish itself from the Klan, partly because it recognized that any association with the renegade group would harm its efforts to gain credibility. The Klan struggled to secure lasting influence among organized workers. Local Klan chief Walter Groves was an insurance salesman and had never worked in any of Louisville's manufacturing plants. Groves was also in conflict with Kentucky grand dragon Phillip Chopper, whom he accused of misusing Klan money.[56]

Some black union members tried to stop their dues being used to fight busing. Their actions reflected the fact that the black community in Louisville had a long tradition of political mobilization. When Judge Gordon's order was handed down, surveys indicated that around 61 percent of blacks favored busing.[57] Despite threats and violence, most black students continued to ride the buses. "I like the school," declared one black eighth grader who was being transported to the suburbs. "I like the kids. I don't mind having to get up earlier to catch my bus. . . . I even like the ride. If it just weren't for the fighting [outside], it would be all right." While some parents worried for the safety of their children, African American activists were determined to make busing work. As a coalition of local ministers explained, the black community could not back down because they had "waited too long for such an opportunity."[58]

Within Local 761, black members felt that their elected leaders should not have become involved in the antibusing movement. Immediately after the September 4 protests, a group of African American workers wrote to IUE headquarters in Washington to complain about Cassady's actions. "Enclosed are papers of Local 761 Black union members wishing to resign from the union if the President did not curtail his activities in the anti-Busing movement," they explained. The IUE's national leaders had already criticized Local 761's executive board, but they refused to take any further action. Following this, ten African American members wrote Cassady and informed him that they were withdrawing from the union. "Black members were not represented at these rallies," they noted, "but spokesmen for these anti-busing individuals stated they were representing all of 761 IUE, which is not true."[59]

A worker in his mid-forties who claimed to have grown up alongside blacks, Cassady consistently denied that he was racist. He argued, however, that his behavior reflected the wishes of the "majority" of his members, and he reiterated that it was not to the "children's benefit" to bus. "Our position," he explained, "is that the money used for 'forced busing' would or could be better used by repairing or building schools and paying teachers higher wages so that quality teachers could be found." He also insisted that Gordon's order was hurting the black community. "We feel," he wrote, "the Black children who have to ride a bus for eight years are being discriminated against."[60]

Despite Cassady's rebuffs, African American union members continued to fight to get their views heard. Opposition from black workers helped to narrowly overturn an endorsement that the local had given to Republican gubernatorial candidate Robert Gable. The president of a mining company, Gable opposed busing, but he also disliked unions. In October black members also introduced a motion to limit union spending on antibusing literature to $10,000, but the white majority voted this effort down.[61]

Antibusing protesters faced some formidable foes. Although busing clearly aroused strong opposition among many whites, it also had powerful supporters. The U.S. Supreme Court refused to hear challenges to Judge Gordon's order, and Congress was reluctant to pass legislation that could pave the way for an antibusing constitutional amendment. In November 1976, Jimmy Carter, who was less opposed to busing than his predecessor, replaced Gerald Ford as president. While Ford had criticized the court order in Louisville, Carter refused to do so. During the 1976 presidential election, he endorsed busing as a "last resort" and criticized Ford for "aggravating volatile situations" in Louisville and Boston.[62]

In Louisville busing also had many supporters, including African American leaders and many middle-class whites. In October white civil rights activist Anne Braden helped to organize a pro-busing rally that featured the folk singer Pete Seeger. A local resident, Braden also helped to establish Progress in Education, a predominantly white organization that worked with black groups to fight racism in the schools.[63] Breaking ranks with other metropolitan unions, a local of the American Federation of Teachers continued to endorse busing, as did a heavily black branch of the Laborers and Service Employees Union. With federal politicians refusing to change tack, some Louisville residents began to see further protests as futile. Although ULAB talked of organizing another march in Washington, by the spring of 1977 the group was concentrating on lobbying and legal action. Jack Shore still believed busing would eventually be "turned around," but he no longer thought demonstrations could accomplish this end. In the 1980s, plant closures and mass layoffs also led to a weakening of the Louisville labor movement, undermining its ability to fight busing.[64]

As the demonstrations subsided, liberal whites tried to see Louisville as proof that even virulent opposition to school integration could be overcome. As early as June 1976, the *New York Times* asserted that Louisville was "a place where busing seems to work," pointing out that the violent protests of the early school year had now subsided. The *Times* had a point, as there were whites who came to realize that they could not overturn Gordon's decree.[65] By early 1977, some union members were taking part in Community for Educational Excellence, an interracial discussion group that was dedicated to improving the local school system. A former ULAB supporter, IAM activist Robert DePrez admitted that "We're all looking for better ways to educate children, and if busing stopped tomorrow we'd still have to deal with the poor schools we have here."[66] Busing in Louisville certainly produced some positive results. Over time the facilities at some formerly all-black schools were upgraded and students' achievement scores consequently improved.[67]

There is also evidence, however, that busing failed to work. Many whites never accepted Gordon's edict, and they frequently reacted to it by taking their children away from the public schools. By January 1976, at least five private schools had been started as a result of the court order, while seven established Christian schools had also reported a 40 percent increase in enrollment.[68] After a year of busing, almost 16 percent of local parents with preschool-age children declared that they did not intend to send their offspring to the public schools. In June 1976, Judge Gordon revised his original edict, requiring more black students to be bused for a longer period. He explained that busing more whites would only have caused even greater numbers to leave the school system.[69]

Even as street demonstrations declined, they were replaced by tensions in the classroom. In the spring of 1977, racial brush fires erupted in many Louisville-area schools as black and white students fought to establish dominance over one another.[70] Many observers doubted whether race relations had improved at all. "You get the feeling that somebody is always watching you if you shake a white person's hand," commented black student Zachary Royal in 1978. "But look at our parents, they feel the same way." By 1978 the *New York Times* had scaled back its position and admitted that busing in Louisville had brought only "mixed results."[71]

Many residents also believed that busing had caused a decline in educational standards.[72] Into the 1990s Kentucky's schools remained some of the worst in the nation, and both blacks and whites questioned the wisdom of Gordon's order. Busing took a heavy toll on blacks, as they were bused for more years than whites and over longer distances. Some students had to get up before 5 a.m. to attend distant schools, forcing extracurricular activities to be cancelled. By 1991 many black parents supported a proposal to ban mandatory busing in elementary grades and advocated well-equipped local schools, even if they were predominantly black. "Integration," claimed black pastor Rev. Kevin Cosby, "has resulted in the disintegration of our institutions." The aging activists who had brought the original desegregation suit, however, continued to argue that separate schools could only harm the black community.[73]

Through the 1980s and 1990s, busing divided African Americans across the country, and many grew disillusioned with the results of the tactic. In many respects, Louisville's experience was similar to that of other cities where the tactic was used. In both north and south, busing evoked violent opposition, often accelerated the rate of white flight, and left schools troubled by racial divisions.

Over time, however, resistance did subside, and once parents realized that the busing plans were not going to be rescinded, most worked to maximize the educational benefits of mixed schools. As was the case elsewhere, busing left a complicated legacy, with supporters and opponents both able to find examples to support their claims. The tactic was most effective, however, when civic and political leaders remained committed to the process, and when well-conceived court orders encouraged whites to keep their children in the public school system.[74]

In the fall of 1975, the disturbances in Louisville made front-page headlines. Like Boston, Louisville was viewed as an example of the "massive turmoil" that busing could cause. Despite this, the Kentucky community has received little scholarly coverage in comparison to its Massachusetts counterpart.[75] The story outlined here shows that the protests did not simply reflect racism but also drew on deep-seated fears about educational quality and opposition to federal interference. Both the Boston and Louisville protests also occurred in cities with reputations for racial tolerance. They are reminders that racial conflict was not unique to the Deep South, as narratives of the "classic" phase of the civil rights movement often suggest. The Louisville crisis underlined that whites and blacks continued to fight over school integration well into the 1970s. Blacks remained determined to secure an equal education, but even twenty years after *Brown* they were still struggling to realize this.[76]

Busing was one of the most controversial issues of the 1970s, and it often had a disproportionate impact on blue-collar workers.[77] As was the case in Louisville, the tactic could easily divide union members from their leaders. In Boston busing was also deeply opposed by many rank and filers. As Al Kehrer reported after a December 1975 trip to the Massachusetts city, "many of the individual crafts are involved in the anti-busing movement." Despite Kehrer's efforts, the situation in Boston also remained tense. "Most of the leadership I talked to," reported Kehrer nervously, "were of the opinion that the best we could do would be to keep the busing issue off the floor of our union meetings." Events in Boston were also widely reported in the Louisville press, encouraging union activists to believe that they could build a national antibusing movement.[78]

Louisville's strong labor movement contributed greatly to the crisis, as local unions provided an organizational focus for antibusing sentiment. The situation revealed the large gap that still existed between the AFL-CIO's civil rights policies and actual practices on the ground. For many years, labor chiefs had claimed that the autonomy of local unions limited their ability to tackle racial discrimination at the grassroots level. This argument, however, often concealed leaders' failure to confront racism. In Louisville, AFL-CIO heads reminded affiliated unions of national policy but never threatened to punish their subordinates. In fact, local unions were quite willing to defy an aging AFL-CIO president whom they viewed as out of touch and ineffective.[79]

In a broader context, the conflict revealed how many rank-and-file union members felt alienated from their leaders. From the mid-1960s through the mid-1970s, many unionists defied leaders whom they viewed as remote bureaucrats. In 1970 around two hundred thousand New York City postal workers ignored a ban on federal employee walkouts to launch possibly the largest wildcat strike in the nation's history. Others copied their example, as the 1970s opened with an unlikely surge of labor militancy that received little encouragement from above. Within the Teamsters and the United Mine Workers, rank-and-file groups even pressed for the overthrow of established officials. "Labor leaders," noted historian Joshua Freeman, "often found themselves out of touch with their own members."[80]

Events in Louisville ultimately highlighted some of the broader problems that confronted organized labor's civil rights policies in the 1970s. Throughout the decade, the AFL-CIO supported a racial agenda that many of their white members disliked or opposed. At the same time, labor leaders also came under attack from black activists who felt that unions were not tackling discrimination in their own ranks.[81] Union officials often felt caught in the middle, attacked by black interest groups for not combating racism and by their white members for being too supportive of civil rights.[82] The federation's sole civil rights functionary in the South, Al Kehrer was frequently unable to "turn the issue around." In Louisville he was powerless to stop the local labor movement from becoming a vehicle for powerful antibusing activists who bluntly told him that they would not see "any 'agent' of George Meany." "It would be fair to say," he concluded, "that all of these local leaders responded politically to their highly vocal and angry members." Incapable of changing how the Louisville workers felt, Kehrer trudged back to his office in Atlanta and continued his efforts to limit the fallout from a severe busing crisis.[83]

Notes

Introduction

1. Thomas A. Johnson, "Georgia March Planned," *New York Times*, May 18, 1970; Thomas A. Johnson, "300 Start a 5-Day Protest March in Georgia, Despite Plea by Maddox," *New York Times*, May 20, 1970; Thomas A. Johnson, "5-Day March in Georgia Ends With Massive Rally," *New York Times*, May 24, 1970.

2. For a pathbreaking study of the Selma civil rights campaign that culminated in the march to Montgomery, see Garrow, *Protest at Selma*. The Selma march is covered in many other studies. See, for example, J. Williams, *Eyes on the Prize*, 251–87; Fairclough, *To Redeem the Soul of America*, 225–51; J. Lewis, *Walking with the Wind*, 335–62. The concentration of civil rights studies on the period before 1968 is covered fully in Eagles, "Toward New Histories," 815–48, 837–39.

3. J. Williams, *Eyes on the Prize*; Powledge, *Free at Last?*; Branch, *Pillar of Fire*; Norrell, "One Thing We Did Right," 65–80. The literature on the civil rights movement is vast and is summarized well in Eagles, "Toward New Histories." Less up to date, Fairclough's "State of the Art" is also useful. Both of these works stress the fact that historians have concentrated on the 1954–65 era.

4. See, for example, Lawson and Payne, *Debating the Civil Rights Movement*, and Salmond, *"My Mind Set on Freedom."* Many studies are King-centered and also terminate in 1968. See Garrow, *Bearing the Cross*; Kirk, *Martin Luther King, Jr.*; D. Lewis, *King*.

5. Examples of this type include Chappell, *A Stone of Hope*; Edds, *Free At Last*; and Korstad, "Daybreak of Freedom." Biblical qualities are also suggested by the titles of Garrow's *Bearing the Cross* and Branch's *Pillar of Fire*, as well as Branch's earlier *Parting the Waters*. See also Norrell, *Reaping the Whirlwind*.

6. Chappell, *A Stone of Hope*, 1–2.

7. Eagles, "Toward New Histories," 838; Hall, "The Long Civil Rights Movement," 1230 (quotations), 1258–61.

8. Jacoway, "*Brown* and the 'Road to Reunion,'" 303–8, quotation on 307.

9. Patterson, *Brown v. Board of Education*, 141–46; Webb, "A Continuity of Conservatism," 329; Davidson and Grofman, eds., *Quiet Revolution in the South*; Minchin, *Hiring the Black Worker*; L. Hill, *The Deacons for Defense*, 270 (King quotation).

10. Civil rights historiography has focused heavily on the fight to break down segregation

in the South, a fight that Eagles terms "the most profound change in southern history"; Eagles, "Toward New Histories," 816. See Edds, *Free at Last*, xi–xv.

11. In developing this argument I am grateful to Thornton's *Dividing Lines*, 500–501.

12. This scholarship has been heavily influenced by Korstad and Lichtenstein's pathbreaking "Opportunities Lost and Found." For other important studies in this vein, see Bates, *Pullman Porters*; Korstad, *Civil Rights Unionism*; Sullivan, *Days of Hope*; Honey, *Southern Labor and Black Civil Rights*; M. Reed, *Seedtime for the Modern Civil Rights Movement*.

13. Several older studies also stress the importance of the period after 1965. For works that do give due attention to the long trajectory of the movement, see Goldfield, *Black, White, and Southern*; Marable, *Race, Reform and Rebellion*; Lawson, *Running for Freedom.* Some community studies by political scientists and sociologists also pay attention to the ongoing struggle for civil rights. See especially Button, *Blacks and Social Change*, and Wirt, *"We Ain't What We Was."*

14. Crosby, *A Little Taste of Freedom*; Fleming, *In the Shadow of Selma*; Greene, *Our Separate Ways*; Lovett, *The Civil Rights Movement in Tennessee*; Moye, *Let the People Decide*; Tyson, *Blood Done Sign My Name*.

15. Crosby, *A Little Taste of Freedom*, xiv; Fleming, *In the Shadow of Selma*, 312; Moye, *Let the People Decide*, 39, 204.

16. Tyson, *Blood Done Sign My Name*, 128–29 (first quotation), 252 (second quotation).

17. This quote comes from the title of Carroll's, *It Seemed Like Nothing Happened*.

18. For a summary of the activism that occurred, see Schulman, *The Seventies*; Hurup, ed., *The Lost Decade*; B. Bailey, *America in the Seventies*. My focus is on African Americans in the South, chiefly because the civil rights legislation of the mid-1960s was aimed at southern blacks. This was especially true of the 1964 Civil Rights Act. As economists John J. Donohue III and James Heckman have commented, "The 1964 Civil Rights Act was directed toward the South." Donohue and Heckman, "Continuous Versus Episodic Change," 1604.

19. Adrian DeWind, "LDF: 'Robust' Civil Rights Veteran," *New York Times*, January 24, 1979; Chambers interview.

20. Frederickson, "Four Decades of Change"; MacLean, *Freedom Is Not Enough*, 76–90; Minchin, *The Color of Work*, 1–5.

21. For an overview of the SRC's early years, see Egerton, *Speak Now Against the Day*, 307–12.

22. General and Narrative Descriptions of Soul City, n.d., folder 1746a, box 80, Floyd B. McKissick Papers, held at the Southern Historical Collection, UNC–Chapel Hill, hereafter cited as "McKissick Papers." Recently processed, McKissick's papers are richly detailed and are the best source for Soul City.

23. Moreno, *Black Americans and Organized Labor*, 259–84; Weiss, *"We Want Jobs,"* ix–xiii, 235–47; Donohue and Heckman, "Continuous Versus Episodic Change," 1641 (statistic).

24. MacLean, *Freedom Is Not Enough*, 4; Katznelson, *When Affirmative Action Was White*, 170; Donohue and Heckman, "Continuous Versus Episodic Change," 1641.

25. Donohue and Heckman, "Continuous Versus Episodic Change," 1607–10; U.S. Commission on Civil Rights, *Above Property Rights*, 7–11; U.S. Commission on Civil Rights, *The Federal Civil Rights Enforcement Effort*, 1–13. For an overview of the "under-class" debate, see Chafe, *The Unfinished Journey*, 439–50; Hodgson, *More Equal Than Others*, 186–91.

26. For some fine examples of recent scholarship, see Ransby, *Ella Baker and the Black Freedom Movement*; Collier-Thomas and Franklin, eds., *Sisters in the Struggle*; Kelley, *Freedom Dreams*.

27. In *Swann* the Supreme Court approved the use of busing to achieve racial balance in schools. See Douglas, *Reading, Writing, and Race*, 206–12. On busing, see Heale, *Twentieth-Century America*, 247; Cataldo, Giles, and Gatlin, *School Desegregation Policy*, 54. The quotation is from U.S. Commission on Civil Rights, *State of Civil Rights*, 18.

28. "U.S. Judge Orders Full Desegregation of Louisville Schools," *New York Times*, July 31, 1975; R. Williams, "What Louisville Has Taught Us About Busing."

29. "The Need for Expanded EEOC Conciliation Efforts under Title VII," n.d., folder 1, box 1592, AFL-CIO Civil Rights Department Southern Office Records, 1964–1979, held at the Southern Labor Archives, Georgia State University, Atlanta, hereafter cited as "AFL-CIO Civil Rights Papers." Although this document is not dated, all the material in the folder comes from 1974. For an examination of the relationship between organized labor and the civil rights movement, see Draper, *Conflict of Interests*; Zieger, "Recent Historical Scholarship."

30. Patterson, *Brown v. Board of Education*, 184–85.

31. National Institute of Education, *School Desegregation in the 1970s*, 1–2.

32. Two particularly fine studies of the impact of black voting are Bass and DeVries, *The Transformation of Southern Politics*, and Davidson and Grofman, *Quiet Revolution in the South*. Lawson's *In Pursuit of Power* is also crucial.

33. Some of these essays do summarize developments after 1980, but my main focus is on the 1965–80 period. Sources for this period are stronger, and after 1980 the civil rights issue increasingly expanded to involve Latinos and other groups. This struggle, while very important, is too broad to cover here. The political climate also shifted dramatically after Ronald Reagan's election to the presidency in the fall of 1980.

34. For insight into black economic conditions, see "NAACP Report on Labor is Grim," *New York Times*, January 18, 1976, and "Study Traces Progress of Blacks Since 1790," *New York Times*, June 19, 1979.

35. "Economic Survey Cites Black Loss," *New York Times*, July 29, 1975.

36. Report cited in Bennett Jr., "Have We Overcome?" 195.

37. "Job-Equality Complaints Piling Up," *New York Times*, June 14, 1976.

38. Couto, *Ain't Gonna Let Nobody Turn Me Around*, 3–5, 19.

39. Thomas A. Johnson, "In Six Years, Evers Has Lifted Mississippi County to Prosperity," *New York Times*, December 29, 1975.

40. Ruby C. Clayton to Jimmy Carter and Andrew Young, January 17, 1977, folder 4, box 1592, AFL-CIO Civil Rights Papers.

41. Moye, *Let the People Decide*, 155–65; Lee, *For Freedom's Sake*, 147–62.

42. Roy Reed, "Southern Blacks Shift Goals From Rights to Economics," *New York Times*, January 24, 1977.

43. "Abernathy Will Lead March Against Hunger," flyer dated March 18, 1975, folder 7356, box 333, McKissick Papers; "Dr. King's 48th Birthday Is Celebrated At Church Where He Was Co-Pastor," *New York Times*, January 16, 1977; Mrs. Martin Luther King Jr. to E. T. Kehrer, March 31, 1977, folder 173, box 1604, and Mrs. Martin Luther King Jr. to George Meany, November 18, 1975, folder 171, box 1604, both AFL-CIO Civil Rights Papers.

44. "Hill Quitting NAACP Labor Job," *New York Times*, August 14, 1977.

45. Roy Reed, "Southern Blacks Shift Goals From Rights to Economics," *New York Times*, January 24, 1977; "Remembering Martin Luther King," *New York Times*, January 15, 1979; Hugh B. Price, "Whither the Civil Rights Movement?" *New York Times*, April 9, 1979; "King Celebration Changes Its Tune: Jobs Big Issue Now," *Atlanta Journal*, January 15, 1976.

46. In the era after Martin Luther King Jr.'s death in 1968, media reports often overlooked just how much remained to be done and hurriedly declared that a "New South" had suddenly arrived. In 1976 northern writer Bryant Rollins spoke of "the crash of racial barriers falling throughout the South," while three years later the *New York Times'* Howell Raines spoke of "great progress" in race relations in Birmingham, "a city once regarded as the citadel of segregation." "Black Passage: From Civil Rights to the Ballot Box," *New York Times*, November 14, 1976; "'New South' Encounters Troubles of Old North," *New York Times*, April 29, 1979.

47. "Poverty Still Pinches Rural Alabama Blacks," *New York Times*, December 30, 1975 (Grant quotation); "Making It in Atlanta," *New York Times*, April 7, 1974.

48. J. Williams, *Eyes on the Prize*, 213–18; Dittmer, *Local People*, 138–42.

49. Leuchtenburg, "The White House and Black America," 140.

50. Roland quoted in Wiebe, "White Attitudes and Black Rights," 171; Bennett quoted in Namorato, "Introduction," *Have We Overcome?* xix.

51. Floyd McKissick, "Economic Issues in the Black Community," May 4, 1978, folder 7482, box 337, McKissick Papers; Ralph David Abernathy to SCLC Contributor, December 1973, folder 170, box 1604, AFL-CIO Civil Rights Papers.

52. Lovett, *The Civil Rights Movement in Tennessee*, 304; Franklin, *Back to Birmingham*, 94, 132–33.

53. "New Governor of Georgia Urges End of Racial Bias," *New York Times*, January 13, 1971; "New Era in Georgia," *New York Times*, January 14, 1971; Dumbrell, *The Carter Presidency*, 88.

Chapter 1. Beyond the Dominant Narrative

1. Of the King-centered studies, the most influential are Garrow, *Bearing the Cross*; Fairclough, *To Redeem the Soul of America*; Branch, *Parting the Waters* and *Pillar of Fire*. Garrow's *Bearing the Cross* and Branch's *Parting the Waters* won the Pulitzer Prize. The vast civil rights literature is effectively summarized in Eagles, "Toward New Histories."

2. Important case studies include Chafe, *Civilities and Civil Rights*; Rabby, *The Pain and the Promise*; Norrell, *Reaping the Whirlwind*; and Kirk, *Redefining the Color Line*. Standard general histories include Weisbrot, *Freedom Bound*; Salmond, *"My Mind Set on Freedom"*; and J. Williams, *Eyes on the Prize*.

3. Hall, "The Long Civil Rights Movement," 1230.

4. Important works that call for a broader chronological focus and stress black activism before 1955 include Sitkoff, *A New Deal for Blacks*; Korstad and Lichtenstein, "Opportunities Lost and Found"; Sullivan, *Days of Hope*; and Korstad, *Civil Rights Unionism*.

5. Norrell, *The House I Live In*, xvii. Many studies do emphasize the events of the classic phase but also identify the long trajectory of the movement. See Marable, *Race, Reform and Rebellion*; Tuck, *Beyond Atlanta*.

6. Despite steady out-migration, the 1970 Census showed that the South was still home to 53 percent of the African American population, down from 77 percent in 1940. See Jack Rosenthal, "Negro Migration to North," *New York Times*, March 4, 1971.

7. As J. Mills Thornton has put it in his detailed history of the civil rights movement in three southern communities, "the presumed decline of the civil rights movement is far more an artifact of the recounting of history from a national perspective than it is an accurate portrayal of the experience of southerners. . . . In that sense, the death of the civil rights movement has been greatly exaggerated. While the national movement's influence was being curtailed, at this local level the movement remained as significant as ever." Thornton, *Dividing Lines*, 500.

8. Reginald Stuart, "Black Prosperity Image Found to be Superficial," *New York Times*, May 31, 1976; Robert Reinhold, "Study Traces Progress of Blacks Since 1790," *New York Times*, June 19, 1979; Heale, *Twentieth-Century America*, 249–50.

9. Roy Reed, "Dr. King's Followers Modify His Approach," *New York Times*, January 7, 1972; Fairclough, *To Redeem the Soul of America*, 389–94; Carson, *In Struggle*, 296–98.

10. Paul Delaney, "NAACP Official Asserts Labor is an Enemy," *New York Times*, June 29, 1977; Jerry Flint, "Hill Quitting NAACP Labor Job," *New York Times*, August 14, 1977; Albin Krebs, "Roy Wilkins, 50-Year Veteran of Civil Rights Fight, is Dead," *New York Times*, September 9, 1981.

11. Spence quoted in Blauner, *Black Lives, White Lives*, 175.

12. Mary E. Mebane, "The Black and White Bus Lines," *New York Times*, January 2, 1971; John Herbers, "Blacks Returning to Southern Cities," *New York Times*, July 5, 1981; Davidson and Grofman, eds., *Quiet Revolution in the South*; White, *Black Leadership*, 179.

13. Reginald Stuart, "Black Prosperity Image Found to be Superficial," *New York Times*, May 31, 1976.

14. B. Drummond Ayers Jr., "Civil Rights Groups in the South," *New York Times*, December 21, 1974; Paul Delaney, "Economic Survey Cites Black Loss," *New York Times*, July 29, 1975; Chafe, *The Unfinished Journey*, 446–48; Norton et al., *A People and A Nation*, 921, 929.

15. Fairclough, *To Redeem the Soul of America*, 394–96; Thornton, *Dividing Lines*, 500–564.

16. Tyson, *Blood Done Sign My Name*, 198–214, quotation on 213–14; Hill, *The Deacons for Defense*, 44–47.

17. Tyson, *Blood Done Sign My Name*, 318; Davidson and Grofman, eds., *Quiet Revolution in the South*, 38–39, 108–9, 138, 200, 211–12; Bernard M. Porche to E. T. Kehrer, November 26, 1974, folder 2, box 1592, AFL-CIO Civil Rights Papers (second quotation).

18. James T. Wooten, "1200 Guardsmen Ring Augusta Area," *New York Times*, May 13, 1970; Tuck, *Beyond Atlanta*, 234–35.

19. Ibid.

20. For the Perry-Atlanta march, see *New York Times*, May 18–20, 1970.

21. Roy Reed, "Widespread Racial Violence Persists in Eastern Arkansas Farming Area," *New York Times*, October 10, 1971.

22. Richard D. Lyons, "Killing of Black by Trooper Stirs Protests and Violence in North Carolina Town," *New York Times*, November 22, 1971; Richard D. Lyons, "Carolina Marchers Seized in Protest Against Slaying," *New York Times*, November 30, 1971.

23. Tyson, *Blood Done Sign My Name*, 197–217.

24. Thomas A. Johnson, "Arms Race Over in a Georgia Area," *New York Times*, October 17, 1971; Howell Raines, "Georgia Town, in a Replay of 60's, Holds a Meeting to Ease Tensions," *New York Times*, May 24, 1980; Goldfield, *Black, White, and Southern*, 211; *Durham Morning Herald*, December 16, 1979, clipping in folder 515, box 15, Greensboro Civil Rights Fund Papers, held at the Southern Historical Collection, UNC–Chapel Hill; Waller, *Love and Revolution*, xv–xvii.

25. Roy Reed, "Blacks Start Wide Protest on Police Killings in South," *New York Times*, May 18, 1970; Martin Waldron, "Panel Told Mississippi Negroes Are Prepared for Self-Defense," *New York Times*, August 13, 1970.

26. Crooks, *Jacksonville*, 86–107.

27. Jon Nordheimer, "4 in Baton Rouge are Slain in Clash," *New York Times*, January 11, 1972; Jon Nordheimer, "Racial Tension Rises in Baton Rouge," *New York Times*, January 12, 1972; Howell Raines, "Changes Cost Birmingham Its Feeling of Security," *New York Times*, September 7, 1979.

28. Although there is no recent scholarly account of the Wilmington disturbances, the events are covered in several polemical works. See Thomas, *The True Story Behind the Wilmington Ten*; Myerson, *Nothing Could Be Finer*; Godwin, *Black Wilmington and the North Carolina Way*. The events in Wilmington are also vividly portrayed in Tyson, *Blood Done Sign My Name*, 256–73. Tyson was a high school student in Wilmington during the integration crisis.

29. Quoted in Thomas, *The True Story Behind the Wilmington Ten*, 36.

30. *Raleigh News and Observer*, February 9 and 10, 1971 and *Time*, May 23, 1977, clippings in the North Carolina Collection Clipping File through 1975, filed under "Wilmington–Race Relations," held at the Wilson Library, UNC–Chapel Hill, hereafter cited as "NCC Clipping File." These events are also covered well in Tyson's *Blood Done Sign My Name*, 256–75.

31. Lennox S. Hinds to Robert Malson, March 14, 1978, "Wilmington 10 (North Carolina Civil Rights, 1/78–2/78)" folder, box 35, Public Liaison Files, Jimmy Carter Library and Museum, Atlanta, Georgia, hereafter cited as "Carter Library"; *The Financial Times*, June 9, 1977, clipping in "Wilmington 10 (2)" folder, box 107, Louis Martin Files, Carter Library; *Greensboro Daily News*, November 14, 1976; *Raleigh News and Observer*, January 20, 1976, December 1, 1977, and January 24, 1978; *Charlotte Observer*, December 15 and 16, 1977; *Durham Morning Herald*, December 30, 1979, all clippings filed under "Wilmington, N.C.—Wilmington Ten," NCC Clipping File, 1976–89.

32. Louis Martin to Anne Wexler, September 13, 1978, "Wilmington 10 (1)" folder, box 107, Louis Martin Files; Margaret Costanza to Jimmy Carter, February 10, 1978, "Wilmington 10 (North Carolina Civil Rights 1/78–2/78)" folder, box 35, Public Liaison Files; "President Carter: It's Time To End This Disgrace!," n.d., "Wilmington 10 Petitions (14)" folder, box 45, Public Liaison Files, all Carter Library.

33. Lennox S. Hinds to Robert Malson, March 14, 1978, "Wilmington 10 (North Carolina Civil Rights 1/78–2/78)" folder, box 35, Public Liaison Files; "Confidential Note," January 9, 1978, "Wilmington 10" folder, box 35, Domestic Policy Staff Files, both Carter Library; Godwin, *Black Wilmington and the North Carolina Way*, 3.

34. "Curfew in Southern Pines Ordered in Racial Violence," *New York Times*, October 25, 1971; Fairclough, *To Redeem the Soul of America*, 394–95.

35. Patterson, *Brown v. Board of Education*, xx (quotation), 141–55; Webb, "A Continuity of Conservatism," 329.

36. Patterson, *Brown v. Board of Education*, 154–55, 173 (quotation); Interview with James E. Ferguson II, March 3 and 17, 1992, 25–30, interview J-4, Southern Historical Collection, UNC–Chapel Hill; *Louisville Times*, September 6, 1975.

37. Pride, *The Political Use of Racial Narratives*, 124; Wilkinson, *From Brown to Bakke*, 151–52.

38. "Private Schools Seem to be the Coming Modern Day Thing," n.d., 14, 37, reel 168; "The New Dual School Systems of the South: A Case Study," May 1972, 4, reel 168; SRC Press Release, May 3, 1970, reel 161; "White Flight: The Segregation Academy Movement," reel 220, all in Southern Regional Council Papers, held at Robert W. Woodruff Library, Atlanta University Center, Atlanta, Georgia, hereafter cited as "SRC Papers."

39. "The New Dual School Systems of the South: A Case Study," May 1972, 4, reel 168, SRC Papers; "Statement on Metropolitan School Desegregation: A Report of the United States Commission on Civil Rights," February 1977, "Metropolitan School Desegregation—Report 2/77" folder, box 90, Public Liaison Files, Carter Library.

40. Institute for Educational Leadership, "*Brown v. Board of Education*: 25 Years Toward Equal Educational Opportunity," February 1979, "Brown v. Board of Education" folder, box 14, Louis Martin Files, Carter Library (quotation on ii); Patterson, *Brown v. Board of Education*, 189.

41. Fairclough, *To Redeem the Soul of America*, 395–96; Minchin, *Fighting Against the Odds*, 112–13; "Abernathy Will Lead March Against Hunger," press release dated March 18, 1975, folder 7356, box 333, McKissick Papers; "Rights Group Urges Marches in U.S. and State Capitols," *New York Times*, August 12, 1980.

42. "Dr. King's 48th Birthday Is Celebrated at Church where he was Co-Pastor," *New York Times*, January 16, 1977; "Thousands March," *New York Times*, March 9, 1975 (quotation); Mrs. Martin Luther King Jr. to George Meany, November 18, 1975, folder 171, box 1604, AFL-CIO Civil Rights Papers.

43. For the historiographical emphasis on protest, see Norrell, "One Thing We Did Right," 65–80.

44. Adrian DeWind, "LDF: 'Robust' Civil Rights Veteran," *New York Times*, January 24, 1979; Thomas A. Johnson, "Black Legal Group Honors Greenberg," *New York Times*, November 29, 1979.

45. Jerry Flint, "Washington Plans Affirmative Action Push in '79," *New York Times*, December 24, 1978.

46. "Decision," July 18, 1966, *John W. Norman et al. v. Missouri Pacific Railroad Company*, papers of the NAACP, part 23, series A, section 1, reel 14 (microfilm copy in author's possession); 398 F. Supp. 1107 at 1111, 1117, 1119, 1120; 495 F.2d 398 at 410–11 (1974); Minchin, *Hiring the Black Worker*, 3; Bass, *Taming the Storm*, 373–82, 373, 377.

47. U.S. Commission on Civil Rights, *Five Communities* (quotation in title). For another example of the commission's work, see "Statement on Metropolitan School Desegregation:

A Report of the United States Commission on Civil Rights," February 1977, "Metropolitan School Desegregation—Report 2/77" folder, box 90, Public Liaison Files, Carter Library.

48. Reginald Stuart, "Black Prosperity Image Found to be Superficial," *New York Times*, May 31, 1976.

49. Rev. Jesse L. Jackson, "Speech at the Regular Saturday Community Meeting of Operation PUSH," September 13, 1980, "Speeches (1)" folder, box 94, Louis Martin Files; Jack Watson to Jimmy Carter, September 16, 1977, "9/19/77 (2)" folder, box 50, Presidential Handwriting File; "Congressional Black Caucus Legislative Agenda," n.d., "Congressional Black Caucus 7/77–9/78" folder, box 6, Martha Mitchell Files, all Carter Library.

50. White, *Black Leadership*, 183–86; Marable, *Race, Reform and Rebellion*, 214–17.

51. J. Lewis, *Walking With The Wind*, 434–37; Roy Reed, "Dr. King's Followers Modify His Approach in Their Continuing Pursuit of Social Change," *New York Times*, January 7, 1972; Thomas A. Johnson, "In Six Years, Evers Has Lifted Mississippi County to Prosperity," *New York Times*, December 29, 1975.

52. Bayard Rustin to E. T. Kehrer, January 28, 1974, folder 85, box 1598; Norman Hill and Bayard Rustin to Brothers and Sisters, April 18, 1975, folder 86, box 1598; Bayard Rustin et al. to Brothers and Sisters, November 8, 1976, folder 87, box 1598, all AFL-CIO Civil Rights Papers.

53. Important recent works on black power include Self, "'To Plan Our Liberation'"; K. Woodard, *A Nation Within a Nation*; and Cleaver and Katsiaficas, eds., *Liberation, Imagination, and the Black Panther Party*.

54. Moreno, *From Direct Action to Affirmative Action*; Hill and Jones, eds., *Race in America*; Graham, *Collision Course*.

55. Evans, "Beyond Declension"; Woloch, *Women and the American Experience*, 348; Evans, *Born for Liberty*, 290–301; Brinkley, *American History*, 867–68, 870–71; Escoffier, "Fabulous Politics"; Strange and Loo, "Holding the Rock."

56. Goldfield, *Black, White, and Southern*, 209.

57. Floyd B. McKissick, Untitled Speech, n.d., 1, folder 7487, box 337 (first quotation); "Speech by F. B. McKissick, Snr.," June 23, 1978, 10, 15, folder 7481b, box 337, (second and third quotations), both McKissick Papers.

58. "Economic Issues in the Black Community," May 4, 1978, folder 7482, box 337, McKissick Papers; *New York Times*, April 2, 1978. For an example of press coverage writing off the civil rights movement, see Hugh B. Price, "Whither the Civil Rights Movement?" *New York Times*, April 9, 1979. For an angry response to this article by a civil rights leader, see Vernon E. Jordan, "The Unsolved Problem of Blacks," *New York Times*, April 19, 1979.

59. Chappell, *A Stone of Hope*, 1–3; Chafe, *The Unfinished Journey*, 146 (first quotation); Chafe, "The End of One Struggle," 138.

60. Johnson interview. Many new archival collections on the civil rights struggle have become available in recent years, including Floyd McKissick's Papers at the University of North Carolina and new additions to the NAACP's Papers. See note 22, introduction, and note 46, chapter 1.

Chapter 2. "They didn't want you around them"

1. Trawick interview.

2. Dr. Vivian W. Henderson, president of Clark College in Atlanta, declared in 1967 that

"The textile industry in the South has an extremely poor record on Negro employment. The industry has a vicious history of outright exclusion and sheer discrimination regarding Negroes from the workforce in the various plants." Transcript of EEOC Textile Employment Forum Proceedings, January 12–13, 1967, 26, 32, part 2, reel 2, Civil Rights During the Johnson Administration Papers, material microfilmed from the Lyndon Baines Johnson Presidential Library and held at Cambridge University library, hereafter cited as "LBJ Papers."

3. Brattain, *The Politics of Whiteness*, 47. The term "whiteness" is much debated in the field of labor history. For an influential discussion, see Roediger, *The Wages of Whiteness*. For an overview of the debate about the usefulness of the term, see the various contributions to a special issue of *International Labor and Working-Class History* in October 2001 (Volume 60). The discussions of whiteness cover 1–92 of this issue.

4. Charge of Discrimination, April 16, 1970, *Hicks v. Cannon Mills*, 2, U.S. District Court records held at the National Archives and Records Administration, Atlanta, Georgia, hereafter cited as "NARA-Atlanta"; Gordon interview.

5. Congressional testimony of Herbert Hill and B. Tartt Bell, January 15, 1962, *Proposed Federal Legislation*, 719, 762.

6. "The Negro and Employment Opportunities in the South: Chattanooga," 1961, 5, reel 219, SRC Papers.

7. "A Status Study of Negro Employment and Training Opportunities in Four Southern Cities (Houston, Atlanta, Chattanooga, and Miami)," July 16, 1961; "The Negro and Employment Opportunities in the South: Atlanta," 1961, both reel 219, SRC Papers.

8. "The Negro and Employment Opportunities in the South: Chattanooga," 1961, 4, 16, reel 219, SRC Papers. For a very similar conclusion, see "The Negro and Employment Opportunities in the South: Houston," November 1961, 22, reel 219, SRC Papers.

9. Nathan, *Jobs and Civil Rights*, 13–16.

10. For the support that Nixon gave to the EEOC, see Berman, *America's Right Turn*, 11. For Nixon's broader approach to civil rights, see Frymer and Skrentny, "Coalition-Building and the Politics of Electoral Capture"; Kotlowski, "Nixon's Southern Strategy Revisited"; Kotlowski, *Nixon's Civil Rights*, 1–14.

11. U.S. Commission on Civil Rights, *Statement on Affirmative Action*, 2–3; Adrian DeWind, "LDF: 'Robust' Civil Rights Veteran," *New York Times*, January 24, 1979; Congressional testimony of William Robinson, December 1, 1969, *Bills to Promote Equal Employment Opportunities*, 92.

12. "Textile Production in South Soars," *Greensboro Daily News*, April 17, 1963; EEOC Press Release, December 14, 1966, copy in series 3, box 316, Textile Workers Union of America (TWUA) Papers, held at the State Historical Society of Wisconsin, Madison, Wisconsin, hereafter cited as "TWUA Papers"; Phyllis A. Wallace and Maria Beckles, "1966 Employment Survey in the Textile Industry of the Carolinas," EEOC Research Report 1966–11, December 19, 1966, 1, copy in series 3, box 316, TWUA Papers; MacLean, *Freedom Is Not Enough*, 77. MacLean uses textiles as her case study of how black activists fought for job rights in the South.

13. Northrup, "The Negro in the Paper Industry," 11, 14–15, 17.

14. A. Eaton and Kriesky, "Collective Bargaining in the Paper Industry," 30–31; Northrup, "The Negro in the Paper Industry," 22–25; Hodges, *New Deal Labor Policy*, 32–34.

15. Rowan, "The Negro in the Textile Industry," 54; Hall et al., *Like A Family*, 66.

16. Gibson interview; "Interview with Mr L. A. Combs, Vice President, Container Corp. of America," September 27, 1968, folder 16, box 45, Wharton School Industrial Research Unit papers, held at the University Archives and Records Center, University of Pennsylvania, Philadelphia, hereafter cited as "Wharton School Papers (WSP)"; Pretrial Memorandum, July 16, 1971, *Moody v. Albemarle Paper Company*, 12, NARA-Atlanta (quotation). For the exclusion of black women from southern industries before 1965, see Cobb, *The Selling of the South*, 119.

17. In most southern paper mills, promotions were awarded on the basis of job and department seniority, discriminating against black workers who were segregated into low-paying jobs and departments. For black workers' complaints about the discriminatory impact of seniority provisions, see, for example, Deposition of Moses K. Baker, June 10, 1971, *Miller v. Continental Can*, 30–31; Trial Testimony of Ed Young, August 21–September 20, 1973, *Miller v. Continental Can*, 328, both NARA-Atlanta.

18. Alphonse Williams interview.

19. Paul Swaity to President Pollock, June 29, 1970, box 652, TWUA Papers; Pope interview. Illustrating the way that the TWUA recruited black support after 1970, in 1973 the union even won a long strike at Oneita Knitting Mills in Andrews, South Carolina, by drawing heavily on support from blacks in the workforce and broader community. For an overview of the Oneita strike, see Ashbaugh and McCurry, "On the Line at Oneita."

20. Raynor interview; Complaint, n.d., *Ellison v. Rock Hill Printing and Finishing Company*, NARA-Atlanta.

21. H. Hill, "Lichtenstein's Fictions," 83.

22. Rowan, "The Negro in the Textile Industry," 54; Frederickson, "Four Decades of Change," 62–82, statistic drawn from 62.

23. "Reasonable Workforce Analysis," February 17, 1998, data supplied by the United Paperworkers International Union, Nashville, Tennessee (copy in author's possession).

24. Glover interview.

25. Little interview; West Point Pepperell visit, July 14, 1969, folder 18, box 13, WSP; DuPont Visit, May 16, 1969, folder 75, box 12, WSP.

26. Deposition of Henry Wilson, February 10, 1970, *Adams v. Dan River Mills*, 13–14, U.S. District Court records held at the National Archives and Records Administration, Philadelphia, Pennsylvania, hereafter cited as "NARA-Philadelphia"; Order on Final Pre-Trial Conference, September 28, 1978, *Seibles v. Cone Mills*, 2, NARA-Atlanta.

27. Sylvester quoted in Thomas D. Finney Jr. to William Gittens, May 10, 1967, folder 12, box 45, WSP.

28. Winn I. Newman to Franklin D. Roosevelt, December 16, 1965, folder 26, box 45, WSP; Hicks interview.

29. Funk interview; Gill interview.

30. Trial Testimony of James H. Coil, January 29, 1973, *Watkins v. Scott Paper*, 1272–73, NARA-Atlanta.

31. M. Taylor interview; Johnson interview.

32. Robert H. Foster to Harris A. Williams of EEOC, November 20, 1975, *Foster v. Fieldcrest*; Geraldine Lindsay to the EEOC, January 3, 1974, *Lindsay v. Cone Mills*, both NARA-Atlanta.

33. Long interview.

34. Joann W. Calhoun to Mr. Foster, n.d., *Lewis v. Bloomsburg Mills*, NARA-Atlanta.

35. Beck interview; Johnson interview.

36. Celanese Plant Visit, July 28–29, 1969, folder 18, box 13, WSP; Waldrep interview.

37. Plaintiffs' Proposed Findings of Fact and Conclusions of Law, September 16, 1974, *Adams v. Dan River Mills*, 7, 9, NARA-Philadelphia; Plaintiffs' Proposed Findings of Fact and Conclusions of Law, June 11, 1980, *Lewis v. J. P. Stevens*, 100, NARA-Atlanta.

38. Deal interview; Gaines interview.

39. Plaintiffs Proposed Findings of Fact and Conclusions of Law, February 18, 1975, *Sherrill v. J. P. Stevens*, 17; Deposition of A. C. Sherrill, March 18, 1974, *Sherrill v. J. P. Stevens*, 58, 116–17, both NARA-Atlanta.

40. Details of the landmark decision can be found at *United States v. Local 189, United Papermakers and Paperworkers, et al.*, 282 F. Supp. 39. The records of the case are held at the National Archives and Records Administration, Fort Worth, Texas, hereafter cited as "NARA-Fort Worth." For an excellent overview of the case, see Northrup, "The Negro in the Paper Industry," 95–104.

41. Trial remarks of Jim Youngdahl, February 7, 1972, *Rogers v. International Paper*, 24–25, NARA-Fort Worth; "3 Unions, Paper Firm Enter Landmark Collective Bargaining Agreement to Increase Negro Job Opportunities," *Labor Press Service*, August 12, 1968, folder 74, box 19, AFL-CIO Civil Rights Department Papers, held at the George Meany Memorial Archives, National Labor College, Silver Spring, Maryland, hereafter cited as "AFL-CIO Papers"; G. S. Young to R. M. Hendricks, December 16, 1969, filed as Exhibit 7, *Gantlin v. Westvaco*, NARA-Atlanta.

42. Edward C. Sylvester to Ralph W. Kittle, May 20, 1968; Ward McCreedy to Ralph W. Kittle, June 28, 1968, both folder 35, box 45, WSP.

43. Spence interview; Bragg interview.

44. Current Status Re-Cap of Affected Class Employees, September 1, 1972, filed as Exhibit 28, *Stevenson v. International Paper*, NARA-Atlanta.

45. Trial Testimony of Martin Mador, February 8, 1972, 309–10, 376; EEOC Decision, September 11, 1978, 19, both *Rogers v. International Paper*, NARA-Fort Worth.

46. Gill interview; Transcript of Trial Testimony, September 5, 1972, 739, 750; Copy of Fifth Circuit Court of Appeals Decision, July 16, 1975, 6521, both *Stevenson v. International Paper*, NARA-Atlanta.

47. U.S. Court of Appeals for the Eighth Circuit Decision, January 7, 1975, *Rogers v. International Paper*, 31, NARA-Fort Worth.

48. Arthur Williams interview.

49. Stewart interview; Calhoun interview.

50. Gill interview; Arthur Williams interview; Calhoun interview.

51. McCullough interview.

52. Testimony of George B. Williams before the Hearing on Class Certification, July 28–29, 1980, 163; Transcript of Class Certification Hearing, September 22–October 10, 1980, 688–720, quotations on 714, 720, both *Gilley v. Hudson Pulp and Paper*, NARA-Atlanta.

53. McCall interview.

54. Ford interview; Langham interview.

55. In the textile case of *Lea v. Cone Mills*, for example, the main issue was that a Cone Mills

plant in Hillsborough, North Carolina, had never hired a black woman, even though 30–35 percent of its workforce was female. In 1971 the U.S. Court of Appeals ruled that the *Lea* case, brought by a group of black women who had been refused jobs at the mill, had "opened the way for employment of Negro women in the Cone Mills plant." U.S. Court of Appeals for the Fourth Circuit Decision, January 29, 1971, *Lea v. Cone Mills*, 4, NARA-Atlanta.

56. Memoranda from Project Director to TEAM Aides, July 12, 1968, reel 163, SRC Papers.

57. For the way that litigation led to the abandonment of many discriminatory practices and an increased amount of integration, see, for example, Trial Transcript, July 10, 1975, *Lewis v. J. P. Stevens*, 576–79; Deposition of Leroy Ellison, August 17, 1972, *Ellison v. Rock Hill Printing and Finishing Company*, 18; Deposition of Edward Earl Benson Jr., November 22, 1977, *Garrett v. Weyerhauser*, 28; R. M. Hendricks to Charles E. Smith, November 25, 1969, filed as Exhibit 85, *Gantlin v. Westvaco*, all NARA-Atlanta.

58. Sawyer interview. In November 1972, the district court ruling in *Boles v. Union Camp* was critical of the company's affirmative action program, forcing Union Camp to make improvements. See *Boles v. Union Camp*, 57 F.R.D. 46 (S.D. Ga. 1972).

59. J. U. Blacksher to William B. Hand, September 15, 1972, *Watkins v. Scott Paper*; Proposed Findings of Fact and Conclusions of Law, May 12, 1980, *Myers v. Gilman Paper*, 22–23, both NARA-Atlanta.

60. Goldfield, *Black, White, and Southern*, 204.

61. "Employment, Hours, and Earnings from the Current Employment Statistics Survey," U.S. Department of Labor, Bureau of Labor Statistics, http://data.bls.gov/PDQ/servlet/SurveyOutputservlet (accessed October 13, 2004).

62. Ibid.

63. Amy Joyce, "The Bias Breakdown," *Washington Post*, December 9, 2005; MacLean, *Freedom Is Not Enough*, 2.

Chapter 3. "Soberly, responsibly, never noisily"

1. *New South* 1, no. 1 (January 1946): 1, complete run held at the SRC's Atlanta Headquarters; Egerton, *Speak Now Against the Day*, 307–12.

2. Garrow, *Bearing the Cross*, 161–63, 233. The fact that the SRC needs a complete history to be written was the main theme of a conference organized by Professor Brian Ward at the University of Florida in October 2003. At the conference, a variety of speakers gave papers outlining the important work that the SRC has carried out in a variety of areas. I delivered an earlier version of this paper at the conference.

3. Most studies have focused on groups that led direct-action protests, such as SCLC and SNCC. For examples of such studies, see Fairclough, *To Redeem the Soul of America*; Carson, *In Struggle*; Meier and Rudwick, *CORE*. As noted previously (see note 1, chapter 1), there has also been a considerable concentration on Rev. Martin Luther King Jr. The quotation comes from George S. Mitchell to Neil Hickey, December 14, 1955, reel 31, SRC Papers.

4. Eskew, *But For Birmingham*; "Economic Issues in the Black Community," May 4, 1978, folder 7482, box 337, McKissick Papers; Dittmer, *Local People*, 126–28.

5. The literature on the civil rights movement is vast. Important case studies include Norrell, *Reaping the Whirlwind*; Colburn, *Racial Change and Community Crisis*; and Chafe, *Civili-*

ties and Civil Rights. On the struggle for voting rights, see in particular Lawson, *Black Ballots*, and Garrow, *Protest at Selma*. A good overview of scholarship is provided in Robinson and Sullivan, eds., *New Directions in Civil Rights Studies*, and Ward and Badger, eds., *The Making of Martin Luther King*. The SRC is only given treatment within broader studies. See especially Egerton, *Speak Now Against the Day*, and Sosna, *In Search of the Silent South*.

6. Stein, *Running Steel, Running America*, 39; Minchin, *The Color of Work*, 19–25. While rather dated, Northrup et al., *Negro Employment in Southern Industry*, offers a full discussion of the causes of segregation in the southern work place, with a wealth of data drawn from several industries.

7. "The Durham Conference Statement," and "The Atlanta Conference Statement," extracted in *New South* 19:1, January 1964, 3–15, quotation on 12, reel 168, SRC Papers.

8. Hall et al., *Like A Family*, 66; Minchin, *Hiring the Black Worker*, 16–23.

9. W. Hardin Hughes, "The Negro In Our Economy," 10–15, quotation on 10, reel 218, SRC Papers; H. Hill, *Black Labor and the American Legal System*, 378.

10. Chafe, *The Unfinished Journey*, 112–13; Sosna, *In Search of the Silent South*, 159–60.

11. Roscoe E. Lewis to George Mitchell, January 11, 1946, reel 189, SRC Papers.

12. See, for example, Horace A. Bohannon to Dr. Mitchell, March 11, 1946, reel 188, SRC Papers.

13. Adams, *The Best War Ever*, 145–46.

14. Harry L. Wright to George S. Mitchell, December 31, 1946, reel 188, SRC Papers.

15. Emory F. Via to the Executive Committee of the Southern Regional Council, January 3, 1959, folder 9, box 3367, Emory Via Papers, held at the Southern Labor Archives, Georgia State University, Atlanta, hereafter cited as "Via Papers."

16. "Summary of Southern Regional Council's Labor Conference," n.d., reel 31, SRC Papers.

17. "List of attendants at SRC Labor Conference," May 7, 1957; "Summary of Southern Regional Council's Labor Conference," n.d., both reel 31, SRC Papers.

18. Draper, *Conflict of Interests*, 15–16; Local Union Questionnaire, Granite Local 1113, and Local Union Questionnaire, Columbia Local 253, both folder 11, box 1277, Via Papers.

19. "Summary of Southern Regional Council's Labor Conference," n.d., reel 31, SRC Papers.

20. Emory F. Via to Harold Fleming, January 4, 1959, folder 9, box 3367, Via Papers; "Directors' Report for Third NILE Southern Union Staff Institute," n.d., reel 167, SRC Papers.

21. "Labor Education Project," n.d., folder 8, box 3369, Via Papers.

22. Coley interview.

23. Emory F. Via to Ray Marshall, September 26, 1966; Emory F. Via to Herbert Hill, October 18, 1966; "Breaking the Barrier in the Building Trades Unions," n.d., all reel 167, SRC Papers; Zieger and Gall, *American Workers, American Unions*, 223; "Letters to the Editor," *New York Times*, October 20, 1972, clipping in folder 14, box 1593, AFL-CIO Civil Rights Papers.

24. Wilma Bledsoe to Stephen Horn, February 28, 1973, folder 14, box 1593; George Meany to John A. Morsell, June 19, 1974, folder 1, box 1592, both AFL-CIO Civil Rights Papers.

25. Paul Anthony to David S. Packard, February 12, 1969, folder 2, box 3384, Via Papers; Minchin, *Hiring the Black Worker*, 9.

26. Minchin, *Hiring the Black Worker*, 41.

27. "Statement of Emory F. Via at the Textile Employment Forum," January 12–13, 1967, 1, 3, folder 8, box 3369, Via Papers.

28. "Project Report for Year Ending September 1968," September 12, 1968, reel 163, SRC Papers.

29. Jean Fairfax to Samuel Jackson, March 20, 1967, reel 163, SRC Papers.

30. U.S. Census of Population, 1960; 31st Annual Report of the Department of Labor of South Carolina, Tables IV, XXI, and VI, both reel 163, SRC Papers.

31. "Agencies Unite to Increase Textile Industry Employment," *The Afro-American* (South Carolina edition), clipping, November 4, 1967; Unidentified clipping entitled "New Civil Rights Organization Aims at Opening Job Opportunities in S.C.," October 27, 1967, both reel 163, SRC Papers.

32. Four Months Activity Report of Robert M. Ford, September 1968; Project Report for Year Ending September 1968, September 12, 1968, 12–13, 15, 25, both reel 163, SRC Papers.

33. Minutes of TEAM Board Meeting, March 8, 1968, 2–3; William Patrick Flack Reports of August 19–22 and August 31, 1968; Minutes of TEAM Board Meeting of August 28, 1968, 4; "Project Report for Year Ending September 1968," September 12, 1968, 32, 37, 69; Mordecai Johnson to Constance Curry, September 9, 1968, all reel 163, SRC Papers.

34. "The Textile Industry and Negroes in Western South Carolina," TEAM Report, 4, reel 163, SRC Papers; Minchin, *Hiring the Black Worker*, 163, 165.

35. "Project Report for Year Ending September 1968," September 12, 1968, reel 163, SRC Papers, 67–68.

36. Ibid., 48–52.

37. Ibid., 2–4, 48–52, 70; TEAM Summary Report, September 1968, reel 163, SRC Papers, 2–3; Trial Transcript, July 8, 1975, *Lewis v. J. P. Stevens*, 322–26; Deposition of Sallie Pearl Lewis, April 26, 1973, *Lewis v. Bloomsburg Mills*, both NARA-Atlanta.

38. "Report of the Executive Director to the Annual Meeting of the Southern Regional Council," November 13, 1968, 7, 8, reel 169, SRC Papers.

39. "Southern Regional Council: Program for the '70's," November 1972, 1, folder 9, box 3370, Via Papers.

40. E. T. Kehrer to Harry Bowie, October 23, 1973, and E. T. Kehrer to Don Slaiman, November 8, 1973, folder 14, box 1593, AFL-CIO Civil Rights Papers.

41. Bartley, *The New South*, 430–32.

42. "The Southern Regional Council: Annual Report for 1973," quotation on 2, folder 12, box 3366, Via Papers; Gretchen Maclachlan, "The Other Twenty Percent: A Statistical Analysis of Poverty in the South," December 1974, 2, 5, "Poverty" folder, box 49, AFL-CIO Civil Rights Papers.

43. "Southern Regional Council: Program for the '70's," November 1972, 56–57, folder 9, box 3370, Via Papers.

44. "Thresholds: Black Women Employment Program—An Opportunity For Success," January 1974, copy in "Black Workers" folder, box 13, AFL-CIO Civil Rights Papers (Pamphlet Series).

45. For more details of Roosevelt's observation, and the administration-sponsored *Report on Economic Conditions of the South* (1938) that accompanied it, see Bartley, *The New South*, 1–4.

46. "A Southern Declaration: 1976," 6, 14, folder 205, box 1606, AFL-CIO Civil Rights Papers.

47. "Affirmative Inaction: Public Employment in the Rural Black Belt," February 1980, copy held at the SRC's Atlanta Headquarters, copy in author's possession, 2–3, 9–10 (quotation on 2, 3).

48. "The Southern Regional Council Beginning the Fifth Decade: Our Annual Report," *Southern Changes* 7, no. 3 (1985): 21–26, 28–30, http://chaucer.library.emory.edu; "The Climate for Workers in the United States: The Second Biennial Report from the Southern Labor Institute," 1988, report held at the SRC's Atlanta Headquarters, copy in author's possession.

49. Kenny Johnson and Marilyn Scurlock, "The Climate for Workers: Where Does the South Stand?" *Southern Changes* 8, no. 4 (1986): 3–15, http://chaucer.library.emory.edu.

50. Kenny Johnson, "Coalition-Building for a New Labor Climate," *Southern Changes* 9, no. 3 (1987): 8–9, http://chaucer.library.emory.edu.

51. "Hard Labor: A Report on Day Labor Pools and Temporary Employment," 1988, report held at the SRC's Atlanta Headquarters, copy in author's possession, quotations on 11, 15.

52. Ibid., quotation on 10.

53. "The Climate for Workers in the United States: The Second Biennial Report from the Southern Labor Institute," 1988, report held at the SRC's Atlanta Headquarters, copy in author's possession, 3–4, 12; "The Climate for Workers in the United States: The Third Biennial Report from the Southern Labor Institute," 1990, report held at the SRC's Atlanta Headquarters, copy in author's possession, 3, 4, 6, 8, quotations on 6, 7, 8.

54. Wendy S. Johnson, "Using Our Past to Build the Future," *Southern Changes* 22, no. 1 (Spring 2000): 3–4, http://chaucer.library.emory.edu; Ben Stocking, "Life and death at Imperial," *Raleigh News and Observer*, December 8, 1991; "Voices and Choices: Workplace Justice and the Poultry Industry," *Southern Changes* 23, no. 1 (Spring 2001): 3–7, http://chaucer.library.emory.edu.

55. As explained in notes 2 and 3, the SRC has been largely bypassed by the upsurge in studies of the civil rights era. Those studies that have covered the group, such as Egerton, *Speak Now Against the Day*, concentrate more on the group's politics and strategy rather than its efforts to fight for equal employment.

56. W. Hardin Hughes, "The Negro In Our Economy," 13, reel 218, SRC Papers.

Chapter 4. "A brand new shining city"

1. "General Description of Soul City," n.d., 17, folder 1746a, box 80, McKissick Papers; *Addresses and Public Papers of James Eubert Holhouser*, 173; *Profile: North Carolina Counties*, 204.

2. "Soul City, N.C., Is Moving From Dream Stage to Reality," *New York Times*, January 4, 1974.

3. "U.S. Puts $14 Million Behind Black Capitalism Project," *Washington Post*, July 3, 1972, clipping in folder 1752, box 81, McKissick Papers; "H.U.D. Foreclosure on Soul City, Troubled 'New Town' in Carolina," *New York Times*, June 29, 1979.

4. The story of Soul City has received considerable press coverage and has also been the subject of two well-researched undergraduate studies. These are Madison, "Objections Sus-

tained," and Rhee, "Visions, Illusions and Perceptions." To the best of my knowledge, the only other scholarly study is Strain's "Soul City, North Carolina."

5. Eagles, "Toward New Histories," 815–48, quotation on 838. Eagles' article skillfully summarizes a vast literature. As explained in note 1 of chapter 1, much of the scholarship has focused on Martin Luther King Jr., led by Garrow's Pulitzer prize–winning *Bearing the Cross*.

6. "King's Dream: America Still Haunted by Problems of Black Poor," *New York Times*, January 17, 1988; Brochure entitled "Floyd B. McKissick," n.d., folder 1753, box 81, McKissick Papers; Strain, "Soul City," 69 (last quotation).

7. McKissick's CORE career is covered in some detail in Meier and Rudwick, *CORE*, 207, 293–94, 408–25. McKissick's CORE years are also mentioned in other civil rights studies, but he has yet to receive a full-scale biography. See, for example, Garrow, *Bearing the Cross*, 475–76, 484–86. For an unpublished summary of McKissick's career, see H. Woodard, "Floyd McKissick."

8. For McKissick's efforts to integrate the University of North Carolina, see Interview with Floyd B. McKissick Sr., May 31, 1989, Southern Oral History Program, Wilson Library, UNC–Chapel Hill, hereafter cited as "SOHP."

9. Helms quoted in Rhee, "Visions, Illusions and Perceptions," 107; McKissick quoted in "Soul City Plans To Be Given After March 1," *Warren Record*, February 6, 1969.

10. "Analysis of Conclusions in the AVCO Report on Soul City," July 6, 1979, folder 1751, box 80, McKissick Papers. For the persistence of de facto segregation in much of the rural South after 1965, see Goldfield, *Black, White, and Southern*, 206–8.

11. See, for example, "Charts: 1–30 Yr Plan," n.d., folder 1749, box 80, McKissick Papers.

12. "Analysis of Conclusions in the AVCO Report on Soul City," July 6, 1979, folder 1751, box 80, McKissick Papers.

13. "Floyd McKissick, Civil Rights Maverick, Dies at 69," *New York Times*, April 30, 1991, NCC Clipping File, 1989–present, filed under "Floyd Bixler McKissick, Sr."

14. McKissick interview, SOHP, 2–4.

15. Ibid., 5–6; "Judge, civil rights leader Floyd B. McKissick dies," *Raleigh News and Observer*, April 29, 1991, NCC Clipping File, 1989–present, filed under "Floyd Bixler McKissick, Sr." For an illustration of the way that many African American veterans led the subsequent fight for civil rights, see Minchin, *The Color of Work*, 55–57, 90–91.

16. "Floyd McKissick, Civil Rights Maverick, Dies at 69," *New York Times*, April 30, 1991, NCC Clipping File, 1989–present, filed under "Floyd Bixler McKissick, Sr."; Rhee, "Visions, Illusions and Perceptions," 10, 33 (quotation). McKissick's ideas about reforming the economic system are explained further in his *Three-Fifths of a Man*.

17. Interview with Floyd B. McKissick Sr., December 6, 1973, SOHP, 9; Rhee, "Visions, Illusions and Perceptions," 32–42.

18. "Soul City—New Town: Narrative Description," June 18, 1973, 3–4 (quotation on 4), folder 1746a, box 80, McKissick Papers.

19. "General Description of Soul City," n.d., 12, folder 1746a, box 80; "Soul City—New Town: Narrative Description," June 18, 1973, 10, folder 1746a, box 80; "Analysis of Conclusions in the AVCO Report on Soul City," July 6, 1979, folder 1751, box 80, all McKissick Papers; "Skepticism, Fear Of Soul City Abound in Warren County," *Durham Morning Herald*, March 9, 1969, NCC Clipping File through 1975, filed under "Soul City."

20. "General Description of Soul City," n.d., 26–28, 40–42 (quotation on 42); "Soul City—New Town: Narrative Description," June 18, 1973, 6, 10, both folder 1746a, box 80, McKissick Papers.

21. Rhee, "Visions, Illusions and Perceptions," 52–71; Gordon R. Carey to All Staff, February 17, 1977, folder 1749, box 80, McKissick Papers.

22. "Soul City—New Town: Narrative Description," June 18, 1973, 17–18, folder 1746a, box 80, McKissick Papers.

23. "A Paper on Soul City, North Carolina," January 3, 1978, 2, folder 1750, box 80, McKissick Papers.

24. "Soul City—From Wilderness to Camelot," *Daily Tar Heel*, April 16, 1974, NCC Clipping File through 1975, filed under "Soul City" (first quotation); "General Description of Soul City," n.d., 17, folder 1746a, box 80, McKissick Papers.

25. "Soul City: A Fresh Start," (Promotional Brochure), n.d., NCC Clipping File through 1975, filed under "Soul City."

26. "General Description of Soul City," n.d., 13, folder 1746a, box 80; "Division of Cultural Affairs: Ten Point Program," July 27, 1973, folder 1750, box 80, both McKissick Papers.

27. *New York Times*, July 8, 1972; Uncited *Washington Post* article quoted in "Soul City: An Overview," n.d., 1, folder 1758, box 81, McKissick Papers.

28. "State Newspapers Offer Editorial Comment," *Warren Record*, January 23, 1969; Strain, "Soul City," 64.

29. "Soul City Beholds Its Dream Deferred," *Charlotte Observer*, clipping dated "1979," NCC Clipping File, 1976–1989, filed under "Soul City" (first quotation); "An Old 'New Town' Hangs On, Sustained By Federal Money," *Wall Street Journal*, April 19, 1979 (second and third quotations).

30. "Soul City Beholds Its Dream Deferred," *Charlotte Observer*, clipping dated "1979"; "'Why Can't This Be Home?': Founder of Soul City Says That He's an Eternal Optimist," *Winston-Salem Journal*, November 29, 1987, both NCC Clipping File, 1976–1989, filed under "Soul City."

31. "Soul City Seeks To Get Recruits From the North," *New York Times*, June 16, 1979; Robert L. Read to Editor, n.d., folder 1820, box 84, McKissick Papers.

32. "Soul City Converting Skeptics," *Charlotte Observer*, October 8, 1972; "Soul City: No Scoffers Heard Now," *Greensboro Daily News*, June 3, 1973, both NCC Clipping File through 1975, filed under "Soul City." For another example of a largely positive article, see "Soul City Plan on Schedule," *Raleigh News and Observer*, July 29, 1972, also NCC Clipping File through 1975, filed under "Soul City."

33. "Soul City, N.C., Is Moving From Dream Stage to Reality," *New York Times*, January 4, 1974; "McKissick Is Succeeding Although Not 'Supposed To,'" *New York Times*, December 22, 1974.

34 For examples of the *Raleigh News and Observer*'s coverage, see "Soul City: A Tangled Web," *Raleigh News and Observer*, March 2, 1975; "Soul City: A Reward for a Party Switch," *Raleigh News and Observer*, March 3, 1975; "Soul City Needs Thorough Audit," *Raleigh News and Observer*, March 5, 1975, all NCC Clipping File through 1975, filed under "Soul City."

35. Madison, "Objections Sustained," 46; Melvin Margolies to Claude Sitton, April 24, 1975, folder 1752, box 81, McKissick Papers.

36. "History of a free standing new community," 1975, 28–36, folder 1752, box 81 (quotations on 30, 31); "Fact Sheet on the Background and Current Status of Soul City," July 6, 1979, folder 1750, box 80, both McKissick Papers.

37. See, for example, "From the *Raleigh News and Observer*: Rule-Bending For Soul City," *High Point Enterprise*, October 16, 1976, clipping in folder 3018, box 139, McKissick Papers.

38. "Behind the Low Esteem," *Laurinburg Exchange*, June 11, 1975; "Len Sullivan's Shucks," *Mooresville Tribune*, June 5, 1975, both clippings in folder 3004, box 138; "More Tax Aid For Soul City," *Alamance News*, December 9, 1976, clipping in folder 3020, box 139, all McKissick Papers.

39. "The Status and Future of the Soul City New Community," April 12, 1979, 4, folder 2034a, box 94, McKissick Papers.

40. "Soul City Passes State's Scrutiny," *Raleigh News and Observer*, June 19, 1975; "McKissick Claims Soul City Cleared," *Danville (Va.) Bee*, December 18, 1975, both clippings in folder 3005, box 138, McKissick Papers.

41. "Soul City Articles Attacked," *Raleigh News and Observer*, February 10, 1976, clipping in folder 3013, box 138; Emsar Bradford to Floyd McKissick, April 25, 1975, folder 1806, box 83, both McKissick Papers; "North Carolina Blacks Support Troubled New Town," *New York Times*, August 27, 1979, (Helms quotation).

42. "General Description of Soul City," n.d., 21, folder 1746a, box 80, McKissick Papers.

43. "Industrial Site Selection," January 1977, folder 2128, box 99; "Draft Questions and Answers for a 20 Minute Public Affairs Spot on Soul City," n.d., folder 1750, box 80, both McKissick Papers.

44. "General Description of Soul City," n.d., 46, folder 1746a, box 80, McKissick Papers.

45. "Soul City: No Scoffers Heard Now," *Greensboro Daily News*, June 3, 1973, NCC Clipping File through 1975, filed under "Soul City." For similar pledges made by McKissick when he first announced his plans, see also "Plans For Construction of Soul City To Be Announced," *Warren Record*, January 23, 1969.

46. "Analysis of Conclusions in the AVCO Report on Soul City," July 6, 1979, folder 1751, box 80, McKissick Papers; "An Old 'New Town' Hangs On, Sustained By Federal Money," *Wall Street Journal*, April 19, 1979.

47. Cobb, *The Selling of the South*; Hulsemann, "Greenfields in the Heart of Dixie," 228–29; "Many Helped In Bringing New Industry To Norlina Area," *Warren Record*, July 23, 1970.

48. "The Status and Future of the Soul City New Community," April 12, 1979, 13, folder 2034a, box 94, McKissick Papers.

49. "Response to Senator Helms and the *Raleigh News and Observer*'s Accusations Against the Soul City Project," July 17, 1979, 3, folder 1751, box 80 (first quotation); "The Status and Future of the Soul City New Community," April 12, 1979, 11, folder 2034a, box 94 (second quotation); "History of a free standing new community," 1975, 29, folder 1752, box 81; "Industrial Marketing Strategy—Implementation Plan—1975," November 1974, folder 2024, box 94; John W. Edwards to Harvey Gantt, March 8, 1976, folder 537, box 28, all McKissick Papers.

50. "Soul City Industrial Development Report," December 1974, folder 2107, box 98, McKissick Papers. See also "Facts on Soul City," n.d., folder 1750, box 80, McKissick Papers.

51. Chafe, *The Unfinished Journey*, 446–48.

52. "Industrial Marketing Report," n.d., folder 2131, box 100, McKissick Papers. Although

not formally dated, the text of this document establishes that it was written toward the end of 1974.

53. "New Town Blues: HUD abandons a disaster," *Time*, October 16, 1978, clipping in NCC Clipping File, 1976–1989, filed under "Soul City."

54. "An Old 'New Town' Hangs On, Sustained By Federal Money," *Wall Street Journal*, April 19, 1979; F. B. McKissick Sr. to the Editor, April 23, 1979; Julian C. Madison to Ms. Susan Harrigan, April 23, 1979, both folder 1810, box 83, McKissick Papers.

55. "An Old 'New Town' Hangs On, Sustained By Federal Money," *Wall Street Journal*, April 19, 1979.

56. "Its Founder Still Hopes For Revival," *Charlotte Observer*, June 7, 1980, NCC Clipping File, 1976–1989, filed under "Soul City." In February 1979, just a few months before the HUD stopped funding the project, Gast's judgment was confirmed by HUD Secretary Patricia Roberts: "The success of this project rests in attracting jobs, without which the government's investment in Soul City will not be used to fullest advantage"; "HUD News," February 17, 1979, folder 1813, box 83, McKissick Papers.

57. Johnson quoted in "'Why Can't This Be Home?': Founder of Soul City Says That He's an Eternal Optimist," *Winston-Salem Journal*, November 29, 1987, NCC Clipping File, 1976–1989, filed under "Soul City."

58. "Chris" to Floyd B. McKissick, May 22, 1970; "Recommendations on Changing the Name of Soul City," January 24, 1978, both folder 528, box 28, McKissick Papers.

59. "Recommendations on Changing the Name of Soul City," January 24, 1978, folder 528, box 28, McKissick Papers.

60. Gordon R. Carey to Floyd B. McKissick, February 14, 1978, folder 528, box 28, McKissick Papers.

61. Harvey B. Gantt to Floyd B. McKissick Sr., March 7, 1978, folder 528, box 28, McKissick Papers.

62. McKissick claimed that the name of the town came from the bible, citing a passage in Genesis: "And the Lord formed man of the dust of the ground, and breathed into his nostrils the breath of life: and man became a living soul." Passage cited in Floyd B. McKissick Sr. to Arthur Clement Jr., July 31, 1979, folder 1819, box 83, McKissick Papers.

63. "Changing the Name of Soul City," February 17, 1978, folder 528, box 28, McKissick Papers.

64. Schulman, *From Cotton Belt to Sunbelt*, 180–82, 202–3; "Recommendations on Changing the Name of Soul City," January 24, 1978, folder 528, box 28, McKissick Papers.

65. *North Carolina Commerce Report*, January 1979, 13, copy in folder 1753, box 81, McKissick Papers.

66. "Jobs Unevenly Distributed Under State's 'Balanced Growth Policy,'" *Durham Morning Herald*, February 13, 1983, NCC Clipping File, 1976–1989, filed under "Industry-Development"; "New Life in 'Black Belt,'" *Raleigh News and Observer* clipping dated "1979," NCC Clipping File, 1976–1989, filed under "Negroes—History."

67. Gordon R. Carey to Floyd B. McKissick, February 14, 1978, folder 528, box 28 (quotation); Gordon R. Carey to All Staff, February 17, 1977, folder 1749, box 80, both McKissick Papers.

68. "All-Negro City Planned For Warren County Site," *Warren Record*, January 16, 1969.

69. "Citizens Have Mixed Emotions," *Warren Record*, January 23, 1969; "Soul City," *Warren Record*, February 27, 1969; Jones quoted in "Skepticism, Fear Of Soul City Abound in Warren County," *Durham Morning Herald*, March 9, 1969, NCC Clipping File through 1975, filed under "Soul City."

70. Quotation in "'Present at the Creation,'" *Raleigh News and Observer*, November 4, 1973, NCC Clipping File through 1975, filed under "Soul City"; "Soul City," *Warren Record*, February 27, 1969.

71. Goldfield, *Black, White, and Southern*, 206–8.

72. "Board Of Education Rejects Proposal of NAACP Attorneys," *Warren Record*, May 15, 1969; "Negro Percentage In Warren Schools Highest," *Warren Record*, July 10, 1969.

73. "Fact Sheet: Current Status of Development in Soul City," July 6, 1979, folder 1750, box 80, McKissick Papers.

74. Janice R. Crump to The Editor, August 23, 1979, folder 1818, box 83, McKissick Papers; "An Old 'New Town' Hangs On, Sustained By Federal Money," *Wall Street Journal*, April 19, 1979.

75. "General Description of Soul City," n.d., 61, folder 1746a, box 80 (first quotation); "Analysis of Conclusions Found in the AVCO Report on Soul City," July 6, 1979, folder 1751, box 80, both McKissick Papers. For the annoyance of Soul City staff with press portrayals of their community as racially exclusive, see "'All-Black Label Hit," *Durham Morning Herald*, August 4, 1972, NCC Clipping File through 1975, filed under "Soul City."

76. Gordon R. Carey to All Staff, February 17, 1977, folder 1749, box 80; "Soul City—New Town: Narrative Description," June 18, 1973, 8–10, folder 1746a, box 80, both McKissick Papers.

77. H. Woodard, "Floyd McKissick," 43.

78. "New Towns: Realities Dim Dreams," *Washington Post*, January 12, 1975.

79. Quotations in Shirley F. Weiss, "New Town Development in the United States: Experiment in Private Entrepreneurship," March 1973, iv, 4, 8, folder 2140, box 100; "The Status and Future of the Soul City New Community," April 12, 1979, 10, folder 2034a, box 94, both McKissick Papers.

80. "Analysis of Conclusions Found in the AVCO Report on Soul City," July 6, 1979, folder 1751, box 80, McKissick Papers.

81. "'Soul City' A Total Loss," *Richmond News Leader*, April 25, 1981, NCC Clipping File, 1976–1989, filed under "Soul City."

82. Floyd B. McKissick to Hillie Jackson, August 3, 1979; Walter Larke Sorg to Patricia Roberts Harris et al., June 27, 1979, both folder 1819, box 83, McKissick Papers.

83. Clarence E. Lightener to Patricia Roberts Harris, July 9, 1979, folder 1751, box 80 (first two quotations); "Resolution in Support of Soul City, NC, By the North Carolina Black Leadership Caucus," July 7, 1979, folder 1751, box 80 (third quotation); Leon White and Irving Joyner to Patricia Harris, June 29, 1979, folder 1821, box 84, all McKissick Papers; "North Carolina Blacks Support Troubled New Town," *New York Times*, August 27, 1979.

84. "Soul City and McKissick 'are not failures,'" *Durham Sun*, March 10, 1982; Daniel H. Pollitt to President Jimmy Carter, May 31, 1979, folder 1820, box 84, McKissick Papers.

85. "Settlement Reached on Soul City," May 17, 1980, folder 1855, box 85, McKissick Papers.

86. "New Life in 'Black Belt,'" *Raleigh News and Observer*, clipping dated "1979"; "Exploring a Changed Landscape," *Charlotte Observer*, March 14, 1982, both NCC Clipping File, 1976–1989, filed under "Negroes—History."

87. "Fact Sheet on the Background and Current Status of Soul City," July 6, 1979, folder 1750, box 80, McKissick Papers.

88. "U.S. to Acquire Soul City in January," *Raleigh News and Observer*, June 27, 1980; Quotation in "Dream Community of Soul City Has All But Faded Away," *Raleigh News and Observer*, June 26, 1988, both NCC Clipping File, 1976–1989, filed under "Soul City."

89. "Lofty Vision Gives Way To Quiet Life," *Raleigh News and Observer*, July 26, 1995; "'Dream Town' Tries to Shake Aura of Failure," *Durham Morning Herald*, August 31, 2003, both NCC Clipping File, 1989–present, filed under "Soul City."

90. "'Why Can't This Be Home?': Founder of Soul City Says That He's an Eternal Optimist," *Winston-Salem Journal*, November 29, 1987, NCC Clipping File, 1976–1989, filed under "Soul City"; "Lofty Vision Gives Way to Quiet Life," *Raleigh News and Observer*, July 26, 1995, NCC Clipping File, 1989–present, filed under "Soul City."

91. "'Why Can't This Be Home?': Founder of Soul City Says That He's an Eternal Optimist," *Winston-Salem Journal*, November 29, 1987, NCC Clipping File, 1976–1989, filed under "Soul City"; "McKissick Named Judge of 9th District," *Durham Morning Herald*, June 30, 1990; "Judge, Civil Rights Leader Floyd B. McKissick Dies," *Raleigh News and Observer*, April 29, 1991, both NCC Clipping File, 1989–present, filed under "Floyd Bixler McKissick, Sr."

92. "Lofty Vision Gives Way to Quiet Life," *Raleigh News and Observer*, July 26, 1995; "'Dream Town' Tries to Shake Aura of Failure," *Durham Morning Herald*, August 31, 2003, both NCC Clipping File, 1989–present, filed under "Soul City."

93. "Soul City—New Town: Narrative Description," June 18, 1973, 12, folder 1746a, box 80, McKissick Papers.

94. Rhee, "Visions, Illusions and Perceptions," 6–7.

95. Wiebe, "White Attitudes and Black Rights," 156, 160.

96. Chafe, "The End of One Struggle," 127–48, 137–39; Ralph, *Northern Protest*, 5–6.

97. Wiebe, "White Attitudes and Black Rights," 158.

98. Quotation in "Industry Gives Its Stamp of Approval to N.C.," undated *Raleigh News and Observer* clipping; "Jobs Unevenly Distributed Under State's 'Balanced Growth Policy,'" *Durham Morning Herald*, February 13, 1983, both NCC Clipping File, 1976–1989, filed under "Industry-Development"; "Textile losses highest in N.C.," *Winston-Salem Journal*, October 5, 2001, NCC Clipping File, 1989–present, filed under "Textile Industry."

99. "Economic Issues in the Black Community," May 4, 1978, folder 7482, box 337, McKissick Papers; "McKissick Is Succeeding Although Not 'Supposed To,'" *New York Times*, December 22, 1974; "'Why Can't This Be Home?': Founder of Soul City Says That He's an Eternal Optimist," *Winston-Salem Journal*, November 29, 1987, NCC Clipping File, 1976–1989, filed under "Soul City."

Chapter 5. "They don't care nothing for Blacks"

1. J. P. Stevens 1973 Annual Report, 2, "J. P. Stevens and Co. Inc. Annual Reports—1967–1981," folder, box 677, ACTWU Papers, Kheel Center for Labor-Management Documentation and Archives, School of Industrial and Labor Relations, Cornell University, Ithaca, New

York, hereafter cited as "ACTWU-Cornell"; "Stevens Workers Vote Tie to Union," *New York Times*, September 1, 1974; "Stevens Pact is Ratified, Encouraging Unions in the South," *New York Times*, October 20, 1980. National coverage of Roanoke Rapids continued even after the union's campaign was over. See, for example, William Serrin, "Union at Stevens, Yes; Upheaval, No," *New York Times*, December 5, 1985. The town is also the focus of Conway's *Rise, Gonna Rise*, which is largely based on oral history accounts.

2. Hodges, "The Real Norma Rae," 251–56; "How J. P. Stevens and the Union Reached a Truce," *Charlotte Observer*, October 25, 1980, NCC Clipping File under "Stevens, J.P. and Co.-Unionization"; "Great Labor War Gains Tallied," *Washington Post*, October 26, 1980.

3. 585 F.2d 625.

4. "Notice: To All Roanoke Rapids Employees," July 13, 1976, *Sledge v. J. P. Stevens*, NARA-Atlanta; http://www.lieffcabraser.com/practice_areas.htm#employment; Seymour quoted in "Brief," June 12, 2002, *Mary Beck v. The Boeing Company* (U.S. Court of Appeals for the Ninth Circuit), 16, accessed at http://www.tlpj.org/briefs/06-12-02_beck_brief.htm.

5. Congressional testimony of Jack Greenberg, October 6, 1971, *Equal Employment Opportunities Enforcement Act of 1971*, 248; Congressional testimony of William Robinson, December 1, 1969, *Bills to Promote Equal Employment Opportunities for American Workers*, 92.

6. "Court Orders Stevens To End Racial Job Bias," *Charlotte Observer*, June 30, 1976; Findings of Fact and Conclusions of Law, December 22, 1975, *Sledge v. J. P. Stevens*, 12–24, NARA-Atlanta.

7. Chambers interview.

8. Henry Leiferman, "Trouble in the South's First Industry: The Unions Are Coming," *New York Times Magazine*, August 5, 1973.

9. Goldfield, *Black, White, and Southern*, 204; J. Williams, *Eyes on the Prize*, 13; Hall et al., *Like A Family*, 66–67.

10. Hunter, "'The Women Are Asking for BREAD,'" 62–65; Gordon interview; Pope interview.

11. As Ed Rankin, public relations director of Cannon Mills, admitted in 1982 as he settled a class action, "This type of suit has been initiated against every major textile company . . . so it's not the first of its kind." "Discrimination Suit Settled by Cannon," *Daily News Record*, January 13, 1982, clipping in *Hicks v. Cannon Mills*, NARA-Atlanta. The *Daily News Record* was a trade publication for the textile industry. It is still published out of New York City.

12. Transcript of EEOC Textile Forum, January 12–13, 1967, 94, part 2, reel 2, LBJ Papers; Plaintiffs' Proposed Findings of Fact and Conclusions of Law, June 11, 1980, *Lewis v. J. P. Stevens*, 1; Plaintiffs Proposed Findings of Fact and Conclusions of Law, February 18, 1975, *Sherrill v. J. P. Stevens*, both NARA-Atlanta.

13. Transcript of EEOC Textile Forum, January 12–13, 1967, 47–50, 94, part 2, reel 2, LBJ Papers; "Discrimination Suit Settled by Cannon," *Daily News Record*, January 13, 1982, clipping in *Hicks v. Cannon Mills*, NARA-Atlanta.

14. Trial Transcript, November 6, 1972, *Sledge v. J. P. Stevens*, 4–5, NARA-Atlanta.

15. Sarah Herbin to Jean Fairfax, June 26, 1962, "Southern Program: High Point, Employment on Merit, 1962" folder, "Community Relations 1962, Southern Program" box, American Friends Service Committee Papers, held at the AFSC headquarters, Philadelphia; Conway, *Rise, Gonna Rise*, 101–5, 119.

16. Alston interview; B. Taylor interview.

17. Trial Transcript, November 6, 1972, *Sledge v. J. P. Stevens*, 397, 737, NARA-Atlanta.

18. Ibid., 522, 666.

19. Ibid., 670–73.

20. "Stevens Employees Hear Talk on Decertification," *Roanoke Rapids Daily Herald*, October 4, 1976; Deposition of James B. Miller, September 8, 1971, 54–60; Hearing before Judge Franklin T. Dupree Jr., May 4, 1976, 17, both *Sledge v. J. P. Stevens*, NARA-Atlanta.

21. Moody interview. Many blacks in Roanoke Rapids refer to "Stevens" as "Stephenson," a reflection of the fact that the latter is a common surname in the area. See Conway, *Rise, Gonna Rise*, 19.

22. B. Taylor interview.

23. Purnell interview.

24. Alston interview; Back Pay Questionnaire and Claim Form of Jasper Daniel Jr., April 8, 1981, *Sledge v. J. P. Stevens*, NARA-Atlanta.

25. Goldfield, *Black, White, and Southern*, 199–200.

26. Back Pay Questionnaire and Claim Forms of Denise Johnson and Jo Ann S. Hicks, April 12, 1981 and May 14, 1981, both *Sledge v. J. P. Stevens*, NARA-Atlanta; "Workers Win Battle Against J. P. Stevens," *Raleigh News and Observer*, February 18, 1995; Conway, *Rise, Gonna Rise*, 110.

27. Complaint, October 2, 1970, 6; Victoria Nicholson to Rich Leonard, February 16, 1981, both *Sledge v. J. Stevens*, NARA-Atlanta.

28. Alston interview; Crittenden interview; Defendant's Discovery Deposition of Ray Tate, March 29, 1966, *Hall v. Werthan Bag*, 40–41, NARA-Atlanta.

29. Moody interview; 474 F.2d 134 (4th Cir. 1973); 422 U.S. 405 (1975).

30. Trial Transcript, November 6, 1972, *Sledge v. J. P. Stevens*, 124, NARA-Atlanta.

31. Affidavit of Richard T. Seymour, n.d., *Sledge v. J. P. Stevens*, 1–2, NARA-Atlanta; Moody interview; "Court Leaves J. P. Stevens Ruling Intact," *Durham Morning Herald*, April 3, 1979.

32. Complaint, October 2, 1970, *Sledge v. J. P. Stevens*, 7, NARA-Atlanta.

33. Brief for Plaintiffs-Appellants, December 15, 1976, *Sledge v. J. P. Stevens*, 10, NARA-Atlanta. The district court certified the class as "all Negroes employed at all the Roanoke Rapids plants of J. P. Stevens and Company, Inc., on and after October 2, 1967," and "all Negroes who have applied for employment at said Roanoke Rapids plants since October 2, 1967, who claim to have been affected by the alleged racially discriminatory employment practices of the defendant." See 585 F.2d 625.

34. Findings of Fact and Conclusions of Law, December 22, 1975, *Sledge v. J. P. Stevens*, 16–17, NARA-Atlanta.

35. Ibid., 34.

36. Ibid., 20; Trial Transcript, November 6, 1972, *Sledge v. J. P. Stevens*, 700, NARA-Atlanta.

37. Findings of Fact and Conclusions of Law, December 22, 1975, *Sledge v. J. P. Stevens*, 24, NARA-Atlanta.

38. Trial Transcript, November 6, 1972, *Sledge v. J. P. Stevens*, 805–20, NARA-Atlanta.

39. 1975 WL 278 (E.D. N.C.)

40. Trial Transcript, November 6, 1972, *Sledge v. J. P. Stevens*, 822, NARA-Atlanta.

41. Hearing before Judge Franklin T. Dupree Jr., May 4, 1976, *Sledge v. J. P. Stevens*, 74–75, 82, 142–45, NARA-Atlanta.

42. Moody interview.

43. Trial Transcript, November 6, 1972, 496 (quotation); Findings of Fact and Conclusions of Law, December 22, 1975, 16–17, both *Sledge v. J. P. Stevens*, NARA-Atlanta.

44. Findings of Fact and Conclusions of Law, December 22, 1975, *Sledge v. J. P. Stevens*, 14–15, NARA-Atlanta; 1989 WL 168011 (E.D. N.C).

45. "Court Orders Stevens To End Racial Job Bias," *Charlotte Observer*, June 30, 1976; Findings of Fact and Conclusions of Law, December 22, 1975, 14–15; Decree, February 23, 1976, both *Sledge v. J. P. Stevens*, NARA-Atlanta.

46. Brief for the United States Equal Employment Opportunity Commission as Amicus Curiae, December 15, 1976, *Sledge v. J. P. Stevens*, 9, NARA-Atlanta.

47. 1976 WL 623 (E.D. N.C.); "Notice: To All Roanoke Rapids Employees," July 13, 1976; Hearing before Judge Dupree, February 24, 1976, 82, both *Sledge v. J. P. Stevens*, NARA-Atlanta.

48. "Memorandum for the Defendant and Analysis of Decree Tendered by the Plaintiffs," March 7, 1976 (first quotation); Hearing before Judge Dupree, February 24, 1976, 65 (second quotation), both *Sledge v. J. P. Stevens*, NARA-Atlanta.

49. Testimony of the Textile Workers Union of America Before the House of Representatives Committee on Education and Labor, Subcommittee on Labor-Management Relations, March 15, 1976, "House Subcommittee" folder, box 390, ACTWU-Cornell.

50. *Decisions and Orders of the National Labor Relations Board*, vol. 220, case 34, 220, copy held at the library of the School of Industrial and Labor Relations, Cornell University, Ithaca, New York; Si Lippa, "Stevens Looks on Union as Third-Party Intruder," *Daily News Record*, August 28, 1967, clipping in "Stevens J.P. and Company General Labor, 1966–71" folder, box 678, ACTWU-Cornell; David Leonhardt, "James Finley, Textile Executive, Dies at 86," *New York Times*, April 10, 2003; "J. P. Stevens and Co., Inc. Annual Report 1972," 4, and "J. P. Stevens and Co., Inc. Annual Report 1971," 4, both "J. P. Stevens and Company Inc. Annual Reports, 1967–1981" folder, box 677, ACTWU-Cornell.

51. Swaity interview, tape 3, side 2, Textile Workers Union of America Oral History Project, State Historical Society of Wisconsin, Madison; Joe Pedigo to William Pollock, May 3, 1959, "J. P. Stevens-Newspaper Clippings" folder, box 34, ACTWU Southern Textile Regional Office Papers, Southern Labor Archives, Georgia State University Library, Georgia State University, Atlanta, hereafter cited as "ACTWU-SRO"; Bush interview; "Brief for Plaintiff-Intervenor-Appellee," November 29, 1976, *Sledge v. J. P. Stevens*, 6 (quotation), NARA-Atlanta.

52. See, for example, Weekly Reports by Lou Agre, September 30 and November 11, 1978, box 58; Weekly Report by Mel Tate, October 27, 1977, box 57; Weekly Report by Susan Sachen, May 12, 1979, box 49, all ACTWU-SRO.

53. J. P. Stevens and Co. Inc., to All Employees, April 25, 1973, "Stevens, J.P. and Company Inc., General Labor, 1972–74" folder, box 678, ACTWU-Cornell.

54. Boone interview; Lambert quoted in "Target J. P. Stevens," *Sixty Minutes*, March 1977; Smith quoted in "J. P. Stevens," *The MacNeill/Lehrer Report*, December 22, 1976, videotape copies held at the Kheel Center for Labor-Management Documentation and Archives, School of Industrial and Labor Relations, Cornell University, Ithaca, New York; Brief for Plaintiff-Intervenor-Appellee, November 29, 1976, *Sledge v. J. P. Stevens*, 5, NARA-Atlanta; Purnell interview.

55. "Court Leaves J. P. Stevens Ruling Intact," *Durham Morning Herald,* April 3, 1979; 1976 WL 3791 (4th Cir.).

56. Plaintiffs' Submission in Response to the March 7, 1980 Direction of the Court, March 15, 1980, *Sledge v. J. P. Stevens,* NARA-Atlanta.

57. Plaintiffs' First Compliance Report Pursuant to Paragraph 37 (c) of the Amended Decree, January 5, 1981; Amended Consent Decree, April 4, 1980, both *Sledge v. J. P. Stevens,* NARA-Atlanta.

58. Amended Consent Decree, April 4, 1980, *Sledge v. J. P. Stevens,* NARA-Atlanta.

59. Plaintiffs' Third Compliance Report Pursuant to Paragraph 37 (c) of the Amended Decree, December 1, 1981, *Sledge v. J. P. Stevens,* 2, NARA-Atlanta.

60. J. P. Stevens Compliance Report, October 16, 1980; Males by Plant for Salaried Employees, February 2, 1981; Defendant's Reply Brief in No. 76–1988 and Answering Brief in No. 76–2150, December 16, 1976, 7; Tandy W. Fitts to J. Rich Leonard, April 13, 1982; Tandy W. Fitts to J. Rich Leonard, January 14, 1985, all *Sledge v. J. P. Stevens,* NARA-Atlanta.

61. Plaintiffs' Third Compliance Report Pursuant to Paragraph 37 (c) of the Amended Decree, December 1, 1981, *Sledge v. J. P. Stevens,* 1, 2, NARA-Atlanta.

62. Back Pay Questionnaire and Claim Forms of Hattie F. Lewis, David L. Burnette, and Larry Cornelius Dowton, February 14, 1981, February 16, 1981, and March 5, 1981, all *Sledge v. J. P. Stevens,* NARA-Atlanta.

63. 1989 WL 168011 (E.D. N.C.); 108 S.Ct. 2777.

64. "J. P. Stevens Closings," *New York Times,* June 2, 1981; "J. P. Stevens Mill," *New York Times,* August 19, 1982; Stevens 1977 Annual Report, "J. P. Stevens and Co. Inc. Annual Reports—1967–1981" folder, and Stevens 1987 Annual Report, "J. P. Stevens and Co. Inc. Annual Reports—1982–1988" folder, both box 677, ACTWU-Cornell.

65. 1989 WL 180701 (E.D. N.C.); Leslie Wayne, "Buyout Bid is Received by Stevens," *New York Times,* February 9, 1988.

66. "Westpoint Stevens Plans to Close Two Plants," *New York Times,* October 7, 2000; Boone interview.

67. Alston interview; Boone interview; B. Taylor interview; Bush interview.

68. Findings of Fact and Conclusions of Law, July 29, 1969, *Lea v. Cone Mills,* 9; Deposition of Janie Belle Ashmore, May 24, 1973, *Lewis v. Bloomsburg Mills,* 6–12; Deposition of Sallie Pearl Lewis, April 26, 1973, *Lewis v. Bloomsburg Mills,* 9–10, 11–13, all NARA-Atlanta.

69. Complaint, October 24, 1969, *Adams v. Dan River Mills,* NARA-Philadelphia; Complaint, n.d., *Ellison v. Rock Hill Printing and Finishing Company,* NARA-Atlanta; Boger interview; Ellison interview; "Workers Pleased with Cannon Settlement," *Charlotte News,* January 13, 1982.

70. Congressional testimony of Jack Greenberg, October 6, 1971, *Equal Employment Opportunities Enforcement Act,* 248; Chambers interview.

71. For a full discussion of *Griggs,* see Moreno, *From Direct Action to Affirmative Action.*

72. Heale, *Twentieth-Century America,* 248–49; Boger interview; Graham, *Collision Course.* For a good insight into the polarization produced by affirmative action, see Anderson, *The Pursuit of Fairness,* esp. x–xii.

73. Tyson, *Blood Done Sign My Name,* 249–52; Cecelski, *Along Freedom Road.*

74. Strain, "Soul City," 57–62.

75. Godwin, *Black Wilmington*, 233; "Troops Called to Keep Curfew in North Carolina Racial Strife," *New York Times*, November 8, 1970.

76. Jon Nordheimer, "Guard Is Ordered to Wilmington, N.C.," *New York Times*, February 8, 1971; Wayne King, "The Case Against the Wilmington Ten," *New York Times Magazine*, December 3, 1978; Richard D. Lyons, "Killing of Black by Trooper Stirs Protests and Violence in North Carolina Town," *New York Times*, November 22, 1971; Tyson, *Blood Done Sign My Name*, 317–21.

77. Purnell interview.

Chapter 6. "We were trying to get equal employment"

1. Charge of Discrimination, n.d., *Myers v. Gilman Paper Company*, NARA-Atlanta; 527 F. Supp. 647 (first quotation); Deposition of George Jones, January 28, 1974, *Myers v. Gilman Paper Company*, 4, NARA-Atlanta.

2. 392 F. Supp. 413; Findings of Fact and Conclusions of Law, February 18, 1981, *Myers v. Gilman Paper Company*, 19–21, NARA-Atlanta.

3. 544 F.2d 837 at 845; Benjamin Wyle to Ben L. Wooten, August 20, 1982, series 3, folder 10, box 9, UPIU Local 446 Papers, held at the Southern Labor Archives, Georgia State University Library, Georgia State University, Atlanta, hereafter cited as "Local 446 Papers."

4. Hall, "The Long Civil Rights Movement," 1235; Brinkley, *American History*, 878; Evans, *Born for Liberty*, 290–301; Schulman, *The Seventies*, 62–68, 179–82.

5. Joseph Tonelli to Noel D. Lewis, August 7, 1970, series 1, box 4, folder 15, Local 446 Papers.

6. Benjamin Wyle to Wayne E. Glenn et al., April 7, 1980, series 3, box 9, folder 10, Local 446 Papers; Stein, *Running Steel, Running America*.

7. Findings of Fact and Conclusions of Law, December 16, 1982, *Myers v. Gilman Paper Company*, 2, series 3, folder 8, box 9, Local 446 Papers.

8. Benjamin Wyle to Ben L. Wooten, August 20, 1982, series 3, folder 10, box 9, Local 446 Papers.

9. Findings of Fact and Conclusions of Law, December 16, 1982, *Myers v. Gilman Paper Company*, 5–6, series 3, folder 8, box 9, Local 446 Papers.

10. Draper, *Conflict of Interests*, 3–16, quotation on 15; Zieger, "Recent Historical Scholarship"; Sugrue, "Affirmative Action from Below"; MacLean, "The Hidden History of Affirmative Action."

11. Schuck and Wellford, "Democracy and the Good Life in a Company Town," quotations on 56, 58. Over time, women also gained access to a limited number of production jobs. As late as 1999, however, women composed just 23 of the plant's 580 workers. PACE Negotiation Report, June 6, 1999, "Durango-Georgia PACE Local 3–0446" file, papers held at the office of the USW, Mobile, Alabama, hereafter cited as "PACE-Mobile Papers." In 2004 PACE, a successor to the UPIU that was created in 1999, merged with the United Steelworkers to form the new United Steel, Paper and Forestry, Rubber, Manufacturing, Energy, Allied Industrial and Service Workers Union (USW).

12. "Gilman Facing $60 Million Bias Suit," *Camden County (Ga.) Tribune*, September 7, 1972.

13. "St. Marys Kraft Mill Began Operations Last Week," *Southeast Georgian*, September 4, 1941; Northrup, "The Negro in the Paper Industry," 11, 14–15, 17; Findings of Fact and Conclusions of Law, February 18, 1981, *Myers v. Gilman Paper Company*, 6, NARA-Atlanta.

14. Findings of Fact and Conclusions of Law, February 18, 1981, *Myers v. Gilman Paper Company*, 7–9, NARA-Atlanta.

15. 544 F.2d 837 at 844.

16. Hall interview; Answers and Objections of Defendant United Paperworkers International Union to Plaintiffs' First Remand Interrogatories to Defendant Unions, April 12, 1978, series 3, folder 4, box 9, Local 446 Papers.

17. Charge of Discrimination, n.d.; Findings of Fact and Conclusions of Law, February 18, 1981, 10, both *Myers v. Gilman Paper Company*, NARA-Atlanta.

18. Claim Forms of Thomas L. McGauley and Anthony Jackson, December 5 and 12, 1981, *Myers v. Gilman Paper Company*, NARA-Atlanta.

19. In the paper industry, jobs were organized into lines of progression, collections of related jobs that were theoretically ranked according to the skill and experience necessary to perform each job. As workers became skilled and experienced in the lowest job in the line, they built seniority. When a vacancy occurred in the next highest job in the line of progression, the worker with the most seniority in that line of progression received the job, provided they had the skill to perform that job.

20. Findings of Fact and Conclusions of Law, February 18, 1981, *Myers v. Gilman Paper Company*, 12–13, NARA-Atlanta; Roberts interview.

21. Trial Testimony of John M. Love, May 14, 1980, *Myers v. Gilman Paper Company*, 156, 158, NARA-Atlanta; Brooker interview; H. L. Brookins to Jerry Ridenhour, February 12, 1980, series 3, box 2, folder 5, Local 446 Papers.

22. Hamilton interview; Roberts interview.

23. Claim Forms of Harvey Jordan and Jeff W. Brewton, December 2 and 31, 1981, *Myers v. Gilman Paper Company*, NARA-Atlanta.

24. Trial Testimony of Anthony Jackson, May 14, 1980, 105; Findings of Fact and Conclusions of Law, February 18, 1981, 18, both *Myers v. Gilman Paper Company*, NARA-Atlanta.

25. Claim Form of Nathaniel Joseph, December 2, 1981, *Myers v. Gilman Paper Company*, NARA-Atlanta.

26. Claim Forms of Earnest Baker and George E. Jones, December 2 and 3, 1981, *Myers v. Gilman Paper Company*, NARA-Atlanta.

27. McGauley interview.

28. Hamilton interview; McGauley interview.

29. Affidavit of Madison Jenkins, November 18, 1978, series 3, box 9, folder 5, Local 446 Papers.

30. "Demands of Local 616," August 1963, series 3, box 10, folder 2, Local 446 Papers.

31. M. C. Peterson to Charles L. Ridenhour, November 14, 1963, series 1, box 5, folder 6, Local 446 Papers.

32. S. M. Rollinson to John Robinson, August 31, 1965, series 3, folder 8, box 4, Local 446 Papers.

33. Local 616 Minutes, April 7, 1963 and June 3, 1963, series 3, folder 3, box 10, Local 446 Papers.

34. Jonnie L. Robinson and Hayman B. Brown to John Burke, June 17, 1963, *Myers v. Gilman Paper Company*, NARA-Atlanta; McGauley interview.

35. Paul L. Phillips to International Executive Board, January 27, 1969, series 3, box 11, folder 3, Local 446 Papers.

36. Minutes of Local 616, March 4 and May 5,1968, series 3, box 10, folder 3, Local 446 Papers; Wilkes interview.

37. McGauley interview; Hamilton interview.

38. Wilkes interview; McGauley interview.

39. 61 LA 416–418, quotation on 418.

40. 392 F.Supp. 413 at 419.

41. Charge of Discrimination of Lawrence E. Brown, Jarone Smith, Eddie Lee Smith, and Theodore R. Williams, 1969–70, *Myers v. Gilman Paper Company*, NARA-Atlanta.

42. Claim Form of Elmo V. Myers, December 3, 1981, *Myers v. Gilman Paper Company*, NARA-Atlanta; "$60 Million Suit Served Against Gilman," *Camden County (Ga.) Tribune*, September 14, 1972.

43. For influential recent works on Black Power, see Tyson, *Radio Free Dixie*; Self, "'To Plan Our Liberation'"; K. Woodard, *A Nation Within a Nation*; Cleaver and Katsiaficas, eds., *Liberation, Imagination, and the Black Panther Party*.

44. Trial Testimony of Elmo Myers, December 5, 1974, 643; Petition, May 5, 1970; Trial Testimony of Don Walker, December 4, 1974, 515–16, 541, all *Myers v. Gilman Paper Company*, NARA-Atlanta.

45. 544 F.2d 837 at 845; McGauley interview.

46. Trial Testimony of Elmo Myers, December 5, 1974, 633–34, 662, *Myers v. Gilman Paper Company*, NARA-Atlanta; Roberts interview.

47. Order Determining Liability for Discrimination, January 14, 1975, 2–3, series 3, box 9, folder 2, Local 446 Papers.

48. Charge of Discrimination, September 1972, and Deposition of George Jones, January 28, 1974, 4, both *Myers v. Gilman Paper Company*, NARA-Atlanta.

49. Findings of Fact and Conclusions of Law, February 18, 1981, *Myers v. Gilman Paper Company*, 13–14, NARA-Atlanta; 544 F.2d 837 at 845–846 (1977).

50. 392 F. Supp. 413 at 419, 420.

51. "Work Stoppage Report," September 14, 1970, series 2, box 1, folder 33, Local 446 Papers; "Statement from Gilman Paper Company," *Camden County (Ga.) Tribune*, August 13, 1970 (quotation), and August 20, 1970; Trial Testimony of Elmo Myers, December 5, 1974, *Myers v. Gilman Paper Company*, 647, NARA-Atlanta; 392 F. Supp. 413 at 417.

52. 544 F.2d 837 at 846–847.

53. UPIU Defendants Post-Trial Memorandum, June 9, 1980, *Myers v. Gilman Paper Company*, 1, 30–31, NARA-Atlanta.

54. Ibid., 40 (quotation); Supplemental Labor Agreement, September 1972, *Myers v. Gilman Paper Company*, NARA-Atlanta; 544 F.2d 837 at 846–847; 392 F. Supp. 413 at 419; Benjamin Wyle to Jesse W. Whiddon, March 9, 1979, series 3, box 9, folder 10, Local 446 Papers.

55. Jesse W. Whiddon to Joseph Tonelli, October 31, 1977 and Ben Wooten to Jesse W. Whiddon, January 2, 1982, both series 3, box 12, folder 4, Local 446 Papers.

56. Findings of Fact and Conclusions of Law, February 18, 1981, *Myers v. Gilman Paper Company*, 1, NARA-Atlanta.

57. Joseph Tonelli Memos of July 25, 1975 and May 12, 1975, both series 3, box 11, folder 4, Local 446 Papers.

58. George O'Bea to John H. Powell, February 11, 1975, series 3, box 11, folder 5, Local 446 Papers.

59. Report of Gilman Paper Company Pursuant to Decree For Period of April 15, 1977 to April 15, 1978, series 3, box 9, folder 5, Local 446 Papers.

60. Claim Form of Wilbert Sibley, December 1, 1981, *Myers v. Gilman Paper Company*, NARA-Atlanta; Roberts interview; McGauley interview.

61. Claim Forms of Nathaniel Way, Elmo Myers, Elvridge Lawrence, Richard Spells, and Arthur Dawson Sr., December 1–4, 1981, all *Myers v. Gilman Paper Company*, NARA-Atlanta.

62. Benjamin Wyle to Jesse W. Whiddon, May 6, 1975, series 3, box 9, folder 10, Local 446 Papers.

63. Complaint, January 7, 1983, *Jones v. Gilman Paper Company*, series 3, box 12, folder 1; Affidavit of Clay Kemp, n.d., series 3, box 12, folder 2, both Local 446 Papers.

64. Deposition of Jerry Ridenhour, March 30, 1983, *Jones v. Gilman Paper Company*, 22, series 3, box 12, folder 2, Local 446 Papers.

65. Deposition of Leroy Hamilton, March 30, 1983, *Jones v. Gilman Paper Company*, 6, 29, series 3, box 12, folder 2, Local 446 Papers.

66. McGauley interview.

67. Roberts interview.

68. Ferguson II interview.

69. As mentioned in the introduction, textbooks often propagate the view that 1965 was the climax of the civil rights movement. For two good examples, see Powledge, *Free At Last?* and J. Williams, *Eyes on the Prize*. Neither of these histories of the civil rights movement covers beyond 1965. See note 3, introduction.

70. Adrian DeWind, "LDF: 'Robust' Civil Rights Veteran," *New York Times*, January 24, 1979; Chambers interview; Douglas, *Reading, Writing, and Race*, 108–9, 120–31; Patterson, *Brown v. Board of Education*, 155–59, 172–83.

71. Chambers interview; Douglas, *Reading, Writing, and Race*, 108.

72. Whiddon interview; "The AFL-CIO and Civil Rights," 1977, folder 4, box 1592; Coretta Scott King to E. T. Kehrer, March 31, 1977, folder 173, box 1604; Mrs. Martin Luther King Jr. to George Meany, folder 171, box 1604, all AFL-CIO Civil Rights Papers.

73. Bluestone and Harrison, *The Deindustrialization of America*, 54–55; Honey, *Black Workers Remember*, 322–26, 359–64.

74. Payne interview; "Employment, Hours, and Earnings from the Current Employment Statistics Survey," October 13, 2004, U.S. Department of Labor, Bureau of Labor Statistics, http://data.bls.gov/PDQ/servlet/SurveyOutputServlet.

75. Brooker interview; James L. Johnson to Michael E. Dees, September 13, 2002, "Durango-Georgia Paper Company" file, PACE-Mobile Papers.

76. McGauley interview.

Chapter 7. "They over there and we over here"

1. "Golden Anniversary Celebration, Gulf County, Florida, June 6–14, 1975," unpublished manuscript, Port St. Joe Public Library, Port St. Joe, Florida; Zieger, *Rebuilding the Pulp and Paper Workers' Union*, 142–43.

2. Jeffery A. Drobney highlighted how southern labor history has concentrated in the textile and coal industries at the expense of other important southern industries; see Drobney, "Company Towns and Social Transformation." For excellent studies over the last decade that have concentrated on workers in southern Florida, see Cindy Hahamovitch, "Standing Idly By"; Lichtenstein "'Scientific Unionism' and the 'Negro Question'"; Wilkens, "Gender, Race, Work Culture." Historical scholarship on the paper industry is limited, especially in book form; see Northrup, "The Negro in the Paper Industry"; Zieger, *Rebuilding the Pulp and Paper Workers' Union*; Kaufman, "The Emergence and Growth of a Nonunion Sector." Loveland's new *Under The Workers' Caps* recounts the story of a group of North Carolina workers who purchased a paper mill in order to save their jobs. For a recent study of labor relations at a northern paper firm, see Hillard, "Labor at 'Mother Warren.'"

3. In 2004 environmental writers Kathryn Ziewitz and June Wiaz published *Green Empire*. This study focuses on Port St. Joe, but its main emphasis is on the company's efforts to redevelop the land in the area for residential and tourist purposes following the 1999 closure of the mill. At the time of the closure, St. Joe Paper Company owned 3 percent of the state's land, making it Florida's largest private landowner. Much of this land was prime beachfront property, and the mill closure occurred partly because residential development was more lucrative than making paper. The *Winfield* lawsuit and race relations in the area are hardly covered in *Green Empire*, however. Ziewitz and Wiaz, *Green Empire*, 6, 89–90.

4. Michael Hamilton to Lynn Agee, December 21, 1995; Motion for Further Relief for Violation of the Consent Decree, July 31, 1992; Ben Wyle to Wayne E. Glenn, February 2, 1988; "Significant Legal Developments," Report to UPIU Executive Board, August 1, 1979, all in Legal Files, UPIU Papers, held at the headquarters of the USW, Nashville, Tennessee, hereafter cited as "UPIU Papers." UPIU is a predecessor of the current-day USW. In 1982 a union document noted the seriousness of the union's concern over the *Winfield* case: "The Paperworkers are Defendants in *Winfield v. St. Joe Paper Company*. The exposure in this case is overwhelming. This racially discriminatory system is going to cost us a lot of bucks." Kent Spriggs to Lynn Agee, November 9, 1982, Legal Files, UPIU Papers.

5. Goldfield, *Black, White, and Southern*, 204.

6. Nelson, "'CIO Meant One Thing for the Whites and Another Thing For Us'"; Stein, *Running Steel, Running America*; MacLean, *Freedom Is Not Enough*, 76–90.

7. The historiographical emphasis on protest prior to 1965 is brought out well in Norrell, "One Thing We Did Right," and Fairclough, "State of the Art," 387–90. Specific examples of the concentration on protest include Garrow, *Protest at Selma*; Garrow, *Bearing the Cross*; Fairclough, *To Redeem the Soul of America*; Sitkoff, *The Struggle for Black Equality*; Carson, *In Struggle*; and J. Williams, *Eyes on the Prize*. In the 1990s, several studies also stressed the continuity of black protest after 1965. See, for example, Cecelski, *Along Freedom Road*; Payne, *I've Got the Light of Freedom*; Fairclough, *Race and Democracy*.

8. Neglect of the economic aspects of the movement has been highlighted well by Wright

in "Economic Consequences of the Southern Protest Movement." In the 1990s, two main studies explored the links between organized labor and the civil rights movement, although both concentrated on the period before the mid-1960s. See Honey, *Southern Labor and Black Civil Rights*, and Draper, *Conflict of Interests*. For recent studies that do look at the impact of Title VII litigation on the workforce, see Stein, *Running Steel, Running America*; Moreno, *From Direct Action to Affirmative Action*; Skrentny, *The Minority Rights Revolution*; Graham, *Collision Course*.

9. "Preliminary Results of API Equal Employment Survey," September 21, 1967, folder 12, box 45, WSP; Trial Remarks of Kent Spriggs, November 30, 1977, *Winfield v. St. Joe Paper Company*, 305, NARA-Atlanta. For the amount of litigation that occurred in the southern paper industry and the strength of white resistance to change, see Deposition of Christopher Jenkins, June 6–7, 1971, *Gantlin v. Westvaco*, 85, NARA-Atlanta; "Significant Legal Developments to Report to UPIU Executive Board," August 1, 1979, Legal Files, UPIU Papers; Amended Pre-Trial Order, January 10, 1973, *Watkins v. Scott Paper*, 1, NARA-Atlanta; Northrup, "The Negro in the Paper Industry," 54–126.

10. Spriggs interview (quotation); Findings of Fact and Conclusions of Law, August 23, 1973, *Watkins v. Scott Paper*, 15–20; Proposed Findings of Fact and Conclusions of Law, May 12, 1980, *Myers v. Gilman Paper Company*, 12–14; Proposed Findings of Fact and Conclusions of Law, n.d., *Moody v. Albemarle Paper Company*, 12, all NARA-Atlanta; William H. Brewster to Ellsworth M. Pell, January 21, 1966, folder 11, box 45, WSP. For overviews of cases brought at other small mills, see *Moody v. Albemarle Paper Company* 422 U.S. 405 (1975); *Suggs v. Container Corporation of America*, Case Number 7058–72, U.S. District Court for the Southern District of Alabama, 1972, NARA-Atlanta; *White v. Carolina Paperboard*, Case Number CC-73–255, U.S. District Court for the Western District of North Carolina, 1973, NARA-Atlanta; *Myers v. Gilman Paper Company* 392 F. Supp. 413 (1975).

11. "Golden Anniversary Celebration, Gulf County, Florida, June 6–14, 1975," unpublished manuscript, Port St. Joe Public Library, Port St. Joe, Florida, 33; Spriggs interview; Langham interview; Ziewitz and Wiaz, *Green Empire*, 6, 38, 59–90 (quotation on 60). Howard's testimony in the case was extremely evasive, making it difficult to substantiate the degree to which he may have been carrying out Ball's instructions; see Trial Testimony of John Howard, July 20, 1978, *Winfield v. St. Joe Paper Company*, 32–44, NARA-Atlanta.

12. "Golden Anniversary Celebration," 33; Spriggs interview; Larry interview. This paragraph also draws on my own reflections after visiting Port St. Joe.

13. Memorandum Opinion, June 25, 1979, *Winfield v. St. Joe Paper Company*, 34–42, 57, NARA-Atlanta.

14. Findings of Fact and Conclusions of Law, August 5, 1985, *Winfield v. St. Joe Paper Company*, 11–20, 23, NARA-Atlanta.

15. Trial testimony of M. D. Yon, December 1, 1977, 100–120; Opening Remarks of Kent Spriggs before the Non-Jury Trial, February 13, 1984, 24; Plaintiffs' Exhibit 3, July 26, 1954, all *Winfield v. St. Joe Paper Company*, NARA-Atlanta.

16. Trial testimony of Ellis Dunning, December 2, 1977, 76; Affidavit of Willie James Jenkins, February 12, 1974; Trial Testimony of Alphons Mason, December 2, 1977, 203, all *Winfield v. St. Joe Paper Company*, NARA-Atlanta.

17. Gantt interview; Deposition of Jason Lewis, November 9 1983, *Winfield v. St. Joe Paper Company*, 4, NARA-Atlanta.

18. Bryant interview.

19. Larry interview; Trial testimony of Ellis Dunning, December 2, 1977, *Winfield v. St. Joe Paper Company*, 78–79, NARA-Atlanta.

20. Walker interview.

21. Deposition of Colbert Bryant, October 25, 1979, *Winfield, v. St. Joe Paper Company*, 5, NARA-Atlanta; Bailey interview.

22. Yon interview; Order, August 22, 1979, *Winfield v. St. Joe Paper Company*, 5–6, NARA-Atlanta.

23. Trial testimony of Lawrence Martin, November 30, 1977, 8–19; Trial testimony of M. D. Yon, December 1, 1977, 121–25; Findings of Fact and Conclusions of Law, December 18, 1995, 44, all *Winfield v. St. Joe Paper Company*, NARA-Atlanta.

24. Trial testimony of Capers Allen, December 2, 1977, *Winfield v. St. Joe Paper Company*, 99–102, NARA-Atlanta.

25. Findings of Fact and Conclusions of Law, December 18, 1995, *Winfield v. St. Joe Paper Company*, 44, NARA-Atlanta; Bryant interview; Larry interview.

26. Gantt interview.

27. Trial testimony of Draughton Bass, November 30, 1977, *Winfield v. St. Joe Paper Company*, 40–54, NARA-Atlanta.

28. Deposition of Jason Lewis, November 9, 1983, 7–8; Trial testimony of Draughton Bass, November 30, 1977, 40–54, both *Winfield v. St. Joe Paper Company*, NARA-Atlanta.

29. List of separate locals in folder 56, box 19, AFL-CIO Papers; Whiddon interview; Spence interview.

30. Zieger, *Rebuilding the Pulp and Paper Workers' Union*, 116; Wayne E. Glenn Affidavit, September 16, 1980, *Miller v. Continental Can*, 16, NARA-Atlanta. On the establishment of segregated locals and their lack of bargaining power, see Deposition of Joseph Hooker, October 25, 1977, *Garrett v. Weyerhauser*, 5–9; Deposition of Charles Jenkins, June 6, 1973, *Gantlin v. Westvaco*, 151, both NARA-Atlanta. It is clear that the experience of the segregated local at Port St. Joe was not unusual, as many other black locals also found that they had to bargain through white unions. At the Crown-Zellerbach Mill in Bogalusa, Louisiana, for example, Robert Hicks, who served as president of the black local, remembered how he had to negotiate through the white local and was never able to secure positive changes. He dismissed the negotiating process as no more than "a little show." Hicks later played a key role in bringing Title VII litigation against the company; Hicks interview.

31. Trial testimony of Howard Garland, December 1, 1977, *Winfield v. St. Joe Paper Company*, 201, NARA-Atlanta.

32. Trial testimony of John Lewis, December 1, 1977, *Winfield v. St. Joe Paper Company*, 178, 182–83, NARA-Atlanta.

33. Trial testimony of Howard Garland, December 1, 1977, 209–10; Trial testimony of Herman Williams, December 1, 1977, 249–51, both *Winfield v. St. Joe Paper Company*, NARA-Atlanta.

34. Trial testimony of Herman Williams, December 1, 1977, *Winfield v. St. Joe Paper Company*, 251–52, NARA-Atlanta.

35. Trial testimony of Howard Garland, December 1, 1977, 210–11; Trial comments of Kent Spriggs, November 30, 1977, 221, both *Winfield v. St. Joe Paper Company*, NARA-Atlanta.

36. Robinson interview; Alphonse Williams interview.

37. Trial testimony of Herman Williams, December 1, 1977, *Winfield v. St. Joe Paper Company*, 248–49, 260, NARA-Atlanta.

38. Deposition of Alfonso Lewis, October 24, 1979, *Winfield v. St. Joe Paper Company*, 42, NARA-Atlanta.

39. Alton Fennell, quoted in Plaintiffs' Proposed Findings of Fact and Conclusions of Law, October 16, 1978, 29–30; Trial testimony of Thaddeus Russ, May 16, 1978, 42–43, both *Winfield v. St. Joe Paper Company*, NARA-Atlanta.

40. Speights interview.

41. Charge of Discrimination, June 1968, *Winfield v. St. Joe Paper Company*, NARA-Atlanta.

42. Willie James Jenkins, Grievance No. 210, February 13, 1970; Local 379, Request for Adjustment of Grievance, April 28, 1975; Otis Walker, Request for Adjustment of Grievance, February 11, 1977, all *Winfield v. St. Joe Paper Company*, NARA-Atlanta.

43. EEOC Charge of Discrimination of Willie James Jenkins, June 22, 1972; Affidavit of Willie James Jenkins, February 12, 1974; Otis Walker, Request for Adjustment of Grievance, February 11, 1977; C. E. Garland, Request for Adjustment of Grievance, June 19, 1975, all *Winfield v. St. Joe Paper Company*, NARA-Atlanta.

44. Trial Testimony of Donald Langham, July 20, 1978, *Winfield v. St. Joe Paper Company*, 120–46, NARA-Atlanta.

45. Ibid., 139–40; EEOC Charge of Discrimination of UPIU Local 379, November 24, 1975, *Winfield v. St. Joe Paper of Company*, NARA-Atlanta.

46. Minutes of Local 379 Meeting, July 29, 1976, *Winfield v. St. Joe Paper Company*, NARA-Atlanta; Spriggs interview.

47. Testimony of Clyde E. Garland before the Non-Jury Trial, February 16, 1984, 21–26; Testimony of James Winfield before the Non-Jury Trial, February 16, 1984, 121, both *Winfield v. St. Joe Paper Company*, NARA-Atlanta.

48. Opening Statement of Kent Spriggs before the Non-Jury Trial, February 13, 1984, 17–27, 30–31; Plaintiffs' Exhibit 4, both *Winfield v. St. Joe Paper Company*, NARA-Atlanta.

49. Testimony of David W. Rasmussen before the Non-Jury Trial, February 15, 1984, *Winfield v. St. Joe Paper Company*, 37, 83, 88, NARA-Atlanta.

50. Testimony of David J. Lewis before the Non-Jury Trial, February 17, 1984, 77–80; Testimony of Thomas Sims before the Non-Jury Trial, February 15, 1984, 194–205, both *Winfield v. St. Joe Paper Company*, NARA-Atlanta.

51. Larry interview.

52. Ibid.

53. Testimony of Howard Garland Jr., before the Non-Jury Trial, February 14, 1984, *Winfield v. St. Joe Paper Company*, 155–56, NARA-Atlanta.

54. Opening Statement of Kent Spriggs before the Non-Jury Trial, February 13, 1984, 30–31; Deposition of A. D. Fennell, December 1, 1983, 4, both *Winfield v. St. Joe Paper Company*, NARA-Atlanta.

55. Testimony of Mark Anthony Williams before the Non-Jury Trial, February 20, 1984,

169–239, quotation on 207; Testimony of Daniel Sims before the Non-Jury Trial, February 20, 1984, 16, 22–23, both *Winfield v. St. Joe Paper Company*, NARA-Atlanta.

56. Motion for Further Relief for Violation of the Consent Decree, July 31, 1992; Mark Brooks to Robert Sugarman, September 29, 1989, both Legal Files, UPIU Papers; Spriggs interview.

57. Gantt interview; Walker interview.

58. A list compiled in January 1979 by the UPIU showed that there were twenty-three class action Title VII cases concerning southern paper mills; see Minutes of Executive Board Sessions, February 5–9, 1979, Shelf Item, UPIU Papers, 63–64, 72–75. For evidence of the long struggle to integrate other southern mills, see especially *Stevenson v. International Paper Company*, 516 F.2d 103 (1975). Among the important Title VII cases that involved Florida paper mills were *Gilley v. Hudson Pulp and Paper Company* and *Roberts v. St. Regis Paper Company*, both NARA-Atlanta.

59. For studies that have reached similar conclusions to my own, see Nelson, "Working-Class Agency and Racial Inequality"; H. Hill, *Black Labor and the American Legal System*; H. Hill, "Lichtenstein's Fictions." For an overview of some influential scholarship on southern black workers, see Halpern, "Organized Labour."

60. Hamilton interview.

61. Young interview.

62. Bailey interview. In 1997 R. C. Larry emphatically proclaimed that "St. Joe is the worst place in the world for prejudice"; Larry interview.

Chapter 8. "Meany doesn't sign my check"

1. "Union Members Urged to March Against Busing," *Louisville Times*, October 20, 1975; "March-March-March," flyer dated September 27, 1975, folder 120, box 1601; E. T. Kehrer to William Pollard, January 30, 1976, folder 4, box 1592, both AFL-CIO Civil Rights Papers.

2. Draper, *Conflict of Interests*, 3–22. According to the pathbreaking work of David Roediger, "whiteness" initially served as a way for antebellum northern workers to come to terms with industrial wage work. More recently, historians have shown that in the South white racial identity was central to determining access to the industrial working class. See Roediger, *The Wages of Whiteness*, 13–14; Brattain, *The Politics of Whiteness*, 3–4. For an overview of the impact of whiteness studies upon labor history, see Nelson, "Class, Race, and Democracy."

3. Zieger, "Recent Historical Scholarship," 3. As Zieger opens his article, "In the past two decades, historians have produced a substantial body of work on the theme of race and labor. Most of it has dealt with the period from the 1840s through the 1950s and has emphasized two key themes; the 'Wages of Whiteness' and 'Black Agency'"; ibid.

4. Hall, "The Long Civil Rights Movement," 1230. For an overview of recent scholarship on the post-1965 era, most of which has concentrated on the northern states, see note 54, chapter 1.

5. As James T. Patterson has noted, "until the late 1960s Jim Crow continued to flourish in southern schools"; Patterson, *Brown v. Board of Education*, xx (quotation), 157–58.

6. "Absenteeism High as Jefferson Schools Open," *Louisville Courier-Journal*, September 5, 1975. Studies of busing include Pride and Woodard, *The Burden of Busing*; Mills, ed., *Busing*

U.S.A.; Bolner and Shanley, *Busing*; and Formisano, *Boston Against Busing*. While not exclusively concerned with busing, Gaillard's *The Dream Long Deferred* covers busing in Charlotte in detail. While scholars have written recent books on the busing crises in Boston, Charlotte, and Nashville, Louisville has not received the same attention. The most detailed study of the crisis comes from interviews collected by sociologists J. B. McConahay and W. D. Hawley during the crisis. See McConahay and Hawley, "Reactions to Busing in Louisville." Broader works also give some coverage to the crisis in Louisville. See Hochschild, *The New American Dilemma*, 52, 184, 185; Rossell and Hawley, eds., *The Consequences of School Desegregation*, 19, 24, 25, 36–37, 42–49.

7. Heale, *Twentieth-Century America*, 247; Cataldo, Giles, and Gatlin, *School Desegregation Policy*, 54.

8. Pride and Woodard, *The Burden of Busing*, 6.

9. Formisano, *Boston Against Busing*, xi–xii.

10. The reaction of unions to the Boston busing crisis is briefly covered in Formisano, *Boston Against Busing*, 83–84. Other important studies of school desegregation and busing fail to cover the reaction of unions. See Douglas, *Reading, Writing, and Race*; Pride, *The Political Use of Racial Narratives*; Pride and Woodard, *The Burden of Busing*; Kellar, *Make Haste Slowly*; Gaillard, *The Dream Long Deferred*; Baker, *The Second Battle of New Orleans*. None of these works details the reaction of organized labor to school integration and busing. Busing is also not mentioned in standard general labor history works such as Zieger and Gall's *American Workers, American Unions* and Dubofsky and McCartin, eds., *American Labor*.

11. Coretta Scott King to Friends of the Center, n.d., folder 173, box 1604, AFL-CIO Civil Rights Papers.

12. "The AFL-CIO and Civil Rights," ca. 1977, folder 4, box 1592, AFL-CIO Civil Rights Papers.

13. "What's Right With Busing: A Handbook for People Concerned About School Integration," June 1972, folder 120, box 1601; Mrs. Martin Luther King Jr. to George Meany, November 18, 1975, folder 171, box 1604; Ralph David Abernathy to SCLC Contributor, December 1973, folder 170, box 1604; Coretta Scott King to Friend, January 13, 1977, folder 174, box 1604, all AFL-CIO Civil Rights Papers.

14. "The AFL-CIO and Civil Rights," ca. 1978, folder 6, box 1592, AFL-CIO Civil Rights Papers.

15. "Remarks of William E. Pollard," March 10, 1976, folder 2, box 1592; George Meany to Leonard L. Smith, October 23, 1975, folder 120, box 1601, both AFL-CIO Civil Rights Papers; Zieger and Gall, *American Workers*, 204–5.

16. IUE Press Release, September 3, 1975; George Meany to Leonard S. Smith, both folder 120, box 1601, AFL-CIO Civil Rights Papers; *School Desegregation in the 1970s*, 6–7; "Readers' Views," *Louisville Courier-Journal*, September 9, 1975.

17. "Quiet Louisville Accepting Busing," *New York Times*, September 11, 1975; E. T. Kehrer to Sam Ezelle, December 10, 1965, folder 44, box 1595; "Statement Opposing Anti-Desegregation Amendments," October 28, 1975, folder 120, box 1601, both AFL-CIO Civil Rights Papers; K'Meyer, "'The Gateway to the South'" 43–52.

18. K'Meyer, "'The Gateway to the South,'" 46.

19. "Whose Kentucky Home?" *Newsweek*, May 1, 1967.

20. "Louisville Still Among Most Segregated Cities," November 7, 1974; "More Housing Segregation Than Ever in Louisville and Jefferson County," both folder 120, box 1601, AFL-CIO Civil Rights Papers.

21. "Louisville School System Retreats to Segregation," March 1972; "Southern Cities—Except Louisville—Desegregate Schools," November 1972, both folder 120, box 1601, AFL-CIO Civil Rights Papers; R. Williams, "What Louisville Has Taught Us About Busing."

22. "U.S. Judge Orders Full Desegregation of Louisville Schools," *New York Times*, July 31, 1975; "A Curb on Racial Busing—Impact of 'Detroit Decision,'" *U.S. News and World Report*, August 5, 1974; "School Districts in Louisville, Ky., Fail Desegregation Test," *Christian Science Monitor*, January 4, 1974. In North Carolina the Charlotte-Mecklenburg County school system also implemented a desegregation plan encompassing both the city and suburbs, but it was a single school district to start with. In Louisville cross-district busing between separate city and suburban systems took place for the first time.

23. "Louisville, Suburbs Integrate Schools," *New York Times*, September 5, 1975; "Violence Breaks Out in Louisville After 2nd Peaceful Day of Cross-District Busing," *New York Times*, September 6, 1975; "Louisville School System Retreats to Segregation," March 1972, folder 120, box 1601, AFL-CIO Civil Rights Papers.

24. "Louisville, Suburbs Integrate Schools," *New York Times*, September 5, 1975; "8,000 in Louisville March to Protest School Bus Order," *New York Times*, September 28, 1975. Detailed school attendance figures are available in "First-Day School Attendance Figures," *Louisville Times*, September 5, 1975.

25. "Clashes at Protests Bring Injuries, Arrests," *Louisville Courier-Journal*, September 6, 1975; "Violence Breaks Out in Louisville After 2nd Peaceful Day of Cross-District Busing," *New York Times*, September 6, 1975; R. Williams, "What Louisville Has Taught Us About Busing," 7; "Officer Hurt in Riot Bears No Grudge," *Louisville Times*, September 11, 1975.

26. "Carroll Statement on Deploying the National Guard," *Louisville Courier-Journal*, September 7, 1975; "Guard Called Out in Louisville Riot," *New York Times*, September 7, 1975; "Jefferson County School Buses to Carry Armed Guards," *Louisville Courier-Journal*, September 8, 1975.

27. "Hundreds Attend Two Calm Rallies"; "Armed Guards Ride Buses," both *Louisville Times*, September 8, 1975; "Charges Dismissed Against 92 Busing Protesters," *Louisville Times*, September 22, 1975. The law that Sloane invoked was Chapter 39 of the Kentucky Revised Statutes, which was intended to meet situations such as natural disasters or civil disturbances brought about because of a catastrophe. Jefferson County judge Todd Hollenbach later ruled that Sloane's use of Chapter 39 was unconstitutional and all those arrested under the statute had the charges against them dropped.

28. "Louisville Visit," October 9, 1975, "Ford Quotes-Busing" folder, box 98, Records of the 1976 Presidential Campaign, Carter Library; "Louisville Trip Canceled by Ford," *New York Times*, October 10, 1975 (quotation).

29. "Shots Fired at Busing Rally," *New York Times*, October 14, 1975; "Police Use Tear Gas to End Louisville Antibusing Rally," *New York Times*, October 13, 1975; "Tear Gas Used in Protest Over Busing in Louisville," *New York Times*, November 28, 1975.

30. "Testimony of Harvey I. Sloane," October 29, 1975, 3–12 (quotations on 3, 11), "Busing" folder, box 103, Records of the 1976 Presidential Campaign, Carter Library.

31. "After Three Months of Busing, Louisville Schools Still Tense," *New York Times*, December 9, 1975; "Louisville: Underlying Issue Remains Race," *New York Times*, November 6, 1977; McConahay and Hawley, "Is It The Buses or The Blacks?" 9–12. Conducted for McConahay and Hawley, the Harris poll surveyed 1,049 persons living in both metropolitan Louisville and Jefferson County.

32. "A Tale of Two Cities," *New York Times*, May 8, 1983; "Plants Plan Normal Business," *Louisville Courier-Journal*, September 3, 1975.

33. "Leaders of Union Join Two Groups in Busing Protest," undated *Louisville Courier-Journal* clipping; IUE Press Release, September 3, 1975, both folder 120, box 1601, AFL-CIO Civil Rights Papers; "GE Union Urged to Abandon Opposition to School Busing," *Louisville Times*, September 3, 1975.

34. "Absenteeism at Local Plants Runs High," *Louisville Times*, September 4, 1975; "Louisville, Suburbs Integrate Schools," *New York Times*, September 5, 1975; "Ford Disciplines Workers Absent During Boycott," *Louisville Courier-Journal*, October 30, 1975.

35. "Testimony of Harvey I. Sloane," October 29, 1975, 12, "Busing" folder, box 103, Records of the 1976 Presidential Campaign, Carter Library; R. Williams, "What Louisville Has Taught Us About Busing," 8.

36. R. Williams, "What Louisville Has Taught Us About Busing," 7–8.

37. "March-March-March," flyer dated September 27, 1975; "Busing Foes Hear Plan for Marches," *Louisville Courier-Journal*, undated clipping, both folder 120, box 1601, AFL-CIO Civil Rights Papers; "8,000 in Louisville March to Protest School Bus Order," *New York Times*, September 28, 1975. The *Louisville Courier-Journal* was the morning paper while the *Louisville Times* was published in the afternoon. Barry Bingham Jr. edited both. See "The Media," *Louisville Courier-Journal*, September 11, 1975.

38. "Union Members Urged to March Against Busing," *Louisville Times*, October 20, 1975.

39. William E. Pollard to Tom Donohue, September 5, 1975, folder 120, box 1601, AFL-CIO Civil Rights Papers; "Protest Sparked 2 Major Incidents," *Louisville Times*, September 5, 1975.

40. "The AFL-CIO and Civil Rights," ca. 1977, folder 4, box 1592; George Meany to Leonard L. Smith, October 23, 1975, folder 120, box 1601, both AFL-CIO Civil Rights Papers; "Group of Union Members Denounces Meany For His Stance on Busing Issue," *Louisville Courier-Journal*, November 14, 1975.

41. "Meany, AFL-CIO Disown Anti-Busing Pilgrimage by Louisville Unionists," *Louisville Times*, October 25, 1975.

42. "Group of Union Members Denounces Meany For His Stance on Busing Issue," *Louisville Courier-Journal*, November 14, 1975.

43. E. T. Kehrer to William Pollard, November 5, 1975, folder 2, box 1592, AFL-CIO Civil Rights Papers.

44. Ibid.

45. "Quiet Louisville Accepting Busing," *New York Times*, September 11, 1975 (first quo-

tation); K'Meyer, "'The Gateway to the South,'" 46–53; "Solely For Integration," *Louisville Times*, September 11, 1975 (second quotation).

46. E. T. Kehrer to William Pollard, November 5, 1975, folder 2, box 1592; "AFL-CIO Official, Local Union Leaders Discussed Opposition to Busing Orders," *Louisville Courier-Journal*, November 1, 1975, clipping in folder 120, box 1601, both AFL-CIO Civil Rights Papers.

47. E. T. Kehrer to William Pollard, November 5, 1975, folder 2, box 1592, AFL-CIO Civil Rights Papers.

48. "Pipefitters Local Union 522 Oppose Forced Busing"; "Local Union Opposes Busing," both *Louisville Times*, September 2, 1975.

49. "Refinery Workers Local #84 Oppose Court Ordered Forced Busing," *Louisville Courier-Journal*, October 30, 1975. For another example of the same argument, see "Louisville Typographical Union No. 10 Opposes Court Ordered Forced Busing," ibid. In many ways, the union workers reflected broader public opinion, as opinion polls taken in the spring of 1976 highlighted that a slim majority of whites favored racially balanced schools in principle but rejected busing, principally because they saw it as undemocratic and destructive. See McConahay and Hawley, "Reactions to Busing in Louisville," 8–11.

50. "Local Union Opposes Busing"; "Advertisement," both *Louisville Times*, September 2, 1975; Kenneth G. Cassady to Members of Local 761, September 3, 1975, and September 25, 1975, both folder 120, box 1601, AFL-CIO Civil Rights Papers.

51. "Labor Groups Oppose School Busing Plan," *Louisville Courier-Journal*, August 26, 1975; Kenneth G. Cassady to Members of Local 761, September 25, 1975, folder 120, box 1601, AFL-CIO Civil Rights Papers; "Protesters Chants Mar Carroll Speech," *Louisville Courier-Journal*, January 8, 1976.

52. R. Williams, "What Louisville Has Taught Us," 7; "Leaders of Union Join Two Groups in Busing Protest," undated *Louisville Courier-Journal* clipping in folder 120, box 1601, AFL-CIO Civil Rights Papers; "Everyday People," *Louisville Times*, September 6, 1975; "Protests Won't Stop Busing, But Do Serve a Purpose," *Louisville Times*, September 15, 1975.

53. "Testimony of Harvey I. Sloane," October 29, 1975, 11, "Busing" folder, box 103, Records of the 1976 Presidential Campaign, Carter Library; McConahay and Hawley, "Reactions to Busing in Louisville," cited in Rossell, "Desegregation Plans," 19. In its main analysis of the causes of the antibusing violence, the *Louisville Times* also cited the role of blue-collar whites who had moved to the suburbs and vehemently opposed efforts to bus their children back to the city. See "The Rioting in Retrospect," *Louisville Times*, September 11, 1975.

54. Kenneth G. Cassady to Members of Local 761, September 3, 1975, folder 120, box 1601, AFL-CIO Civil Rights Papers; "Liberal Democrats Stir Busing Foes," *New York Times*, November 23, 1975; "McGovern Cautions Party Against Retreat on Busing," *New York Times*, November 24, 1975 (quotation).

55. "Busing Foes Peaceful at 2 Klan Rallies," *Louisville Courier-Journal*, September 7, 1975; "Rift in Ku Klux Klan Aired at Jefferson Rally," *Louisville Courier-Journal*, September 11, 1975.

56. "Protest Sparked 2 Major Incidents," and "White-Supremacist Groves Seeks Nonviolent, Non-Racist Look," *Louisville Times*, September 5 and 20, 1975. As an indication of the Klan's revival, see "Knights of the Ku Klux Klan Are Watching *You!!*" *Louisville Times*, October 29, 1975.

57. K'Meyer, "'The Gateway to the South,'" 46; Rossell, "Desegregation Plans," 45.

58. "Blacks From Core Hesitant to Mix With County Kids," and "Send Pupils to School, Black Ministers Urge," *Louisville Times*, September 8 and 11, 1975. For black reaction to busing, see also "Blacks at J-Town," *Louisville Times*, September 5, 1975.

59. Black Workers' Petition, n.d.; Purnell V. [illegible] to Sir, September 5, 1975, both folder 120, box 1601, AFL-CIO Civil Rights Papers.

60. Kenneth G. Cassady to Members of Local 761, folder 120, box 1601, AFL-CIO Civil Rights Papers.

61. "IUE Local Votes Against Backing Gable," *Louisville Times*, October 13, 1975; Kenneth G. Cassady to Members of Local 761, both folder 120, box 1601, AFL-CIO Civil Rights Papers.

62. R. Williams, "What Louisville Has Taught Us," 10; "Local TV, St. Louis," September 12, 1975, "Ford Quotes-Busing" folder, box 98; "Debate Questions: Busing," n.d., "Busing" folder, box 31, both Records of the 1976 Presidential Campaign, Carter Library.

63. Fosl, *Subversive Southerner*, 323; "500 in Louisville March to Support School Busing," *New York Times*, October 12, 1975.

64. R. Williams, "What Louisville Has Taught Us About Busing," 10, 51; E. T. Kehrer to William Pollard, November 5, 1975, folder 2, box 1592, AFL-CIO Civil Rights Papers; Hart and K'Meyer, "Worker Memory and Narrative," 284–304; "Louisville," *New York Times*, May 8, 1983.

65. "Louisville, A Place Where Busing Seems to Work," *New York Times*, June 6, 1976. For another similar view, see R. Williams, "What Louisville Has Taught Us."

66. Ibid., 10.

67. "Mixed Results of Integration Typified in Louisville School," *New York Times*, March 16, 1978; Mahard and Crain, "Research on Minority Achievement," 117–18.

68. "Testimony of Harvey I. Sloane," October 29, 1975, 7, "Busing" folder, box 103, Records of the 1976 Presidential Campaign, Carter Library; "Quiet Louisville Accepting Busing," *New York Times*, September 11, 1975; "Kentucky Baptists Sue to Bar State From Imposing School Standards," *New York Times*, June 20, 1978; "Parish School Enrollment Up," *New York Times*, September 21, 1975.

69. McConahay and Hawley, "Reactions to Busing in Louisville," cited in Rossell, "Desegregation Plans," 37; "Gordon Approves Plan to Bus 900 More Black Students," *Louisville Times*, June 18, 1976.

70. "Students' Identity Search, Frustration Blamed in Fights," March 2, 1977; "The Shawnee Cluster: Why Did It Get Hot?" March 4, 1977, both *Louisville Courier-Journal*.

71. Patterson, *Brown v. Board of Education*, 187; "Mixed Results of Integration Typified in Louisville School," *New York Times*, March 16, 1978; Wilkinson, *From Brown to Bakke*, 243–44; Rossell, "Desegregation Plans," 43.

72. Eyler, Cook, and Ward, "Resegregation," 157–59; "Mixed Results of Integration Typified in Louisville School," *New York Times*, March 16, 1978.

73. "Louisville Debates Plan to End Forced Grade School Busing," *New York Times*, December 11, 1991.

74. Rossell, "Desegregation Plans," 46–47; Pride and Woodard, *The Burden of Busing*, 3–8, 78–82, 126–43; Douglas, *Reading, Writing, and Race*, 245–54; Armor, "White Flight," 209–14.

For a fine and up-to-date summary of the literature on busing and its contested legacy, see Patterson, *Brown v. Board of Education*, 157–69.

75. Studies of the Boston crisis include Formisano, *Boston Against Busing*; S. Eaton, *The Other Boston Busing Story*; and U.S. Commission on Civil Rights, *School Desegregation in Boston*. General accounts of school desegregation give much more attention to Boston than to Louisville. See Stephan and Feagin, eds., *School Desegregation*, 157–86.

76. Mark Nadler, "Charlotte-Mecklenburg," in Mills, ed., *Busing U.S.A.*, 311 (quotation); "Obeying the Law," *New York Times*, September 12, 1975; "Louisville, Suburbs Integrate Schools," *New York Times*, September 5, 1975; Hall, "The Long Civil Rights Movement," 1233–34.

77. Patterson, *Brown v. Board of Education*, 158.

78. E. T. Kehrer to William Pollard, December 29, 1975, folder 2, box 1592, AFL-CIO Civil Rights Papers. As noted above, only one study of busing covers the reaction of unions in any detail. See Formisano, *Boston Against Busing*, 83–84. As an example of how the Louisville press covered the Boston crisis, see "School Attendance Reported Higher as Boston Busing Starts 2nd Week," *Louisville Times*, September 15, 1975.

79. George Meany to Leonard S. Smith, October 23, 1975, folder 120, box 1601, AFL-CIO Civil Rights Papers; "AFL-CIO Official, Local Union Leaders Discussed Opposition to Busing Orders," *Louisville Courier-Journal*, November 1, 1975; Draper, *Conflict of Interests*, 162–67.

80. Freeman, "Labor During the American Century," 202; Cowie, "'Vigorously Left, Right, and Center.'"

81. For tensions between the NAACP and AFL-CIO, see Bayard Rustin to Roy Wilkins, July 11, 1973, folder 85, box 1598, AFL-CIO Civil Rights Papers; "Month of Victories Marks Herbert Hill's 25th Year as NAACP Labor Director," *New York Times*, December 17, 1974.

82. E. T. Kehrer to William Pollard, January 7, 1977, folder 4, box 1592, AFL-CIO Civil Rights Papers. Highlighting the way that he confronted grassroots opposition to AFL-CIO civil rights policies, at one conference with union members in 1975 Kehrer spoke on the topic, "Labor Views Civil Rights." "What was so amazing and satisfying about the meeting was that it was the first meeting I have been in on this subject where there was no hostility expressed on our position," he noted, ". . . I felt for the first time we might be turning this issue around." E. T. Kehrer to William Pollard, October 21, 1975, folder 2, box 1592, AFL-CIO Civil Rights.

83. E. T. Kehrer to William Pollard, April 30, 1975, and November 5, 1975, folder 2, box 1592, AFL-CIO Civil Rights Papers.

Bibliography

ACTWU Papers. Kheel Center for Labor-Management Documentation and Archives, School of Industrial and Labor Relations, Cornell University, Ithaca, N.Y.

ACTWU Southern Textile Regional Office Papers. Southern Labor Archives, Georgia State University Library, Georgia State University, Atlanta.

Adams, Michael C. C. *The Best War Ever: America and World War II*. Baltimore: The Johns Hopkins University Press, 1994.

Adams v. Dan River Mills. U.S. District Court, Western District of Virginia, 1969. National Archives and Records Administration, Philadelphia.

Addresses and Public Papers of James Eubert Holhouser, Jr., Governor of North Carolina 1973–1977. Raleigh, N.C.: Division of Archives and History, Department of Cultural Resources, 1978.

AFL-CIO (American Federation of Labor–Congress of Industrial Organizations) Civil Rights Department Papers. George Meany Memorial Archives, National Labor College, Silver Spring, Maryland.

AFL-CIO Civil Rights Department Southern Office Records, 1964–1979. Southern Labor Archives, Georgia State University Library, Georgia State University, Atlanta.

Alston, Sammy. Interview with author. Roanoke Rapids, N.C., February 9, 1996.

American Friends Service Committee Papers. Merit Employment Files. AFSC headquarters, Philadelphia, Pennsylvania.

Anderson, Terry H. *The Pursuit of Fairness: A History of Affirmative Action*. New York: Oxford University Press, 2004.

Armor, David J. "White Flight and the Future of School Desegregation." In *School Desegregation: Past, Present, and Future*, edited by Walter G. Stephan and Joe R. Feagin, 187–229. New York: Plenum Press, 1980.

Ashbaugh, Carolyn, and McCurry, Dan. "On the Line at Oneita." In *Working Lives: The Southern Exposure History of Labor in the South*, edited by Marc S. Miller, 205–14. New York: Pantheon Books, 1980.

Bailey, Beth. *America in the Seventies*. Lawrence: University Press of Kansas, 2004.

Bailey, Cleveland. Interview with author. Port St. Joe, Fla., July 24, 1997.

Baker, Liva. *The Second Battle of New Orleans: The Hundred-Year Struggle to Integrate the Schools*. New York: Harper Collins, 1996.

Bartley, Numan V. *The New South, 1945–1980: The Story of the South's Modernization*. Baton Rouge: Louisiana State University Press, 1995.

Bass, Jack. *Taming the Storm: The Life and Times of Judge Frank M. Johnson, Jr., and the South's Fight over Civil Rights*. New York: Anchor Books, 1993.

Bass, Jack, and Walter DeVries. *The Transformation of Southern Politics: Social Change and Political Consequence Since 1945*. New York: Basic Books, 1976.

Bates, Beth Tompkins. *Pullman Porters and the Rise of Protest Politics in Black America, 1925–1945*. Chapel Hill: University of North Carolina Press, 2001.

Beck, Fletcher. Interview with author. Rock Hill, S.C., January 29, 1996.

Bennett, Lerone, Jr., "Have We Overcome?" In *Have We Overcome?: Race Relations Since Brown*, edited by Michael B. Namorato, 189–200. Jackson: University Press of Mississippi, 1979.

Berman, William C. *America's Right Turn: From Nixon to Bush*. Baltimore: Johns Hopkins University Press, 1994.

Blauner, Bob. *Black Lives, White Lives: Three Decades of Race Relations in America*. Berkeley: University of California Press, 1989.

Bluestone, Barry, and Bennett Harrison. *The Deindustrialization of America: Plant Closings, Community Abandonment, and the Dismantling of Basic Industry*. New York: Basic Books, 1982.

Boger, Jake. Interview with author. Rock Hill, S.C., January 30, 1996.

Bolner, James, and Robert Shanley. *Busing: The Political and Judicial Process*. New York: Praeger, 1974.

Boone, James. Interview with author. Roanoke Rapids, N.C., February 9, 1996.

Bragg, Frank. Interview with author. Nashville, Tenn., July 15, 1997.

Branch, Taylor. *Parting the Waters: America in the King Years, 1954–63*. New York: Simon and Schuster, 1988.

———. *Pillar of Fire: America in the King Years, 1963–65*. New York: Simon and Schuster, 1998.

Brattain, Michelle. *The Politics of Whiteness: Race, Workers, and Culture in the Modern South*. Princeton, N.J.: Princeton University Press, 2001.

Brinkley, Alan. *American History: A Survey*. 11th ed. Boston: McGraw Hill, 2003.

Brooker, Larry. Telephone interview with author. June 23, 2005.

Bryant, Robert. Interview with author. Port St. Joe, Fla., July 23, 1997.

Bush, Clyde. Interview with author. Roanoke Rapids, N.C., February 9, 1996.

Button, James W. *Blacks and Social Change: Impact of the Civil Rights Movement in Southern Communities*. Princeton, N.J.: Princeton University Press, 1989.

Calhoun, Myron. Interview with author. Satsuma, Ala., November 12, 2004.

Cannon, Corine Lyttle. Interview with author. Kannapolis, N.C., March 11, 1996.

Carlton, David L. *Mill and Town in South Carolina, 1880–1920*. Baton Rouge: Louisiana State University Press, 1982.

Carroll, Peter N. *It Seemed Like Nothing Happened: America in the 1970s*. New Brunswick, N.J.: Rutgers University Press, 1990.

Carson, Clayborne. *In Struggle: SNCC and the Black Awakening of the 1960s*. Cambridge, Mass.: Harvard University Press, 1981.

Carter, Jimmy. Papers. Jimmy Carter Library and Museum, Atlanta, Georgia.

Cataldo, Everett F., Michael W. Giles, and Douglas S. Gatlin. *School Desegregation Policy: Compliance, Avoidance, and the Metropolitan Remedy*. Lexington, Mass.: Lexington Books, 1978.

Cecelski, David S. *Along Freedom Road: Hyde County, North Carolina, and the Fate of Black Schools in the South*. Chapel Hill: University of North Carolina Press, 1994.

Chafe, William H. *Civilities and Civil Rights: Greensboro, North Carolina and the Black Freedom Struggle*. New York: Oxford University Press, 1980.

———. "The End of One Struggle, The Beginning of Another." In *The Civil Rights Movement in America*, edited by Charles Eagles, 127–48. Jackson: University Press of Mississippi, 1986.

———. *The Unfinished Journey: America since World War II*. 3rd ed. New York: Oxford University Press, 1995.

Chambers, Julius. Interview with author. Durham, N.C., June 28, 1996.

Chappell, David L. *A Stone of Hope: Prophetic Religion and the Death of Jim Crow*. Chapel Hill: University of North Carolina Press, 2004.

Cleaver, Kathleen, and George Katsiaficas, eds. *Liberation, Imagination, and the Black Panther Party: A New Look at the Panthers and Their Legacy*. New York: Routledge, 2001.

Cobb, James C. *The Selling of the South: The Southern Crusade for Industrial Development, 1936–1980*. Baton Rouge: Louisiana State University Press, 1982.

Colburn, David R. *Racial Change and Community Crisis: St. Augustine, Florida, 1877–1980*. New York: Columbia University Press, 1985.

Coley, Allen. Interview with author. Natchez, Miss., October 13, 1997.

Collier-Thomas, Bettye, and V. P. Franklin, eds. *Sisters in the Struggle: African American Women in the Civil Rights–Black Power Movement*. New York: New York University Press, 2001.

Conway, Mimi. *Rise, Gonna Rise: A Portrait of Southern Textile Workers*. Garden City, N.Y.: Doubleday, 1979.

Couto, Richard A. *Ain't Gonna Let Nobody Turn Me Around: The Pursuit of Racial Justice in the Rural South*. Philadelphia: Temple University Press, 1991.

Cowie, Jefferson. "'Vigorously Left, Right, and Center': The Cross Currents of Working-Class America in the 1970s." In *America in the Seventies*, edited by Beth Bailey and David Farber, 75–106. Lawrence: University Press of Kansas, 2004.

Crittenden, Reverna. Interview with author. Columbus, Ga., January 25, 1996.

Crooks, James B. *Jacksonville: The Consolidation Story, From Civil Rights to the Jaguars*. Gainesville: University Press of Florida, 2004.

Crosby, Emilye. *A Little Taste of Freedom: The Black Freedom Struggle in Claiborne County, Mississippi*. Chapel Hill: University of North Carolina Press, 2005.

Davidson, Chandler, and Bernard Grofman, eds. *Quiet Revolution in the South: The Impact of the Voting Rights Act, 1965–1990*. Princeton, N.J.: Princeton University Press, 1994.

Deal, Elboyd. Interview with author. Kannapolis, N.C., March 11, 1996.

Dittmer, John. *Local People: The Struggle for Civil Rights in Mississippi*. Urbana: University of Illinois Press, 1994.

Donohue, John J., III, and James Heckman. "Continuous Versus Episodic Change: The Impact of Civil Rights Policy on the Economic Status of Blacks." *Journal of Economic Literature* 29, no. 4 (December 1991): 1603–43.

Douglas, Davison M. *Reading, Writing, and Race: The Desegregation of the Charlotte Schools.* Chapel Hill: University of North Carolina, 1995.

Draper, Alan. *Conflict of Interests: Organized Labor and the Civil Rights Movement in the South, 1954–1968.* Ithaca, N.Y.: ILR Press, 1994.

Drobney, Jeffrey. "Company Towns and Social Transformation in the North Florida Timber Industry, 1880–1930." *Florida Historical Quarterly* 75 (1996): 121–45.

Dubofsky, Melvyn, and Joseph A. McCartin, eds. *American Labor: A Documentary Collection.* New York: Palgrave MacMillan, 2004.

Dumbrell, John. *The Carter Presidency: A Re-Evaluation.* 2nd ed. Manchester, U.K.: Manchester University Press, 1995.

Eagles, Charles W. "Toward New Histories of the Civil Rights Era." *Journal of Southern History* 66, no. 4 (November 2000): 815–48.

Eaton, Adrienne, and Jill Kriesky. "Collective Bargaining in the Paper Industry: Developments Since 1979." In *Contemporary Collective Bargaining in the Private Sector*, edited by Paula Voos, 25–62. Madison, Wis.: Industrial Relations Research Association, 1994.

Eaton, Susan E. *The Other Boston Busing Story: What's Won and Lost Across the Boundary Line.* New Haven, Conn.: Yale University Press, 2001.

Edds, Margaret. *Free At Last: What Really Happened When Civil Rights Came to Southern Politics.* Bethesda, Md.: Adler and Adler, 1987.

Egerton, John. *Speak Now Against the Day: The Generation Before the Civil Rights Movement in the South.* New York: Alfred A. Knopf, 1994.

Ellison, Leroy. Interview with author. Rock Hill, S.C., January 30, 1996.

Ellison v. Rock Hill Printing and Finishing Company. U.S. District Court, District of South Carolina, 1972. National Archives and Records Administration, Atlanta, Georgia.

Escoffier, Jeffrey. "Fabulous Politics: Gay, Lesbian, and Queer Movements, 1969–1999." In *The World the Sixties Made: Politics and Culture in Recent America*, edited by Van Gosse and Richard Moser, 191–218. Philadelphia: Temple University Press, 2003.

Eskew, Glenn T. *But for Birmingham: The Local and National Movements in the Civil Rights Struggle.* Chapel Hill: University of North Carolina Press, 1997.

Evans, Sara M. *Born for Liberty: A History of Women in America.* New York: Free Press, 1997.

———. "Beyond Declension: Feminist Radicalism in the 1970s and 1980s." In *The World the Sixties Made: Politics and Culture in Recent America*, edited by Van Gosse and Richard Moser, 52–66. Philadelphia: Temple University Press, 2003.

Eyler, Janet, Valerie J. Cook, and Leslie E. Ward. "Resegregation: Segregation Within Desegregated Schools." In *The Consequences of School Desegregation*, edited by Christine H. Rossell and Willis D. Hawley, 126–62. Philadelphia: Temple University Press, 1983.

Fairclough, Adam. *To Redeem the Soul of America: The Southern Christian Leadership Conference and Martin Luther King, Jr.* Athens: University of Georgia Press, 1987.

———. "State of the Art: Historians and the Civil Rights Movement." *Journal of American Studies* 24, no. 3 (December 1990), 387–98.

———. *Race and Democracy: The Civil Rights Struggle in Louisiana, 1915–1972.* Athens: University of Georgia Press, 1995.

Ferguson, James E., II. Interviews, March 3 and 17, 1992. Southern Oral History Project, Southern Historical Collection, Wilson Library, University of North Carolina at Chapel Hill, Chapel Hill.

Flamming, Douglas. *Creating the Modern South: Millhands and Managers in Dalton, Georgia, 1884–1984*. Chapel Hill: University of North Carolina Press, 1992.

Fleming, Cynthia Griggs. *In the Shadow of Selma: The Continuing Struggle for Civil Rights in the Rural South*. Lanham, Md.: Rowman and Littlefield, 2004.

Ford, Willie. Interview with author. Mobile, Ala., October 10, 1997.

Formisano, Ronald P. *Boston Against Busing: Race, Class, and Ethnicity in the 1960s and 1970s*. Chapel Hill: University of North Carolina Press, 1991.

Fosl, Catherine. *Subversive Southerner: Anne Braden and the Struggle for Racial Justice in the Cold War South*. New York: Palgrave MacMillan, 2002.

Foster v. Fieldcrest Mills. U.S. District Court, Middle District of North Carolina, 1977. National Archives and Records Administration, Atlanta, Georgia.

Franklin, Jimmie Lewis. *Back to Birmingham: Richard Arrington, Jr., and His Times*. Tuscaloosa: University of Alabama Press, 1989.

Frederickson, Mary. "Four Decades of Change: Black Workers in Southern Textiles, 1941–1981." In *Workers' Struggles, Past and Present: A "Radical America" Reader*, edited by James Green, 62–82. Philadelphia: Temple University Press, 1983.

Freeman, Joshua B. "Labor During the American Century: Work, Workers, and Unions Since 1945." In *A Companion to Post-1945 America*, edited by Jean-Christophe Agnew and Roy Rosenzweig, 192–210. Malden, Mass.: Blackwell, 2002.

Frymer, Paul, and John David Skrentny. "Coalition-Building and the Politics of Electoral Capture During the Nixon Administration: African Americans, Labor, Latinos." *Studies in American Political Development* 12 (Spring 1998): 131–61.

Funk, Larry. Interview with author. Mobile, Ala., July 21, 1997.

Gaillard, Frye. *The Dream Long Deferred*. Chapel Hill: University of North Carolina Press, 1988.

Gaines, Joe. Interview with author. Opelika, Ala., January 25, 1996.

Gaines, Kevin. "The Historiography of the Struggle for Black Equality since 1945." In *A Companion to Post-1945 America*, edited by Jean-Christophe Agnew and Roy Rosenzweig, 211–34. Malden, Mass.: Blackwell, 2002.

Gantlin v. West Virginia Pulp and Paper Company (Westvaco). U.S. District Court, District of South Carolina, 1972. National Archives and Records Administration, Atlanta, Georgia.

Gantt, Adrian Franklin. Interview with author. Port St. Joe, Fla., July 23, 1997.

Garrett v. Weyerhauser Corporation. U.S. District Court, Eastern District of North Carolina, 1977. National Archives and Records Administration, Atlanta, Georgia.

Garrow, David J. *Protest at Selma: Martin Luther King, Jr., and the Voting Rights Act of 1965*. New Haven, Conn.: Yale University Press, 1978.

———. *Bearing the Cross: Martin Luther King, Jr., and the Southern Christian Leadership Conference*. New York: W. Morrow, 1986.

Gibson, Sidney. Interview with author. Natchez, Miss., October 13, 1997.

Gill, Horace. Interview with author. Mobile, Ala., July 22, 1997.

Gilley v. Hudson Pulp and Paper Company. U.S. District Court, Middle District of Florida, 1976. National Archives and Records Administration, Atlanta, Georgia.

Glover, Sammy. Interview with author. Andalusia, Ala., February 2, 1996.

Godwin, John L. *Black Wilmington and the North Carolina Way: Portrait of a Community in the Era of Civil Rights Protest.* Lanham, Md.: University Press of America, 2000.

Goldfield, David R. *Black, White, and Southern: Race Relations and Southern Culture, 1940 to the Present.* Baton Rouge: Louisiana State University Press, 1990.

Gordon, B. J. Interview with author. Andrews, S.C., April 11, 1996.

Graham, Hugh Davis. *Collision Course: The Strange Convergence of Affirmative Action and Immigration Policy in America.* New York: Oxford University Press, 2002.

Greene, Christina. *Our Separate Ways: Women and the Black Freedom Movement in Durham, North Carolina.* Chapel Hill: University of North Carolina Press, 2005.

Greensboro Civil Rights Fund Papers. Southern Historical Collection, Wilson Library, University of North Carolina at Chapel Hill, Chapel Hill.

Griffith, Barbara S. *The Crisis of American Labor: Operation Dixie and the Defeat of the CIO.* Philadelphia: Temple University Press, 1988.

Hahamovitch, Cindy. "Standing Idly By: 'Organized' Farmworkers in South Florida during the Depression and World War II." In *Southern Labor in Transition, 1940–1995,* edited by Robert H. Zieger, 15–36. Knoxville, University of Tennessee Press, 1997.

Hall, Jacquelyn Dowd. "The Long Civil Rights Movement and the Political Uses of the Past." *Journal of American History* 91, no. 4 (March 2005): 1233–63.

Hall, Jacquelyn Dowd, James Leloudis, Robert Korstad, Mary Murphy, Lu Ann Jones, and Christopher B. Daly. *Like a Family: The Making of a Southern Cotton Mill World.* Chapel Hill: University of North Carolina Press, 1987.

Hall, Russell. Interview with author. Pensacola, Fla., August 4, 1997.

Hall v. Werthan Bag Company. U.S. District Court, Middle District of Tennessee, 1966. National Archives and Records Administration, Atlanta, Georgia.

Halpern, Rick. "Organized Labour, Black Workers and the Twentieth-Century South: The Emerging Revision." *Social History* 19 (October 1994): 359–83.

Hamilton, Leroy. Interview with author. Woodbine, Ga., July 25, 1997.

Hart, Joy L., and Tracy E. K'Meyer. "Worker Memory and Narrative: Personal Stories of Deindustrialization in Louisville, Kentucky." In *Beyond the Ruins: The Meanings of Deindustrialization,* edited by Jefferson Cowie and Joseph Heathcott, 284–304. Ithaca, N.Y.: ILR Press, 2003.

Heale, Michael J. *Twentieth-Century America: Politics and Power in the United States, 1900–2000.* London: Arnold, 2004.

Hicks, Robert. Interview with author. Bogalusa, La., July 22, 1997.

Hicks v. Cannon Mills. U.S. District Court, Middle District of North Carolina, 1970. National Archives and Records Administration, Atlanta, Georgia.

Hill, Herbert. *Black Labor and the American Legal System: Race, Work, and the Law.* Madison: University of Wisconsin Press, 1985.

———. "Lichtenstein's Fictions: Meany, Reuther and the 1964 Civil Rights Act." *New Politics* 7, no. 1 (1998): 82–107.

Hill, Herbert, and James E. Jones, eds. *Race in America: The Struggle for Equality.* Madison: University of Wisconsin Press, 1993.

Hill, Lance. *The Deacons for Defense: Armed Resistance and the Civil Rights Movement.* Chapel Hill: University of North Carolina Press, 2004.

Hillard, Michael. "Labor at 'Mother Warren': Paternalism, Welfarism, and Dissent at S. D. Warren, 1854–1967." *Labor History* 45, no. 1 (February 2004): 37–60.

Hochschild, Jennifer L. *The New American Dilemma: Liberal Democracy and School Desegregation.* New Haven, Conn.: Yale University Press, 1984.

Hodges, James A. *New Deal Labor Policy and the Southern Cotton Textile Industry, 1933–1941.* Knoxville: University of Tennessee Press, 1986.

———. "The Real Norma Rae." In *Southern Labor in Transition, 1940–1995,* edited by Robert H. Zieger, 251–72. Knoxville: University of Tennessee Press, 1997.

Hodgson, Godfrey. *More Equal Than Others: America From Nixon to the New Century.* Princeton, N.J.: Princeton University Press, 2004.

Honey, Michael K. *Southern Labor and Black Civil Rights: Organizing Memphis Workers.* Urbana: University of Illinois Press, 1993.

———. *Black Workers Remember: An Oral History of Segregation, Unionism, and the Freedom Struggle.* Berkeley: University of California Press, 1999.

Hulsemann, Karsten. "Greenfields in the Heart of Dixie: How the American Auto Industry Discovered the South." In *The Second Wave: Southern Industrialization from the 1940s to the 1970s,* edited by Philip Scranton, 219–54. Athens: University of Georgia Press, 2001.

Hunter, Tera W. "'The Women Are Asking for BREAD, Why Give Them Stone?': Women, Work, and Protests in Atlanta and Norfolk during World War I." In *Labor in the Modern South,* edited by Glenn T. Eskew, 62–82. Athens: University of Georgia Press, 2001.

Hurup, Elsebeth, ed. *The Lost Decade: America in the Seventies.* Aarhus, Denmark: Aarhus University Press, 1996.

Jacoway, Elizabeth. "*Brown* and the 'Road to Reunion.'" *Journal of Southern History* 70, no. 2 (May 2004): 303–8.

Johnson, David. Interview with author. Bogalusa, La., July 22, 1997.

Johnson, Lyndon Baines. Papers. Civil Rights During the Johnson Administration (microfilm), Cambridge University Library, Cambridge, U.K.

Katznelson, Ira. *When Affirmative Action Was White: An Untold History of Racial Inequality in Twentieth-Century America.* New York: Norton, 2005.

Kaufman, Bruce E. "The Emergence and Growth of a Nonunion Sector in the Southern Paper Industry." In *Southern Labor in Transition, 1940–1995,* edited by Robert H. Zieger, 295–329. Knoxville: University of Tennessee Press, 1997.

Kellar, William Henry. *Make Haste Slowly: Moderates, Conservatives, and School Desegregation in Houston.* College Station: Texas A&M University Press, 1999.

Kelley, Robin D. G. *Freedom Dreams: The Black Radical Imagination.* Boston: Beacon Press, 2002.

Kirk, John A. *Redefining the Color Line: Black Activism in Little Rock, Arkansas, 1940–1970.* Gainesville: University Press of Florida, 2002.

———. *Martin Luther King, Jr.* Harlow, U.K.: Pearson Education Limited, 2005.

K'Meyer, Tracy E. "'The Gateway to the South': Regional Identity and the Louisville Civil Rights Movement." *Ohio Valley History* 4, no. 1 (Spring 2004): 43–60.

Korstad, Robert. "Daybreak of Freedom: Tobacco Workers and the CIO, Winston-Salem, North Carolina, 1943–1950." PhD diss., University of North Carolina, 1987.

———. *Civil Rights Unionism: Tobacco Workers and the Struggle for Democracy in the Mid-Twentieth-Century South.* Chapel Hill: University of North Carolina Press, 2003.

Korstad, Robert, and Nelson Lichtenstein. "Opportunities Lost and Found: Labor, Radicals, and the Early Civil Rights Movement." *Journal of American History* 75, no. 4 (1988): 786–811.

Kotlowski, Dean J. "Nixon's Southern Strategy Revisited." *Journal of Policy History* 10, no. 2 (1998): 207–38.

———. *Nixon's Civil Rights: Politics, Principle, and Policy.* Cambridge, Mass.: Harvard University Press, 2001.

Langham, Donald L. Interview with author. Mobile, Ala., October 10, 1997.

Larry, R. C. Interview with author. Port St. Joe, Fla., July 23, 1997.

Lawson, Steven F. *Black Ballots: Voting Rights in the South, 1944–1969.* New York: Columbia University Press, 1976.

———. *In Pursuit of Power: Southern Blacks and Electoral Politics, 1965–1982.* New York: Columbia University Press, 1985.

———. *Running for Freedom: Civil Rights and Black Politics in America Since 1941.* New York: McGraw Hill, 1991.

———. "Freedom Then, Freedom Now: The Historiography of the Civil Rights Movement." *The American Historical Review* 96, no. 2 (April 1991), 456–71.

Lawson, Steven F., and Charles Payne. *Debating the Civil Rights Movement, 1945–1968.* Lanham, Md.: Rowman and Littlefield, 1998.

Lea v. Cone Mills. U.S. District Court, Middle District of North Carolina, 1966. National Archives and Records Administration, Atlanta, Georgia.

Lee, Chana Kai. *For Freedom's Sake: The Life of Fannie Lou Hamer.* Urbana: University of Illinois Press, 1999.

Leuchtenburg, William E. "The White House and Black America: From Eisenhower to Carter." In *Have We Overcome?: Race Relations Since Brown,* edited by Michael B. Namorato, 121–45. Jackson: University Press of Mississippi, 1979.

Lewis, David Levering. *King: A Critical Biography.* New York: Praeger, 1970.

Lewis, John. *Walking with the Wind: A Memoir of the Movement.* With Michael D'Orso. San Diego: Harcourt Brace, 1998.

Lewis v. Bloomsburg Mills. U.S. District Court, District of South Carolina, 1973. National Archives and Records Administration, Atlanta, Georgia.

Lewis v. J. P. Stevens. U.S. District Court, District of South Carolina, 1972. National Archives and Records Administration, Atlanta, Georgia.

Lichtenstein, Alex. "'Scientific Unionism' and the 'Negro Question': Communists and the Transport Workers Union in Miami, 1944–1949." In *Southern Labor in Transition, 1940–1995,* edited by Robert H. Zieger, 58–85. Knoxville: University of Tennessee Press, 1997.

Lindsay v. Cone Mills. U.S. District Court, Middle District of North Carolina, 1976. National Archives and Records Administration, Atlanta, Georgia.

Little, Jacob. Interview with author. Columbus, Ga., January 18, 1996.

Long, Willie. Interview with author. Columbus, Ga., January 18, 1996.

Loveland, George W. *Under The Workers' Caps: From Champion Mill to Blue Ridge Paper.* Knoxville: University of Tennessee Press, 2005.

Lovett, Bobby L. *The Civil Rights Movement in Tennessee: A Narrative History.* Knoxville: University of Tennessee Press, 2005.

MacLean, Nancy. "The Hidden History of Affirmative Action: Working Women's Struggles in the 1970s and the Gender of Class." *Feminist Studies* 25, no. 1 (Spring 1999): 42–78.

———. *Freedom Is Not Enough: The Opening of the American Workplace.* Cambridge, Mass.: Harvard University Press, 2006.

MacNeill/Lehrer Report. "J. P. Stevens." Videotape. PBS, December 22, 1976. Copy held at Kheel Center for Labor-Management Documentation and Archives, School of Industrial and Labor Relations, Cornell University, Ithaca, N.Y.

Madison, Emily Webster. "Objections Sustained: The Conception and Demise of Soul City, North Carolina." Undergraduate honors essay, University of North Carolina at Chapel Hill, 1995.

Mahard, Rita E., and Robert L. Crain. "Research on Minority Achievement in Desegregated Schools." In *The Consequences of School Desegregation*, edited by Christine H. Rossell and Willis D. Hawley, 103–25. Philadelphia: Temple University Press, 1983.

Marable, Manning. *Race, Reform and Rebellion: The Second Reconstruction in Black America, 1945–1990.* 2nd ed. Jackson: University Press of Mississippi, 1991.

McCall, Bubba. Interview with author. Nashville, Tenn., July 15, 1997.

McConahay, John B., and Willis D. Hawley, "Is It The Buses or The Blacks?: Self-Interest Versus Symbolic Racism as Predictors of Opposition to Busing in Louisville." Working Paper, Institute of Policy Sciences and Public Affairs, Duke University, 1977.

———. "Reactions to Busing in Louisville: Summary of Adult Opinions in 1976 and 1977." Working Paper, Institute of Policy Sciences and Public Affairs, Duke University, 1978.

McCullough, Joe. Interview with author. Savannah, Ga., October 3, 1997.

McGauley, Thomas. Interview with author. St. Marys, Ga., July 27, 1997.

McKissick, Floyd Bixler. Interviews, December 6, 1973 and May 31, 1989. Southern Oral History Program, Southern Historical Collection, Wilson Library, University of North Carolina at Chapel Hill, Chapel Hill.

———. Papers. Southern Historical Collection, Wilson Library, University of North Carolina at Chapel Hill, Chapel Hill.

———. *Three-Fifths of a Man.* London: MacMillan, 1969.

Meier, August, and Elliott Rudwick. *CORE: A Study in the Civil Rights Movement, 1942–1968.* New York: Oxford University Press, 1973.

Miller v. Continental Can Company. U.S. District Court, Southern District of Georgia, 1971. National Archives and Records Administration, Atlanta, Georgia.

Mills, Nicolaus, ed. *Busing U.S.A.* New York: Teachers College Press, 1979.

Minchin, Timothy J. *Hiring the Black Worker: The Racial Integration of the Southern Textile Industry, 1960–1980.* Chapel Hill: University of North Carolina Press, 1999.

———. *The Color of Work: The Struggle for Civil Rights in the Southern Paper Industry, 1945–1980.* Chapel Hill: University of North Carolina Press, 2001.

————. *Fighting Against the Odds: A History of Southern Labor Since World War II*. Gainesville: University Press of Florida, 2005.

Moody, Joe P. Interview with author. Roanoke Rapids, N.C., March 12, 1996.

Moody v. Albemarle Paper Company. U.S. District Court, Eastern District of North Carolina, 1966. National Archives and Records Administration, Atlanta, Georgia.

Moreno, Paul D. *From Direct Action to Affirmative Action: Fair Employment Law and Policy in America, 1933–1972*. Baton Rouge: Louisiana State University Press, 1997.

————. *Black Americans and Organized Labor: A New History*. Baton Rouge: Louisiana State University Press, 2006.

Moye, J. Todd. *Let the People Decide: Black Freedom and White Resistance in Sunflower County, Mississippi, 1945–1986*. Chapel Hill, University of North Carolina Press, 2004.

Myers v. Gilman Paper Company. U.S. District Court, Southern District of Georgia, 1972. National Archives and Records Administration, Atlanta, Georgia.

Myerson, Michael. *Nothing Could Be Finer*. New York: International Publishers, 1978.

NAACP (National Association for the Advancement of Colored People) Papers. Part 23 (Legal Department Case Files, 1960–1972). Microfilm in author's possession.

Nathan, Richard P. *Jobs and Civil Rights: The Role of the Federal Government in Promoting Equal Opportunity in Employment and Training*. Washington, D.C.: U.S. Commission on Civil Rights, 1969.

Nelson, Bruce. "Class, Race, and Democracy in the CIO: The 'New' Labor History Meets the 'Wages of Whiteness.'" *International Review of Social History* 41 (1996): 351–76.

————. "Working-Class Agency and Racial Inequality." *International Review of Social History* 41 (1996): 407–20.

————. "'CIO Meant One Thing for the Whites and Another Thing For Us': Steelworkers and Civil Rights, 1936–1974." In *Southern Labor in Transition, 1940–1995*, edited by Robert H. Zieger, 113–45. Knoxville: University of Tennessee Press, 1997.

Norrell, Robert J. *Reaping the Whirlwind: The Civil Rights Movement in Tuskegee*. New York: Knopf, 1985.

————. "One Thing We Did Right: Reflections on the Movement." In *New Directions in Civil Rights Studies*, edited by Armstead L. Robinson and Patricia Sullivan, 65–80. Charlottesville: University Press of Virginia, 1991.

————. *The House I Live In: Race in the American Century*. New York: Oxford University Press, 2005.

North Carolina Collection Clipping File. Wilson Library, University of North Carolina at Chapel Hill, Chapel Hill.

Northrup, Herbert R. "The Negro in the Paper Industry." In *Negro Employment in Southern Industry: A Study of Racial Policies in Five Industries*, edited by Herbert R. Northrup, Richard L. Rowan, Darold T. Barnum, and John C. Howard, Part 1. Philadelphia: Industrial Research Unit, Wharton School of Finance and Commerce, University of Pennsylvania, 1970.

Norton, Mary Beth, David M. Katzman, David W. Blight, Howard P. Chudacoff, Thomas G. Paterson, William M. Tuttle Jr., and Paul D. Escott. *A People and A Nation: A History of the United States*. 6th ed. New York: Houghton Mifflin, 2001.

PACE (Paper, Allied-Industrial, Chemical, and Energy Workers International Union) Southern Office Papers. United Steel, Paper and Forestry, Rubber, Manufacturing, Energy, Allied Industrial and Service Workers International Union (USW), Southern Regional Office, Mobile, Alabama.

Patterson, James T. *Brown v. Board of Education: A Civil Rights Milestone and Its Troubled Legacy*. New York: Oxford University Press, 2001.

Payne, Charles M. *I've Got the Light of Freedom: The Organizing Tradition and the Mississippi Freedom Struggle*. Berkeley: University of California Press, 1995.

Payne, Monty. Interview with author. Hattiesburg, Miss., June 22, 2005.

Pope, Laura Ann. Interview with author. Andrews, S.C., April 1, 1996.

Powledge, Fred. *Free at Last?: The Civil Rights Movement and the People Who Made It*. Boston: Little, Brown & Co., 1991.

Pride, Richard A. *The Political Use of Racial Narratives: School Desegregation in Mobile, Alabama, 1954–97*. Urbana: University of Illinois Press, 2002.

Pride, Richard A., and J. David Woodard. *The Burden of Busing: The Politics of Desegregation in Nashville, Tennessee*. Knoxville: University of Tennessee Press, 1985.

Profile: North Carolina Counties. Raleigh: Office of State Budget and Management Research and Planning Services, 1981.

Purnell, Jettie H. Interview with author. Roanoke Rapids, N.C., February 9, 1996.

Rabby, Glenda Alice. *The Pain and the Promise: The Struggle for Civil Rights in Tallahassee, Florida*. Athens: University of Georgia Press, 1999.

Ralph, James R., Jr. *Northern Protest: Martin Luther King, Jr., Chicago, and the Civil Rights Movement*. Cambridge, Mass.: Harvard University Press, 1993.

Ransby, Barbara. *Ella Baker and the Black Freedom Movement: A Radical Democratic Vision*. Chapel Hill: University of North Carolina Press, 2003.

Raynor, Bruce. Interview with author. Greensboro, N.C., July 28, 1995.

Reed, Merl E. *Seedtime for the Modern Civil Rights Movement: The President's Committee on Fair Employment Practice, 1941–1946*. Baton Rouge: Louisiana State University Press, 1991.

Rhee, Foon. "Visions, Illusions and Perceptions: The Story of Soul City." Undergraduate honors thesis, Duke University, 1984.

Roberts, Gerald. Interview with author. St. Marys, Ga., July 15, 1998.

Roberts v. St. Regis Paper Company. U.S. District Court, Middle District of Florida, 1970. National Archives and Records Administration, Atlanta, Georgia.

Robinson, Armstead L., and Patricia Sullivan, eds. *New Directions in Civil Rights Studies*. Charlottesville: University Press of Virginia, 1991.

Robinson, Herman. Interview with author. Moss Point, Miss., October 14, 1997.

Roediger, David R. *The Wages of Whiteness: Race and the Making of the American Working Class*. New York: Verso, 1991.

Rogers v. International Paper Company. U.S. District Court, Eastern District of Arkansas, 1971. National Archives and Records Administration, Fort Worth, Texas.

Rossell, Christine H. "Desegregation Plans, Racial Isolation, White Flight, and Community Response." In *The Consequences of School Desegregation*, edited by Christine H. Rossell and Willis D. Hawley, 13–57. Philadelphia: Temple University Press, 1983.

Rossell, Christine H., and Willis D. Hawley, eds. *The Consequences of School Desegregation*. Philadelphia: Temple University Press, 1983.

Rowan, Richard L. "The Negro in the Textile Industry." In *Negro Employment in Southern Industry: A Study of Racial Policies in Five Industries,* edited by Herbert R. Northrup, Richard L. Rowan, Darold T. Barnum, and John C. Howard, Part 5. Philadelphia: Industrial Research Unit, Wharton School of Finance and Commerce, University of Pennsylvania, 1970.

Salmond, John A. *"My Mind Set on Freedom": A History of the Civil Rights Movement, 1954–1968.* Chicago: Ivan R. Dee, 1997.

Sawyer, George. Interview with author. Savannah, Ga., October 4, 1997.

School Desegregation in Boston. Washington, D.C.: U.S. Commission on Civil Rights, 1975.

School Desegregation in the 1970s: Problems and Prospects. Washington, D.C.: National Institute of Education, 1976.

Schuck, Peter, and Harrison Wellford. "Democracy and the Good Life in a Company Town." *Harper's Magazine* 244 (May 1972): 56–66.

Schulman, Bruce J. *From Cotton Belt to Sunbelt: Federal Policy, Economic Development, and the Transformation of the South, 1938–1980.* New York: Oxford University Press, 1991.

———. *The Seventies: The Great Shift in American Culture, Society, and Politics.* New York: Free Press, 2001.

Seibles v. Cone Mills. U.S. District Court, Middle District of North Carolina, 1977. National Archives and Records Administration, Atlanta, Georgia.

Self, Robert. "'To Plan Our Liberation': Black Power and the Politics of Place in Oakland, California, 1965–1977." *Journal of Urban History* 26, no. 5 (2000): 759–92.

Sherrill v. J. P. Stevens. U.S. District Court, Western District of North Carolina, 1973. National Archives and Records Administration, Atlanta, Georgia.

Sitkoff, Harvard. *A New Deal for Blacks: The Emergence of Civil Rights as a National Issue.* New York: Oxford University Press, 1978.

———. *The Struggle for Black Equality, 1954–1980.* New York: Hill and Wang, 1981.

Sixty Minutes. "Target J. P. Stevens." Videotape. CBS, March 13, 1977. Copy held at Kheel Center for Labor-Management Documentation and Archives, School of Industrial and Labor Relations, Cornell University, Ithaca, N.Y.

Skrentny, John D. *The Minority Rights Revolution.* Cambridge, Mass.: Belknap Press, 2002.

Sledge v. J. P. Stevens. U.S. District Court, Eastern District of North Carolina, 1970. National Archives and Records Administration, Atlanta, Georgia.

Sosna, Morton. *In Search of the Silent South: Southern Liberals and the Race Issue.* New York: Columbia University Press, 1977.

Southern Regional Council (SRC) Papers (microfilm). Robert W. Woodruff Library, Atlanta University Center, Atlanta, Georgia.

Speights, Lamar. Interview with author. Port St. Joe, Fla., July 23, 1997.

Spence, Chuck. Interview with author. Nashville, Tenn., July 17, 1997.

Spriggs, Kent. Interview with author. Tallahassee, Fla., July 20, 1997.

Stein, Judith. *Running Steel, Running America: Race, Economic Policy, and the Decline of Liberalism.* Chapel Hill: University of North Carolina Press, 1998.

Stephan, Walter G., and Joe R. Feagin, eds. *School Desegregation: Past, Present, and Future.* New York: Plenum Press, 1980.

Stevenson v. International Paper Company. U.S. District Court, Southern District of Alabama, 1971. National Archives and Records Administration, Atlanta, Georgia.

Stewart, Grover. Interview with author. Mobile, Ala., November 10, 2004.

Strain, Christopher. "Soul City, North Carolina: Black Power, Utopia, and the African American Dream." *Journal of African American History* 89, no. 1 (Winter 2004): 57–74.

Strange, Carolyn, and Tina Loo, "Holding the Rock: The 'Indianization' of Alcatraz Island, 1969–1999." In *The World the Sixties Made: Politics and Culture in Recent America*, edited by Van Gosse and Richard Moser, 242–64. Philadelphia: Temple University Press, 2003.

Sugrue, Thomas J. "Affirmative Action from Below: Civil Rights, the Building Trades, and the Politics of Racial Equality in the Urban North, 1945–1969." *Journal of American History* 91, no. 1 (June 2004): 145–73.

Sullivan, Patricia. *Days of Hope: Race and Democracy in the New Deal Era.* Chapel Hill: University of North Carolina Press, 1996.

Swaity, Paul. Interview. Textile Workers Union of America Oral History Project, November 15, 1978. State Historical Society of Wisconsin, Madison.

Taylor, Bennett. Interview with author. Roanoke Rapids, N.C., February 9, 1996.

Taylor, Mervin. Interview with author. Bogalusa, La., July 20, 1999.

Thomas, Larry Reni. *The True Story Behind the Wilmington Ten.* Hampton, Va.: U.B. and U.S. Communications, 1993.

Thornton, J. Mills. *Dividing Lines: Municipal Politics and the Struggle for Civil Rights in Montgomery, Birmingham, and Selma.* Tuscaloosa: University of Alabama Press, 2002.

Trawick, Gladys. Interview with author. Andalusia, Ala., February 2, 1996.

Tuck, Stephen G. N. *Beyond Atlanta: The Struggle for Racial Equality in Georgia, 1940–1980.* Athens: University of Georgia Press, 2001.

TWUA (Textile Workers Union of America) Papers. State Historical Society of Wisconsin, Madison.

Tyson, Timothy B. *Radio Free Dixie: Robert F. Williams and the Roots of Black Power.* Chapel Hill: University of North Carolina Press, 1999.

———. *Blood Done Sign My Name: A True Story.* New York: Crown, 2004.

UPIU (United Paperworkers International Union) Papers. USW International Union, Nashville, Tennessee.

UPIU Local 446 Papers, 1941–1998. Southern Labor Archives, Georgia State University Library, Georgia State University, Atlanta.

U.S. Commission on Civil Rights. *The Federal Civil Rights Enforcement Effort: Summary.* Washington, D.C.: U.S. Government Printing Office, 1971.

———. *Above Property Rights.* Washington, D.C.: U.S. Government Printing Office, 1972.

———. *Five Communities: Their Search for Equal Education.* Washington, D.C.: U.S. Government Printing Office, 1972.

———. *Statement on Affirmative Action.* Washington, D.C.: U.S. Government Printing Office, 1977.

———. *State of Civil Rights 1957–1983: The Final Report of the U.S. Commission on Civil Rights.* Washington, D.C.: U.S. Government Printing Office, 1983.

U.S. Congress. House. Special Subcommittee on Labor of the Committee on Education and

Labor, *Proposed Federal Legislation to Prohibit Discrimination in Employment in Certain Cases because of Race, Religion, Color, National Origin, Ancestry, or Sex: Hearings before the Special Subcommittee on Labor of the Committee on Education and Labor*, 87th Cong., 2nd sess., 1962.

————. General Subcommittee on Labor of the Committee on Education and Labor, *Bills to Promote Equal Employment Opportunities for American Workers*, 91st Cong., 1st and 2nd sess., 1970.

U.S. Congress. Senate. Senate Subcommittee on Labor of the Committee on Labor and Public Welfare, *Equal Employment Opportunities Enforcement Act of 1971*, 92nd Cong., 1st sess., 1971.

U.S. District Court Records. National Archives and Records Administration (NARA), Southeastern Region, Atlanta, Georgia.

————. NARA, Mid-Atlantic Region, Philadelphia, Pennsylvania.

————. NARA, Southwestern Region, Fort Worth, Texas.

United States v. Local 189, United Papermakers and Paperworkers. U.S. District Court, Eastern District of Louisiana, 1968. National Archives and Records Administration, Fort Worth, Texas.

Via, Emory F. Papers (1936–1987). Southern Labor Archives, Georgia State University Library, Georgia State University, Atlanta.

Waldrep, G. C., II. Interview with author. Summerfield, N.C., July 24, 1995.

Waldrep, G. C., III. *Southern Workers and the Search for Community: Spartanburg County, South Carolina*. Urbana: University of Illinois Press, 2000.

Walker, Otis. Interview with author. Apalachicola, Fla., July 24, 1997.

Waller, Signe. *Love and Revolution: A Political Memoir. People's History of the Greensboro Massacre, Its Setting and Aftermath*. Lanham, Md.: Rowman and Littlefield, 2002.

Ward, Brian, and Tony Badger, eds. *The Making of Martin Luther King and the Civil Rights Movement*. New York: New York University Press, 1996.

Watkins v. Scott Paper Company. U.S. District Court, Southern District of Alabama, 1971. National Archives and Records Administration, Atlanta, Georgia.

Webb, Clive. "A Continuity of Conservatism: The Limitations of *Brown v. Board of Education*." *Journal of Southern History* 70, no. 2 (May 2004): 327–36.

Weisbrot, Robert. *Freedom Bound: A History of America's Civil Rights Movement*. New York: Norton, 1990.

Weiss, Robert J. *"We Want Jobs": A History of Affirmative Action*. New York: Garland, 1997.

Wharton School of Finance and Commerce, Industrial Research Unit Papers. University Archives and Records Center, University of Pennsylvania, Philadelphia.

Whiddon, Jesse. Interview with author. Mobile, Ala., July 21, 1997.

White, John. *Black Leadership in America: From Booker T. Washington to Jesse Jackson*. 2nd ed. London: Longman, 1990.

Wiebe, Robert H. "White Attitudes and Black Rights from *Brown* to *Bakke*." In *Have We Overcome?: Race Relations Since Brown*, edited by Michael B. Namorato, 147–71. Jackson: University Press of Mississippi, 1979.

Wilkens, Mark. "Gender, Race, Work Culture, and the Building of the Fire Fighters Union in

Tampa, Florida, 1943–1985." In *Southern Labor in Transition, 1940–1995,* edited by Robert H. Zieger, 176–204. Knoxville: University of Tennessee Press, 1997.

Wilkes, Don. Telephone interview with author. June 28, 2005.

Wilkinson, J. Harvie, III. *From Brown to Bakke: The Supreme Court and School Integration: 1954–1978.* New York: Oxford University Press, 1979.

Williams, Alphonse. Interview with author. Mobile, Ala., July 21, 1997.

Williams, Arthur. Interview with author. Theodore, Ala., November 12, 2004.

Williams, Juan. *Eyes on the Prize: America's Civil Rights Years, 1954–1965.* New York: Penguin, 1987.

Williams, Roger M. "What Louisville Has Taught Us About Busing." *Saturday Review,* April 30, 1977, 6–8, 10, 51.

Winfield v. St. Joe Paper Company. U.S. District Court, Northern District of Florida, 1976. National Archives and Records Administration, Atlanta, Georgia.

Wirt, Frederick M. *"We Ain't What We Was": Civil Rights in the New South.* Durham: Duke University Press, 1997.

Woloch, Nancy. *Women and the American Experience: A Concise History.* New York: McGraw Hill, 1996.

Woodard, Harold. "Floyd McKissick: Portrait of a Leader." M.A. diss., University of North Carolina, 1981.

Woodard, Komozi. *A Nation Within a Nation: Amiri Baraka (LeRoi Jones) and Black Power Politics.* Chapel Hill: University of North Carolina Press, 1999.

Wright, Gavin. "Economic Consequences of the Southern Protest Movement." In *New Directions in Civil Rights Studies,* edited by Armstead L. Robinson and Patricia Sullivan, 175–83. Charlottesville: University Press of Virginia, 1991.

Yon, M. D. Interview with author. Wewahitchka, Fla., July 24, 1997.

Young, Boyd. Interview with author. Nashville, Tenn., July 18, 1997.

Zieger, Robert H. *Rebuilding the Pulp and Paper Workers' Union, 1933–1941.* Knoxville: University of Tennessee Press, 1984.

———. "Textile Workers and Historians." In *Organized Labor in the Twentieth-Century South,* edited by Robert H. Zieger, 35–59. Knoxville: University of Tennessee Press, 1991.

———. "Recent Historical Scholarship on Public Policy in Relation to Race and Labor in the Post-Title-VII Period." *Labor History* 46, no. 1 (February 2005): 3–14.

Zieger, Robert H., and Gilbert J. Gall. *American Workers, American Unions.* 3rd ed. Baltimore: Johns Hopkins University Press, 2002.

Ziewitz, Kathryn, and June Wiaz. *Green Empire: The St. Joe Company and the Remaking of Florida's Panhandle.* Gainesville: University Press of Florida, 2004.

Index

Timothy J. Minchin is reader and associate professor of North American history at La Trobe University in Melbourne, Australia. He has authored six books on labor and civil rights history, as well as several articles and pamphlets. He received the Richard A. Lester Prize for the Outstanding Book in Labor Economics and Industrial Relations in 1999 for his *Hiring the Black Worker: The Racial Integration of the Southern Textile Industry, 1960–1980.*